‘You Are a Priest Forever’

Studies on the Texts of the Desert of Judah

Edited by

Florentino García Martínez

Associate editors

Peter W. Flint

Eibert J.C. Tigchelaar

VOLUME 74

‘You Are a Priest Forever’

Second Temple Jewish Messianism and the Priestly Christology of the Epistle to the Hebrews

By

Eric F. Mason

BRILL

LEIDEN • BOSTON
2008

This book is printed on acid-free paper.

Library of Congress Cataloging-in-Publication Data

Mason, Eric Farrel.
You are a priest forever : Second Temple Jewish messianism and the priestly christology of the Epistle to the Hebrews / by Eric F. Mason.
p. cm. — (Studies on the texts of the Desert of Judah, ISSN 0169-9962 ; v. 74)
Includes bibliographical references and index.
ISBN 978-90-04-14987-8 (hardback : alk. paper) 1. Priesthood—Biblical teaching. 2. Jesus Christ—Priesthood. 3. Jesus Christ—Messiahship. 4. Bible. N.T. Hebrews—Criticism, interpretation, etc. 5. Messiah—Judaism—History of doctrines. 6. Judaism—History—Post-exilic period, 586 B.C.–210 A.D. 7. Jesus Christ—History of doctrines—Early church, ca. 30–600. I. Title. II. Series.

BS2775.6.P69M37 2008
227'.8706—dc22

2007048464

ISSN 0169-9962
ISBN 978 90 04 14987 8

PRINTED IN THE NETHERLANDS

FOR

MY WIFE JACQUELINE

AND OUR DAUGHTER ANASTASIA

AND FOR MY PARENTS

DILLARD AND STELLA

CONTENTS

ACKNOWLEDGEMENTS

This monograph is a revised version of my doctoral dissertation, submitted to the Department of Theology at the University of Notre Dame in 2005. I wish to express my enduring gratitude to the university, the department, and the Pew Younger Scholars Program for their generous financial support that made this possible.

Though I certainly am responsible for any deficiencies in this present volume, the influences of numerous mentors from Notre Dame are evident on the following pages. It would be impossible to mention everyone to whom I am indebted, but I wish to thank the following friends in particular. My scholarly interest in Hebrews has its roots in a seminar paper written for Eugene Ulrich on Hebrews' use of biblical citations. My studies with Harold Attridge during the period we both were at Notre Dame unfortunately did not include a seminar on Hebrews, yet no work has been more influential on my own approach to the book than his masterful commentary. I am deeply grateful to the members of my dissertation committee—Gregory Sterling, Jerome Neyrey, and John Meier—both for their insightful critiques as I wrote the dissertation and their respective publications on Hebrews from which I have learned so much. Finally, I am especially indebted to my dissertation director, James VanderKam. Jim is equally acclaimed for his rigorous, careful scholarship and his gracious, gentle manner. Both have left their indelible marks on me in a multitude of ways.

This project began at Notre Dame but was completed—both as a dissertation and now as a monograph—from Judson University in Elgin, Ill. One could scarcely imagine colleagues in biblical and theological studies as supportive and engaging as those with whom I am fortunate to serve. In particular, I wish to thank Laurie Braaten; he has been a constant source of wisdom and encouragement to me since my arrival at Judson. Also, I am indebted to provost Dale Simmons for his support in multiple ways, including funds from the Homer and Margaret Surbeck Summer Research Program for the present work.

Academic research is impossible without the support of libraries and librarians, and this book could not have been completed without the Hesburgh Library at Notre Dame, both during my graduate school years and beyond. Likewise, I am much indebted to the staff of Judson's Benjamin Browne Library. Their dedication to service was perhaps best exemplified in the summer of 2007 as they continued to acquire the many articles and volumes to support my work in the midst of their own relocation to facilities across the campus.

I am very honored that this volume is appearing in the Studies on the Texts of the Desert of Judah series. I am deeply grateful to Florentino García Martínez for accepting my manuscript, offering numerous suggestions for its improvement, and consistently encouraging my work. I am also much indebted to Mattie Kuiper at Brill for her guidance in this process, and to John J. Collins for recommending my manuscript to Florentino.

Numerous persons have enriched my work through their critiques and comments at academic conferences, especially colleagues in the Chicago Society of Biblical Research and the Central States Region Society of Biblical Literature. I was honored to be selected by the latter as its SBL Regional Scholar in April 2006 (and subsequently as a 2007 Regional Scholar by the national SBL Council of Regional Coordinators) for a paper titled "Melchizedek in Hebrews and the Dead Sea Scrolls." A version of this paper was published in *Biblical Research*, the journal of CSBR, as "Hebrews 7:3 and the Relationship between Melchizedek and Jesus," *BR* 50 (2005): 41-62. Much of that article appears in revised form in chapters one, four, and five of the present work; these materials are reprinted with the permission of the editor, David Aune.

I have been much encouraged at various stages in this project by friends including Greg Lucas, Robert Mowery, Fisher Humphreys, Chip Davis, Beulah Coyne, and Shaun Longstreet. My father-in-law and mother-in-law, Jack and Betty Cameron, have consistently supported my work in a multitude of ways.

Ultimately, however, this project could never have been completed without the love, support, and sacrifices of my parents Dillard and Stella Mason, my wife Jacqueline, and my daughter Anastasia. To you I am always grateful, and it is to you that I dedicate this volume.

ABBREVIATIONS

Abbreviations for ancient texts cited in this volume are those of *The SBL Handbook of Style* (ed. Patrick H. Alexander, et al.; Peabody, Mass.: Hendrickson, 1999) and the Discoveries in the Judaean Desert series. Most of the abbreviations below are taken from the *SBL Handbook*, supplemented by the present author's abbreviations as necessary (as for recent publications).

AB	Anchor Bible
ABD	*The Anchor Bible Dictionary* (ed. D. N. Freedman)
ABRL	Anchor Bible Reference Library
AbrN	*Abr-Nahrain*
AbrNSup	Abr-Nahrain: Supplement Series
AGJU	Arbeiten zur Geschichte des antiken Judentums und des Urchristentums
AJT	*American Journal of Theology*
ALBO	Analecta lovaniensia biblica et orientalia
ALD	*Aramaic Levi Document*
ALGHJ	Arbeiten zur Literatur und Geschichte des hellenistischen Judentums
AnBib	Analecta biblica
ANRW	*Aufstieg und Niedergang der römischen Welt: Geschichte und Kultur Roms im Spiegel der neueren Forschung* (eds. H. Temporini and W. Haase)
ANTC	Abingdon New Testament Commentaries
AOT	*The Apocryphal Old Testament* (ed. H. F. D. Sparks)
APOT	*The Apocrypha and Pseudepigrapha of the Old Testament* (ed. R. H. Charles)
ATR	*Australasian Theological Review*
BBR	*Bulletin for Biblical Research*
BDAG	*A Greek-English Lexicon of the New Testament and Other Early Christian Literature*, 3rd. ed. (ed. Frederick William Danker)
BETL	Bibliotheca ephemeridum theologicarum lovaniensium
Bib	*Biblica*
Bijdr	*Bijdragen: Tijdschrift voor filosofie en theologie*
BIS	Biblical Interpretation Series
BJRL	*Bulletin of the John Rylands University Library of Manchester*
BNTC	Black's New Testament Commentaries
BR	*Biblical Research*
CBQ	*Catholic Biblical Quarterly*
CBQMS	Catholic Biblical Quarterly Monograph Series
CC	Continental Commentaries
CQR	*Church Quarterly Review*
CSCO	Corpus scriptorum christianorum orientalium
DJD	Discoveries in the Judaean Desert
DJDJ	Discoveries in the Judaean Desert of Jordan

DNTB	*Dictionary of New Testament Background* (ed. C. A. Evans and S. Porter)
DPL	*Dictionary of Paul and His Letters* (ed. G. F. Hawthorne, R. P. Martin, and D. G. Reid)
DSD	*Dead Sea Discoveries*
DSSSE	*The Dead Sea Scrolls Study Edition* (ed. F. García Martínez and E. J. C. Tigchelaar)
EBib	*Études Bibliques*
ECDSS	Eerdmans Commentaries on the Dead Sea Scrolls
EdF	Erträge der Forschung
EDNT	*Exegetical Dictionary of the New Testament* (ed. H. Balz and G. Schneider)
EDSS	*Encyclopedia of the Dead Sea Scrolls* (ed. L. H. Schiffman and J. C. VanderKam)
EKKNT	Evangelisch-katholischer Kommentar zum Neuen Testament
EV	English version
EvQ	*Evangelical Quarterly*
FRLANT	Forschungen zur Religion und Literatur des Alten und Neuen Testaments
HB	Hebrew Bible
Herm	*Hermathena*
HNT	Handbuch zum Neuen Testament
HTR	*Harvard Theological Review*
HUCA	*Hebrew Union College Annual*
IBC	Interpretation: A Bible Commentary for Teaching and Preaching
ICC	International Critical Commentary
IEJ	*Israel Exploration Journal*
JBL	*Journal of Biblical Literature*
JBR	*Journal of Bible and Religion*
JGRChJ	*Journal of Greco-Roman Christianity and Judaism*
JJS	*Journal of Jewish Studies*
JPS	Jewish Publication Society
JQR	*Jewish Quarterly Review*
JSJ	*Journal for the Study of the Judaism*
JSJSup	Journal for the Study of Judaism: Supplement Series
JSNT	*Journal for the Study of the New Testament*
JSNTSup	Journal for the Study of the New Testament: Supplement Series
JSOTSup	Journal for the Study of the Old Testament: Supplement Series
JSPSup	Journal for the Study of the Pseudepigrapha: Supplement Series
JTS	*Journal of Theological Studies*
KEK	Kritisch-exegetischer Kommentar über das Neue Testament
LCL	Loeb Classical Library
LSJ	*A Greek-English Lexicon*, 9th ed. with revised supplement (ed. H. G. Liddell, R. Scott, and H. S. Jones)
LXX	Septuagint
MM	*The Vocabulary of the Greek Testament* (ed. J. H. Moulton and G. Milligan)
MT	Masoretic Text
MThSt	Marburger Theologische Studien
NAB	New American Bible
NCB	New Century Bible
NIB	*The New Interpreter's Bible* (ed. L. Keck)
NIBC	New International Biblical Commentary

NICNT	New International Commentary on the New Testament
NIDB	*The New Interpreter's Dictionary of the Bible* (ed. K. D. Sakenfeld)
NIGTC	New International Greek Testament Commentary
NIV	New International Version
NIVAC	NIV Application Commentary
NJPS	New Jewish Publication Society
NovT	*Novum Testamentum*
NRSV	New Revised Standard Version
NT	New Testament
NTD	Das Neue Testament Deutsch
NTL	New Testament Library
NTS	*New Testament Studies*
NTT	New Testament Theology
OTL	Old Testament Library
OTP	*Old Testament Pseudepigrapha* (ed. J. H. Charlesworth)
OtSt	*Oudtestamentische Studiën*
PTSDSSP	Princeton Theological Seminary Dead Sea Scrolls Project
PVTG	Pseudepigrapha Veteris Testamenti Graece
RB	*Revue biblique*
RBL	*Review of Biblical Literature*
RevQ	*Revue de Qumran*
RHR	*Revue de l'histoire des religions*
SBLDS	Society of Biblical Literature Dissertation Series
SBLEJL	Society of Biblical Literature Early Judaism and Its Literature
SBLMS	Society of Biblical Literature Monograph Series
SBLSCS	Society of Biblical Literature Septuagint and Cognate Studies
SBLTT	Society of Biblical Literature Texts and Translations
ScrHier	Scripta hierosolymitana
SDSSRL	Studies on the Dead Sea Scrolls and Related Literature
SHR	Studies in the History of Religions
SJLA	Studies in Judaism in Late Antiquity
SNTSMS	Society for New Testament Studies Monograph Series
SP	Sacra pagina
SPhilo	*Studia philonica*
SRivBib	Supplementi alla Rivista Biblica
STDJ	Studies on the Texts of the Desert of Judah
StPB	Studia post-biblica
SVTP	Studia in Veteris Testamenti pseudepigraphica
TDNT	*Theological Dictionary of the New Testament* (ed. G. Kittel and G. Friedrich)
TDOT	*Theological Dictionary of the Old Testament* (ed. G. J. Botterweck, H. Ringgren, and F.-J. Fabry)
THKNT	Theologischer Handkommentar zum Neuen Testament
TS	*Theological Studies*
TZ	*Theologische Zeitschrift*
VT	*Vetus Testamentum*
WBC	Word Biblical Commentary
WDNT	*The Westminster Dictionary of New Testament and Early Christian Literature and Rhetoric* (ed. D. E. Aune)
WTJ	*Westminster Theological Journal*
WUNT	Wissenschaftliche Untersuchungen zum Neuen Testament
ZAW	*Zeitschrift für die alttestamentliche Wissenschaft*
ZTK	*Zeitschrift für Theologie und Kirche*

INTRODUCTION

The epistle to the Hebrews has much in common with its own description of Melchizedek, whose origins and destiny are said to be unknown (Heb 7:3). The identity of the author of Hebrews is elusive, and attempts to determine the date of composition are complicated by a scarcity of relevant clues in the book. Though it contains a tantalizing greeting relayed on behalf of certain Italians, even its destination and the identity of its intended recipients are shrouded in mystery. Other questions about this epistle abound. Not only is the identity of the author of Hebrews unknown, but much disagreement also exists about the background of this author and the influences that affected the distinctive ways he communicated his understanding of Jesus. Also, no scholarly consensus exists for understanding the nature of the problems faced by the recipients. Questions remain even about the genre of the book and its literary unity.

While this is not the place for a thorough discussion of each of these matters, a brief sketch of the issues is appropriate. It is common in many circles today to categorize Hebrews alongside the Catholic Epistles and Revelation—or even *as* a Catholic Epistle—but historically this has not been the case. This approach belies the fact that in the ancient manuscript tradition, the book normally circulated in the Pauline corpus.[1] Indeed, Hebrews ultimately owes its inclusion in the New Testament canon to the insistence in the ancient Eastern churches—and ultimately a compromise consensus with the West, championed by Augustine and Jerome—that Paul was its author. Difficulties with this

---

[1] Pamela M. Eisenbaum is even more emphatic: "While different forms of the *corpus Paulinum* circulated, and some versions did not include Hebrews, there is no evidence that Hebrews circulated with other collections of Christian writings (for instance, with documents that came to be known as the Catholic Epistles)." See her "Locating Hebrews Within the Literary Landscape of Christian Origins," in *Hebrews: Contemporary Methods, New Insights* (ed. G. Gelardini; BIS 75; Leiden: Brill, 2005), 213-37, esp. 218.

identification were long recognized, however.[2] Origin earlier had concluded that only God knew the identity of the author (*Hist. eccl.* 6.25.14), but his caution did not inhibit subsequent speculation, and throughout the centuries numerous alternate proposals for authorship have been offered. Often—but not exclusively—those proposed have been figures in the Pauline orbit, including Barnabas, Apollos, Silas (or Silvanus), and Aquila and Priscilla.[3]

Pauline authorship is rarely defended in modern scholarship for a number of reasons, including literary style, theological emphases, and especially the author's claim in 2:3 to have been evangelized by an earlier generation of believers.[4] Rather than speculate on the personal identity of the author, most modern scholars instead prefer to consider what characteristics about this person may be inferred from the text. The author, with a sophisticated literary style and broad vocabulary, is widely recognized to have produced the finest Greek in the New Testament. In light of this, the author seems almost certainly to have had some level of training in Greek rhetoric.[5] Alongside this, he displays much facility with Jewish exegetical methods and traditions. Virtually all scholars assert that Scripture for the author was the Septuagint.[6] The author is steeped in the texts and exegetical traditions

[2] See Craig R. Koester, *Hebrews* (AB; New York: Doubleday, 2001), 21-27, for a perceptive discussion of the theological issues relevant to positions on authorship of Hebrews in the early church. See also William H. P. Hatch, "The Position of Hebrews in the Canon of the New Testament," *HTR* 29 (1936): 133-51; and Otto Michel, *Der Brief an die Hebräer* (KEK 14; Göttingen: Vandenhoeck & Ruprecht, 1984), 37-39. For broader surveys of background issues, see Werner Georg Kümmel, *Introduction to the New Testament* (rev. ed.; trans. H. C. Kee; Nashville: Abingdon, 1975), 475-502; and Raymond E. Brown, *An Introduction to the New Testament* (ABRL; New York: Doubleday, 1997), 683-704.

[3] For a critique of such proposals, see Harold W. Attridge, *The Epistle to the Hebrews* (Hermeneia; Philadelphia: Fortress, 1989), 3-5.

[4] Scholars typically note the incompatibility of this statement with Paul's insistence in Galatians 1–2 that no human taught him the gospel. See, for example, Attridge, *Hebrews*, 2.

[5] Sophisticated Greek rhetorical methods utilized by the author are catalogued in Attridge, *Hebrews*, 20-21; David E. Aune, "Hebrews, Letter to the," *WDNT* 211-13; and Andrew H. Trotter, Jr., *Interpreting the Epistle to the Hebrews* (Guides to New Testament Exegesis 6; Grand Rapids: Baker, 1997), 163-84. For analysis of such rhetorical skill in a particularly significant passage, see Jerome H. Neyrey, "'Without Beginning of Days or End of Life' (Hebrews 7:3): Topos for a True Deity," *CBQ* 53 (1991): 439-55.

[6] For a recent assessment of Hebrews' use of the Septuagint, see Martin Karrer, "The Epistle to the Hebrews and the Septuagint," in *Septuagint Research: Issues and Challenges in the Study of the Greek Jewish Scriptures* (ed. W. Kraus and R. G.

of Judaism, yet he also draws positively from Greco-Roman mythological and philosophical traditions; his intellectual capacities are profound.[7] Taken together, these characteristics point to a Jewish-Christian author—most likely ethnically Jewish, though a proselyte is possible—whose background was in the Greek-speaking Diaspora.

Hebrews normally is considered an epistle, though it lacks marks of such in its opening section. Increasingly scholars note its homiletic nature.[8] As for the recipients of the book, one can confidently assert little beyond the observation that they had earlier been taught by the author but now faced some crisis of faith.[9] In the early church the book normally was understood as written to Jewish Christians in Jerusalem.[10] Modern scholars, however, almost always assume a Roman destination, in large part due to the statement in Heb 13:24 that 'those from Italy send greetings.'[11] The author's emphasis on exegesis of texts

---

Wooden; SBLSCS 53; Atlanta: Society of Biblical Literature, 2006), 335-53. See also Harold W. Attridge, "The Epistle to the Hebrews and the Scrolls," in *When Judaism and Christianity Began: Essays in Memory of Anthony J. Saldarini* (2 vols.; ed. A. J. Avery-Peck, D. Harrington, and J. Neusner; JSJSup 85; Leiden: Brill, 2004), 2:315-42, esp. 2:316 n. 5, where he notes that the author's correlation of 'rest' in Ps 95 and Gen 2:2 only works in Greek, not Hebrew. Nevertheless some deny that the author of Hebrews normally cited the LXX; see, for example, George Howard, "Hebrews and the Old Testament Quotations," *NovT* 10 (1968): 208-16.

[7] Hans-Friedrich Weiss (among others) cites three common options for understanding the background of Hebrews' thought: Hellenistic-Jewish, Gnostic, and apocalyptic. See his *Der Brief an die Hebräer* (15th ed.; KEK 13; Göttingen: Vandenhoeck & Ruprecht, 1991), 96-114. See also F. F. Bruce, "'To the Hebrews': A Document of Roman Christianity?" *ANRW* 25.4:3496-3521.

[8] Since the late eighteenth century scholars have occasionally argued that Hebrews is a homily rather than an epistle. Similarly, some have argued that the epistolatory ending of Heb 13 is secondary. Attridge (*Hebrews*, 13-14, esp. n. 117) notes, however, that virtually all modern scholars accept the authenticity of Heb 13. See also the discussion of genre and the authenticity of Heb 13 in Udo Schnelle, *The History and Theology of the New Testament Writings* (trans. M. E. Boring; Minneapolis: Fortress, 1998), 372-74.

[9] Several statements imply that the author had previously been among his recipients (Heb 13:19) or at the least knew a great deal about their history (Heb 2:3-4; 5:11-14; 6:9-11; and 10:32-34). See William L. Lane, *Hebrews* (2 vols.; WBC; Dallas: Word, 1991), 1:lv.

[10] This destination is rarely defended today, but see Daniel Stökl Ben Ezra, *The Impact of Yom Kippur on Early Christianity: The Day of Atonement from Second Temple Judaism to the Fifth Century* (WUNT 163; Tübingen: Mohr Siebeck, 2003), 191-92. Stökl Ben Ezra understands Heb 13:13 as a call for Jewish Christians to leave Jerusalem.

[11] Most interpreters have understood the greeting (ἀσπάζονται ὑμᾶς οἱ ἀπὸ τῆς Ἰταλίας) as one sent by Italians back to their homeland, but some have read it to be a greeting sent from Italy or by displaced Italians to persons in a third location. See

from the Jewish Scriptures (especially the Pentateuch, Psalms, and prophets), his frequent use of exemplars (both positive and negative) drawn from these narratives, and his extended comparison of Jesus' activities with aspects of the Jewish sacrificial system typically have been cited by interpreters as evidence that the Jewish identity of the recipients is a key to interpretation of the book. As such, English-language scholarship on Hebrews long was dominated by theories that the author was warning the Jewish Christian recipients not to renounce Christianity and return to their ancestral faith or else was exhorting them finally to make a full break from the synagogue.[12] Alternately, a

---

Attridge, *Hebrews*, 409-10. For discussion of other factors pointing to a Roman destination, see Koester, *Hebrews*, 48-50. Unless otherwise noted, all translations from Hebrews are those of the author, while those of other biblical passages are from the New Revised Standard Version.

[12] Eisenbaum notes this tendency in scholarship on Hebrews but proposes essentially the opposite approach, that Hebrews demonstrates that "the shared experience of persecution during this time [late first-early second centuries C.E.] may have led to a greater sense of commonality among Jews and Christians, or, at the very least, little awareness of any significant differences" ("Locating Hebrews," 236). She assumes a second-century date for the book, in part because of her assertions that the author knew a written gospel and assumes a significant gap of time between the eras of Jesus and his own. On this, see Eisenbaum, "Locating Hebrews," 227-31. Two other essays in the same volume assume Jewish contexts with fascinating but problematic theses. Ellen Bradshaw Aitken interprets Hebrews as a first-century Christian response to the imperial propaganda of the Roman triumph celebrating victory in the first Jewish war. Like Eisenbaum, she presumes that the author addresses both Jews and Jewish Christians, here understood as in solidarity because of threats from this demonstration of imperial power. For Aitken, however, the author's purpose is to counter the images of Roman imperial power and status on a number of points, especially by presenting Jesus "as the triumphator in procession to the temple" where he—not the Flavian emperor—makes the climactic sacrifice. The parallels Aitken suggests are intriguing, but ultimately her proposal suffers from a lack of concrete evidence in Hebrews itself. See Aitken, "Portraying the Temple in Stone and Text: The Arch of Titus and the Epistle to the Hebrews," in *Hebrews: Contemporary Methods, New Insights* (ed. G. Gelardini; BIS 75; Leiden: Brill, 2005), 131-48, esp. 142. Gabriella Gelardini, like Eisenbaum, dates Hebrews to the second century C.E., but she asserts that it is ancient synagogue homily on Exod 31:18-32:35 and Jer 31:31-34 (the *sidrah* and *haphtarah* traditionally associated with the Jewish fast day *Tisha be-Av*) addressed to Jewish slaves exiled to Rome after the second Jewish war. This fast day was associated in Jewish tradition with Israel's violation of the covenant and prohibition from entering Canaan but also (among other things) with the destruction of both Jerusalem temples and Hadrian's transformation of Jerusalem into *Aelia Capitolina*. The Exodus passage, however, is never cited directly in Hebrews, an odd feature is this indeed is the major text for the homily, nor does Gelardini address here the importance of Ps 110 for the author. See Gelardini, "Hebrews, An Ancient Synagogue Homily for *Tisha be-Av*: Its Function, Its Basis, Its Theological Interpretation, in *Hebrews: Contemporary Methods, New Insights* (ed. G. Gelardini; BIS 75; Leiden: Brill, 2005), 107-27. For a more detailed treatment, see her book

few scholars have argued (unpersuasively) that elements in the text demand a Gentile readership. Proposals that the recipients are a congregation of mixed ethnicity also find support.[13]

Ultimately, however, the ethnicity of the recipients is not a determinative factor for interpretation of the book. Views that assume that the author is urging his readers against Judaism are particularly problematic. Instead, the author's comments concern the recipients' fidelity to Christ; the problems addressed are not attraction to alternate teachings but rather the dangers of cessation of faith and disobedience. The author repeatedly warns against or chides the readers for laxity in their commitment to their confession (2:1-4; 3:7–4:13; 5:11–6:8; 10:26-39; 12:18-29), and he notes the failure of some to assemble together (10:25). No restoration is possible for those who abandon their faith (6:4-8), though the author is confident that his addressees have not yet met this dire fate (6:9-12). While persecution seems to be a factor in their wavering (10:32-34), the author notes that no one in the community he addresses has shed blood because of this (12:4).

Though some scholars attempt to date Hebrews quite specifically in the 60s C.E., chiefly in the context of Nero's persecutions, one scarcely can be more precise than to date the book to the last few decades of the first century C.E. As such, most propose a date between 60-100 C.E., with the upper range determined by use of the book in *1 Clement*.[14]

'Verhartet eure Herzen Nicht': Der Hebraer, eine Synagogenhomilie zu Tischa be-Aw (BIS 93; Leiden: Brill, 2007).

[13] Scholars who understand the recipients as primarily Jewish Christians tend to see a possible reversion to Judaism as the problem addressed by the author; those who think the recipients were Gentile Christians or a church of mixed background tend to see apathy or persecution as the problem. For a brief survey of options and identification of major proponents of each view, see Koester, *Hebrews*, 46-48.

[14] Attridge, *Hebrews*, 9. Similarly, Koester (*Hebrews*, 54) dates the book to 60-90 C.E. Lane is bolder, dating the book to 64-68 C.E., the interval between the great fire of Rome and Nero's suicide; see Lane, *Hebrews*, 1:lxvi. F. F. Bruce (*The Epistle to the Hebrews* [rev. ed.; NICNT; Grand Rapids: Eerdmans, 1990], 21) similarly argues for a date just before the outbreak of persecution in 65 C.E. while Barnabas Lindars (*The Theology of the Letter to the Hebrews* [NTT; Cambridge: Cambridge University Press, 1991], 21) supports 65-70 C.E. Ceslas Spicq (*L'Epître aux Hébreux* [2 vols.; Paris: Gabalda, 1952-53], 1:261) argues for 67 C.E., and Paul Ellingworth (*The Epistle to the Hebrews: A Commentary on the Greek Text* [NIGTC; Grand Rapids: Eerdmans, 1993], 33) sees reasons to date it just before either 64 or 70 C.E. David A. DeSilva (*Perseverance in Gratitude: A Socio-Rhetorical Commentary on the Epistle "to the Hebrews"* [Grand Rapids: Eerdmans, 2000], 20-21) is less specific but also prefers a date before 70 C.E. Weiss (*Hebräer,* 77) argues for a later date of 80-90 C.E., as does Mathias Rissi (*Die Theologie des Hebräerbriefs* [WUNT 41; Tübingen: Mohr, 1987],

One cannot even be confident about whether it was written before or after Rome's conquest of Jerusalem in 70 C.E. Attempts to date the book in light of the author's silence about the destruction of the Jewish temple falter because Hebrews' sacrificial discussions consistently address the tabernacle—admittedly sometimes with confusion about its physical arrangement (9:4)—rather than the temple. Similarly, while the author uses language implying a continuing sacrificial system, this too does not assist in dating; like this author, both rabbinic and patristic writers used similar language for centuries. Finally, such attempts are further complicated by the observation that the author seems to know the Jewish sacrificial system chiefly through exegesis, not first-hand experience.

While acknowledging that numerous questions remain, however, one can safely conclude than that the author—an articulate Christian fluent in Greek and the Septuagint, equally comfortable with Jewish exegetical and Greek rhetorical methods—is distressed by the spiritual condition of his friends. He writes to exhort them toward faithfulness to their Christian confession.

Despite—or perhaps because of—these many unanswered questions, Hebrews has not lacked its share of scholarly treatments and commentaries. In English alone three extensive commentaries on this epistle were published in major series between 1989 and 1993. Since they were in preparation at essentially the same time, these offer three largely independent analyses of the book. Two major commentaries incorporating social-scientific and rhetorical criticisms appeared about a decade later, followed shortly by another pair of highly-anticipated volumes.[15] Numerous important monographs on various issues related

13). For further discussion, see Helmut Feld, *Der Hebräerbrief* (EdF 228; Darmstadt: Wissenschaftliche Buchgesellschaft, 1985), 14-18; and Schnelle, *History,* 367-68.

[15] The former three are the aforementioned commentaries by Attridge (Hermeneia), Lane (Word), and Ellingworth (NIGTC). Though written more for the pastor than academician, the earlier commentary by Bruce (NICNT) was also revised during this period. The works by DeSilva (non-serial) and Koester (AB) followed, as did Luke Timothy Johnson, *Hebrews: A Commentary* (NTL; Louisville: Westminster John Knox, 2006); and Alan C. Mitchell, *Hebrews* (SP; Collegeville, Minn.: Liturgical, 2007). Shorter works appearing in recent years include R. McL. Wilson, *Hebrews* (NCB; Grand Rapids: Eerdmans, 1987); Donald A. Hagner, *Hebrews* (NIBC; Peabody, Mass.: Hendrickson, 1990), a revised version of a 1983 commentary in the defunct Good News Commentary series; Victor C. Pfitzner, *Hebrews* (ANTC; Nashville: Abingdon, 1997); Thomas G. Long, *Hebrews* (IBC; Louisville: Westminster John Knox, 1997); Fred B. Craddock, "The Letter to the Hebrews," in *The New Interpreter's Bible* (12 vols.; ed. L. Keck; Nashville: Abingdon, 1998), 12:1-

to Hebrews have also appeared in recent years, testifying to the increased recent interest in this epistle. New program units on Hebrews were added at the annual North American and international meetings of the Society of Biblical Literature, and in 2006 the University of St Andrews hosted an international conference on the book's significance for Christian theology.

Despite this renewed interest in the epistle, relatively little has been written in recent years about its key motif, Jesus as high priest, but this was not the case in previous decades. The centrality of this motif in Hebrews is obvious, but scholars lack a consensus about the currents of thought that influenced the author's conception of Jesus as the priestly messiah. The purpose of this study is to revisit this question, examining past arguments while drawing upon the fruits of decades of scholarship on Second Temple Judaism since the discovery of the Dead Sea Scrolls. The contention advanced here is that currents in Second Temple Judaism—particularly ideas evidenced in the Qumran texts—provide the best background for understanding the presentation of Jesus as priest in Hebrews.

The study unfolds as follows. The first chapter addresses Hebrews' presentation of Jesus, especially as high priest. Each passage in which this is the major subject is examined, and the chapter concludes with a synthesis of Hebrews' thought on the motif. The second chapter is a survey of previous proposals for understanding the conceptual background of Hebrews' priestly thought. The third and fourth chapters include analyses of eschatological or messianic priestly traditions and Melchizedek traditions, respectively, in Second Temple Judaism, with emphasis on texts found among the Dead Sea Scrolls. Finally, the fifth chapter concludes the study with the argument that messianic priestly and Melchizedek traditions at Qumran provide the best sources of shared thought with Hebrews' presentation of Jesus as priest.

173; George H. Guthrie, *Hebrews* (NIVAC; Grand Rapids: Zondervan, 1998); Robert P. Gordon, *Hebrews* (Readings: A New Biblical Commentary; Sheffield: Sheffield Academic, 2000; and Edgar McKnight in Edgar McKnight and Christopher Church, *Hebrews-James* (Smyth & Helwys Bible Commentary; Macon, Ga.: Smyth & Helwys, 2004), 1-320. Though not commentaries, one should also note Lindars, *Theology* (1991); Kenneth Schenck, *Understanding the Book of Hebrews: The Story Behind the Sermon* (Louisville: Westminster John Knox, 2003); and Andrew T. Lincoln, *Hebrews: A Guide* (London: T&T Clark, 2006). A new volume on Hebrews in the International Critical Commentary series has been announced as in preparation; it will replace James Moffatt, *The Epistle to the Hebrews* (ICC; Edinburgh: T & T Clark, 1924).

CHAPTER ONE

HEBREWS' PRESENTATION OF JESUS AS HIGH PRIEST

The author of Hebrews describes Jesus using numerous titles reflecting different roles or christological functions.[1] These include 'Christ'; 'Lord'; 'great shepherd'; 'apostle'; 'pioneer' or 'forerunner'; 'Son' and 'Son of God'; and 'priest' or 'high priest.' Four of these can be discussed briefly and set aside because the author sees no need to develop their implications.

Jesus is called 'Christ' (χριστός) twelve times in the book. Context might lead one to determine that χριστός in Heb 11:26 carries its literal weight as 'messiah' or 'anointed one.' Here Moses is described as having preferred the τόν ὀνειδισμὸν τοῦ χριστοῦ over the riches of Egypt because of his faith. The author correlates the shame of the crucifixion (12:3) with the scorn heaped on God's people; Moses chooses to experience this with his fellow Hebrews, and the recipients of Hebrews are urged in 13:13 to identify clearly with Jesus.[2] In eleven other cases, however, 'Christ' (three times the fuller designation 'Jesus Christ') seems to be used simply as a proper name. Nothing distinctive is to be found in Hebrews' usage of this.

In a similar manner, Jesus is called 'Lord' (κύριος) four times in the epistle.[3] Use of the term 'apostle' (ἀπόστολος) for Jesus in Heb 3:1 ('the apostle and high priest of our confession') is perhaps at first surprising, but the term here obviously is used in its more basic sense of 'messenger' or 'envoy,' not to denote the ecclesial office of

---

[1] Cf. the similar approach by Leopold Sabourin, *Priesthood: A Comparative Study* (SHR 25; Leiden: Brill, 1973), 206-12.

[2] So Johnson, *Hebrews*, 300-01. Johnson finds support for this correlation in Ps 88.

[3] Jesus as 'Lord': Heb 1:10; 2:3; 7:14; 'Lord Jesus': 13:20. In Heb 1:10, a quotation from Ps 101:26 LXX, naturally about God in the Psalter, is cast by the author of Hebrews as referring to Jesus. In several other cases in the epistle (eight certain: Heb 7:21; 8:2, 8, 9, 10, 11; 12:5, 6; three likely: 10:30; 12:14; 13:6), God is called 'Lord,' and many of these also occur in quotations of Scripture. The Holy Spirit is called 'Lord' in Heb 10:16, also a recast quotation of Scripture.

'apostle' as is normally the case elsewhere in the New Testament.[4] In this context, Jesus is presented as the plenipotentiary envoy, representing God with full divine authority.[5]

The appearance in Heb 13:20 of the term 'great shepherd' in the phrase 'the great shepherd of the sheep' (τὸν ποιμένα τῶν προβάτων τὸν μέγαν), so rich with allusions from the Hebrew Scriptures (e.g., Ezek 34, where God is the shepherd and also promises to send a good shepherd), is not stunning, though it appears somewhat unexpectedly since no other 'flock' language (except in sacrificial contexts) has yet been used in the epistle. It seems, however, to be drawn from a liturgical formula; its use in a blessing also invoking covenantal language suggests that the author is adorning his conclusion with traditional language.[6] However, τὸν ποιμένα τῶν προβάτων may be drawn intentionally from Isa 63:11 LXX. There God 'brought up' (ἀναβιβάσας) the shepherd (Moses) from the land to be the leader of Israel during the exodus; in Heb 13:20 God 'brought up' (ἀναγαγών; preferable to the NRSV's 'brought back') the shepherd (Jesus) from the dead, who elsewhere in the book is said to lead his people to salvation (see below). Furthermore, Isa 63:10 evokes Israel's disobedience in the wilderness, a theme also prominent in Hebrews.[7]

The two other roles—Jesus as 'Son,' and Jesus as 'pioneer' or 'forerunner'—need further elaboration before attention is turned to Hebrews' presentation of Jesus as priest. This is especially the case

---

[4] As the first definition, LSJ gives 'messenger, ambassador, envoy' ("ἀπόστολος," 220). Similarly, BDAG renders the most basic definition in the NT as 'delegate, envoy, messenger' ("ἀπόστολος," 122). The phrase 'the apostle and high priest of our confession' has typically been understood in one of two ways. One option is that the author of Hebrews is using the terms to evoke certain aspects of his discussion of Jesus in Heb 2 (esp. 2:12, 17). The other is that he is setting up a contrast between Jesus and both Moses (as one sent by God, based on use of the related verb ἀποστέλλω in Exod 3:10 LXX) and Aaron (the first high priest). Admittedly Aaron is not mentioned in the immediate context (though one might see him implied again in the quotes in Heb 3:7-11, which refer to Israel's disobedience during the Exodus period), but he is named in Heb 5:4. For these interpretative options, see Attridge, *Hebrews*, 107; Lane, *Hebrews*, 1:75-76; and Karl Rengstrof, "ἀπόστολος," *TDNT* 1:407-47. Koester (*Hebrews*, 243) connects the idea of Jesus as ἀπόστολος with his role as ἀρχηγός (see discussion below) on the basis of Num 13:2; Judg 5:15; and Neh 2:9 LXX.

[5] I am indebted to John Meier for this observation.

[6] See the discussion in Attridge, *Hebrews*, 406; and Ellingworth, *Hebrews*, 729.

[7] See Weiss, *Hebräer*, 754-57; and Lane, *Hebrews*, 2:561-62.

because these appellations for Jesus rarely appear in contexts divorced from discussion of Jesus as priest.

1. Jesus as 'Pioneer' or 'Forerunner'

The words ἀρχηγός, typically translated as 'pioneer' or 'author,' and πρόδρομος, usually rendered as 'forerunner,' are relatively rare terms in the New Testament. The former occurs only four times in the NT (Acts 3:15; 5:31; Heb 2:10; 12:2), the latter only in Hebrews (6:20). Both denote the idea of Jesus going before his people and bringing salvation.

In Heb 2:10, Jesus is referred to as 'τὸν ἀρχηγόν of our salvation,' and in Heb 12:2 he is called 'the ἀρχηγόν and perfecter of faith.' Interpreters are divided as to the precise understanding of ἀρχηγός in Hebrews, though they commonly assert that ancient Greek myths of descent, such as those of Heracles and Orpheus, lie behind this imagery.[8] BDAG lists three possible meanings for ἀρχηγός: (1) "one who has a preeminent position, *leader, ruler, prince*;" (2) "*one who begins someth[ing] that is first in a series*" ('instigator' if with a negative connotation); and (3) "one who begins or originates," an 'originator' or 'founder.' The third meaning is preferred for both instances in Hebrews, and LSJ offers a similar opinion.[9] The NRSV and Koester translate the term as 'pioneer' in both occurrences in Hebrews, while Lane prefers 'champion' in both cases.[10] In addition, some commentators, such as Spicq, Weiss, and Attridge, prefer to stress different nuances of the term in its two uses in Hebrews. The French scholar Spicq translates it as 'chef' in Heb 2:10 (making it explicit in his commentary that this is "la moins mauvaise traduction"

---

[8] See, for example, Wilfred L. Knox, "The 'Divine Hero' Christology in the New Testament," *HTR* 41 (1948): 229-49, esp. 245-47; and more recently David E. Aune, "Heracles and Christ: Heracles Imagery in the Christology of Early Christianity," in *Greeks, Romans, and Christians: Essays in Honor of Abraham J. Malherbe* (ed. D. L. Balch, E. Ferguson, and W. A. Meeks; Minneapolis, Fortress, 1990), 3-19, esp. 13-19. See also Attridge (*Hebrews*, 79-82) for a discussion of the Greek origins of this idea and its adaptation by Jewish writers as well as a refutation of suggestions of a Gnostic background to this language.

[9] BDAG 138-39. See also the reference to MM 81, which supports the conclusion in BDAG. Likewise, LSJ 252 offers three definitions: (1) founder; (2) prince, chief, chief captain, leader; and (3) first cause, originator; preferring the last for Heb 2:10.

[10] Koester, *Hebrews*, 228, 523; and Lane, *Hebrews*, 1:56; 2:411.

and combines "les trois idées d'initiateur, prince et guide") but as 'guide' in Heb 12:2.[11] Similarly, Weiss renders it as 'Anführer' in Heb 2:10, stressing Jesus' role as leader, and 'Anfänger' in Heb 12:2, stressing his role as initiator, though here he also offers the former as an alternate translation.[12] Attridge, too, varies his translation of the term, using the clause 'the one who leads the way' in 2:10 but the simpler translation 'initiator' in 12:2.[13]

Detailed discussion of the appearance of this term in Heb 2:10 follows below, as it appears in conjunction with a discussion of Jesus as priest. A priestly theme does not appear when ἀρχηγός is used in Heb 12:2, after the lengthy discussion of prior exemplars of faith in Heb 11. However, it does appear with a discussion of Jesus' suffering and exaltation, themes also prominent when the term is used in Heb 2.

Πρόδρομος is used only once in the NT and is rare in the LXX.[14] In its substantival use, BDAG defines it as 'forerunner,' a translation reflected in the NRSV and generally accepted by commentators.[15] In Heb 6:20 Jesus is called 'a πρόδρομος for us' who has entered the heavenly Holy of Holies as 'a high priest forever according to the order of Melchizedek.' This appears in the context of a discussion in Heb 6:13-20 about the certainty of God's promises; the inviolability of God's oath inspires hope in believers.

These two terms are used by the author of Hebrews to make a significant christological statement in the epistle. Though the precise nuances intended by the author of Hebrews in his use of the former term remain debatable, it is clear that a key characteristic of Jesus in Hebrews is that he leads out or goes before his people. This concept is also seen elsewhere in the epistle, even in the absence of use of these particular terms, especially in passages in which Jesus is described as

---

[11] Spicq, *Hébreux,* 2:39. He rejects ideas that Jesus is the initiator of faith in Heb 12:2 because Heb 11 has shown that many in Israel had faith before Jesus' manifestation (2:386).

[12] Weiss, *Hebräer*, 202, 631.

[13] Attridge, *Hebrews*, 87-88, 356.

[14] Πρόδρομος refers to agricultural first fruits in Num 13:20, Isa 28:4, and Hos 9:10 (Aq., Sm., Th.), a usage not unknown in classical texts, but in Wis 12:8 it has the military connotations most prevalent in its classical usage (see LSJ 1475), referring to God's 'wasps' which served as 'forerunners' of Israel's army during the conquest, and battle imagery is also prominent in Ezek 26:9 Aq.

[15] BDAG 867; Attridge, *Hebrews*, 178; Lane, *Hebrews*, 1:147; Spicq, *Hébreux*, 2:165 ('précurseur'); Koester, *Hebrews*, 330; and Weiss, *Hebräer*, 358 ('Vorläufer'). See also Otto Bauernfeind, "πρόδρομος," *TDNT* 8:235.

high priest.[16] Attridge asserts that the author of Hebrews has received from his tradition the presentation of Jesus' incarnation and redemption in this mythical form but modifies it in light of his presentation of Jesus as high priest.[17] Similarly, Aune argues that "many of the important and vital functions attributed to Heracles as a Hellenistic savior figure were understood by some early Christians as applicable to Jesus."[18] It is clear that these presentations are intertwined, as will be seen more fully below.

2. Jesus as 'Son' and 'Son of God'

Jesus is discussed as 'Son' (υἱός) in seven passages in Hebrews, which should not be surprising given the traditional nature of this confession.[19] Of these, three times (Heb 6:6; 7:3; and 10:29) he is further identified as 'the Son of God' in contexts where this designation is not the primary subject of discussion. Use of the phrase 'Son of God' is far from random in these passages, however, as in each case use of this term heightens the rhetoric of the author or subtly expresses

---

[16] Examples of this motif include Heb 9:12 ('he entered once for all into the Holy Place . . . attaining eternal redemption') and Heb 10:19-20 ('having boldness for entrance into the sanctuary because of the blood of Jesus, a new and living way which he opened for us through the veil').

[17] "Hebrews is hardly being innovative in using a traditional myth of incarnation and redemption. . . . It is rather a part of his tradition, which he goes on to reinterpret and actualize in his priestly christology" (Attridge, *Hebrews*, 82).

[18] Aune, "Heracles," 19.

[19] Certainly this designation is early as it is prominent in the earliest datable Christian written sources, the epistles of Paul. For example, in the undisputed Pauline epistles Jesus is referred to as υἱός (in context, clearly God's Son) in 1 Thess 1:10; Gal 1:16; 4:4, 6; 1Cor 1:9; 15:28; Rom 1:3, 9; 5:10; 8:3, 29, 32; and specifically as υἱὸς (τοῦ) θεοῦ in Gal 2:20; 2 Cor 1:19; and Rom 1:4. Some of these, including Rom 1:3; 8:3; 1 Thess 1:10; and Gal 4:4, 6, are often understood as appearing in older, pre-Pauline formulations. See Jarl Fossum, "Son of God," *ABD* 6:128-37; and Larry W. Hurtado, "Son of God," *DPL* 900-06 (esp. 902). Some scholars sense a discrepancy in Hebrews about when Jesus becomes 'Son.' Some passages seem to imply that Jesus is the preexistent Son (Heb 1:3) while others may suggest that this status (as well as his priesthood) is granted only at the conclusion of his earthly life (Heb 1:4-5; 2:9; 5:5; 6:20; 7:28). See Aune, "Heracles and Christ," 14; Martin Hengel, *The Cross of the Son of God* (trans. J. Bowden; Philadelphia: Fortress, 1976), 86-88; John Knox, *The Humanity and Divinity of Christ* (Cambridge: Cambridge University Press, 1967), 34-49; and James D. G. Dunn, *Christology in the Making: A New Testament Inquiry into the Origins of the Doctrine of the Incarnation* (2nd ed; Grand Rapids: Eerdmans, 1989), 51-56.

Jesus' superiority over an inferior entity. In Heb 6:6 the term climaxes a discussion of the horrors of apostasy. The use in Heb 7:3 is powerful yet playful, occurring just after one reads that Melchizedek, lacking a father, mother, or genealogy, nevertheless resembles a son, the Son of God no less. Likewise, in Heb 7:28 a contrast is offered—the law appoints high priests 'subject to weakness,' but God's oath appoints a Son who has been made perfect (through suffering; cf. Heb 5:8-9). In Heb 10:29, the punishment for spurning the Son of God is compared (or perhaps more accurately, contrasted) to that of breaking the law of Moses in an argument utilizing the *qal wa-ḥomer* technique. In 3:1-6, his status as son *over* God's house makes him superior to Moses, who was faithful *in* God's house.[20]

Most important in regard to Hebrews' presentation of Jesus as priest, however, are Heb 1:1-14 and 4:14-5:10, both of which closely associate Jesus' status as priest with his status as Son. These passages receive significant attention below because of their importance for understanding Hebrews' presentation of Jesus as priest.

3. Jesus as 'Priest' and 'High Priest'

Having surveyed other christological roles of Jesus in Hebrews, attention now turns for the remainder of the chapter to Hebrews' central theme, the presentation of Jesus as priest. Though many have seen priestly overtones in the portrayal of Jesus in other New Testament books, especially the gospel of John, only in Hebrews is Jesus explicitly called 'priest' or 'high priest.'[21] The remainder of this chapter is devoted to examining the key passages in which Jesus is discussed as priest or as having priestly functions.

[20] One might object to examination of Heb 3:1-6 under the motif of Jesus as 'Son' since the argument there is clearly conducted in the realm of figurative language. In light of the great stress the author places at the beginning of the book on Jesus as 'Son of God,' however, it would seem extremely unlikely that he would later discuss Jesus as son without intending to relate it to his previous discussion.

[21] Theories linking Hebrews and John are discussed in the next chapter.

3.1. *Hebrews 1:1-14*

The first hint of Jesus' role as priest, a mention of his cultic activity, appears in the opening sentence of the book, the elegant period that comprises Heb 1:1-4. Here the author's primary focus is on the Son, who is shown in the broader context of 1:1-14 to be superior to the angels.

In Heb 1:1-2, God's revelation of the 'Son' in recent days is contrasted to previous revelations. This is the first of numerous passages in which the author compares Jesus with some figure from the Hebrew Scriptures. This pattern, which effectively advances the author's overall agenda of presenting Jesus as high priest, nevertheless is striking because of the theological backdrop on which it functions—elsewhere (as especially seen in Heb 11-12) the approach of the author is to find continuity in God's actions and the faith of God's people, whether persons of the Hebrew Scriptures or followers of Jesus. Also, it must be noted that while the author contrasts God's various acts of revelation in this passage, these acts ultimately are in continuity because they share a common source. Nevertheless, the author does intend to highlight God's revelation through the Son by contrasting this with previous revelations in a number of ways:

a. the recipients of God's revelation differ; God addressed the 'ancestors' through the prophets, but he has spoken through the Son to 'us';

b. the time frames are contrasted, with the revelation through the prophets occurring 'long ago,' whereas that through the Son has occurred in the 'last days,' a phrase evocative of the eschatological 'Day of the Lord' so prominent in the Hebrew Scriptures;

c. the language and tone used to described God's revelation through the Son imply finality, whereas the revelation through the prophets is described with the incomplete and incremental connotations of 'many parts and ways';

d. the status of the messengers is subtly contrasted, as the status as 'Son' implies greater prestige than even that of noble figures such as 'prophets'; this anticipates the numerous comparisons in the book of Jesus with the institutions of Judaism.[22]

---

[22] See Attridge, *Hebrews*, 37, for a discussion of the author's use of the adverbs πολυμερῶς and πολυτρόπως in Heb 1:1.

One might also notice here the author's preference for 'one' instead of 'many,' a motif prominent later in the book in the comparison of the priesthoods of Jesus and the Levitical order.[23] This tendency also reflects a preference common in Platonism. As Luke Timothy Johnson notes, "In Platonism the choice between the one and the many is always resolved in favor of the one."[24]

As 'Son,' Jesus is described in subsequent verses as:

a. 'heir of all things' (Heb 1:2), an identification not surprising given his Sonship, but also very significant because of what follows in Heb 2:5-14, where it recurs in an interpretation of Ps 8:5-7 LXX;[25]

b. 'through whom also he [God] made the world' (Heb 1:2), a motif strongly reminiscent of descriptions of Wisdom's role in creation in Jewish wisdom literature (for example, Wis 9:9, 'With you is wisdom, she who knows your works and was present when you made the world');[26]

c. 'being the reflection [or radiance] of [God's] glory and the representation of [God's] essence' (Heb 1:3), again drawing on language from the Jewish wisdom tradition (Wis 7:26, 'For she is a reflection of eternal light, a spotless mirror of the working of God, and an image of his goodness') and perhaps as well from Philo's discussion of the Logos;[27]

---

[23] Elsewhere the author emphasizes the 'once for all' nature of Jesus' sacrifice, which may be connected with the once per year occasion of the Day of Atonement sacrifice. On the latter, see Stökl Ben Ezra, *Impact of Yom Kippur*, 181.

[24] Johnson, *Hebrews*, 65.

[25] In the more immediate context, many interpreters have noticed a relationship between the statements about the Son in Heb 1:1-4 and the litany of Scripture quotations in 1:5-14. Thus this statement about the Son as heir would be related to Heb 1:13, a quotation of Ps 110:1 (LXX 109:1). For a discussion of the compositional structure of Heb 1:1-14, see John P. Meier, "Structure and Theology in Heb 1,1-14," *Bib* 66 (1985): 168-89; and "Symmetry and Theology in the Old Testament Citations of Heb 1,5-14," *Bib* 66 (1985): 504-33. For a syntactical defense of the view that exactly seven affirmations are made about Jesus in Heb 1:1-4, see Meier, "Structure," 171-76. See further discussion of Meier's approach below.

[26] See Attridge, *Hebrews*, 40-41; and Lane, *Hebrews*, 1:12. Cf. Ellingworth, *Hebrews*, 96, who lists numerous intermediaries connected with creation in Jewish and Gnostic literature. The verb has been translated here as 'made' rather than 'created' in order to maintain consistency with use of ποιέω below in 1:3.

[27] Interpreters are divided as to whether ἀπαύγασμα denotes 'radiance' or 'reflection' in both Heb 1:3 and Wis 7:26, the only uses of the word in the NT and LXX, respectively. See Attridge, *Hebrews*, 42-44; Lane, *Hebrews*, 1:12-13; and Ellingworth, *Hebrews*, 98-99. Koester (*Hebrews*, 179-80) prefers the active sense of 'radiance' and astutely notes that "the text does not deal primarily with God's relationship *to* the Son, but with the way God communicates *through* the Son." However, 'reflection' also

d. 'sustaining all things by his powerful word' (Heb 1:3), a natural correlative to the Son's role in creation and a task often ascribed to Wisdom and the Logos in Second Temple Jewish literature;[28]

e. 'having in himself made purification for sins' (Heb 1:3), an activity unparalleled in discussions of Wisdom or of the Logos in Philo, yet the first of the many intimations of Jesus as priest in the epistle;[29]

f. 'he sat down at the right hand of the Majesty on high' (Heb 1:3), an allusion to Ps 110 (109 LXX):1, a vitally important psalm for this author;[30] and

g. 'having become as much superior to the angels as the name he had inherited is more excellent than theirs,' an affirmation of the exalted nature of Jesus as Son. This statement also forms the transition, both thematically and grammatically, from the period to the following series of proof texts which stress the Son's superiority over the angels while also reflecting the themes of the previous six statements.

---

seems appropriate because the Son's status is described vis-à-vis his relationship to God, something especially stressed in the second part of this phrase. One is left to decide if this phrase should be understood as making synonymous (so 'reflection') or complementary (thus 'radiance,' expressing a different, more active nuance than 'representation') assertions about the Son.

[28] Attridge, *Hebrews*, 45; and Lane, *Hebrews*, 1:14. See Ellingworth, *Hebrews*, 100-01; and Koester, *Hebrews*, 181, for surveys of options for interpreting φέρω. The translation of the participial form φέρων above is preferable to NRSV's 'he sustains,' which obscures the relationship of the clause with the sentence's finite verb.

[29] The translation 'having in himself made' is an attempt to convey the middle voice of the aorist participle of ποιέω. A similar attempt seems to explain the variant readings of this phrase in very early manuscripts (including P^{46}), such as insertions of δι' ἑαυτοῦ (or αὑτοῦ) to explicate the middle voice or the possessive pronoun ἡμῶν to clarify whose sins Jesus atones. See Bruce M. Metzger, *A Textual Commentary on the Greek New Testament* (2nd ed.; Stuttgart: Deutsche Bibelgesellschaft, 1994), 592. As for the priestly motif, one might argue that this is taken up again in Heb 1:9, where the quotation from Ps 45:8 (LXX 44:8; EV 45:7) mentions anointing, an action associated with the investiture of priests. However, kings (1 Sam 10:1; 16:3; 1 Kgs 1:39; 2 Kgs 9:6; 11:12) also were anointed (as a prophet could be, 1 Kgs 19:16), and the original context of the psalm seems to be royal. While it is certainly true that the author of Hebrews feels free to use quotations of Scripture in ways that do not accord with their original contexts (as evidenced in his habit of recasting statements about God or a Davidic king so that they instead speak of the Son in Heb 1:5-14), here clear evidence for a priestly connotation is lacking, nor would its presence add much of significance to the discussion. Indeed, the last phrase of the quotation, indicating that the anointed has so been honored 'beyond your companions' (παρὰ τοὺς μετόχους σου), is perhaps the part of the quotation most significant for the author of Hebrews (Lane, *Hebrews*, 1:30; cf. Attridge, *Hebrews*, 60).

[30] Attridge, *Hebrews*, 46. For simplicity, in most subsequent references this chapter will be identified only as Ps 110.

Of chief significance for this study are the statements in the second half of Heb 1:3, where one reads that 'having in himself made purification for sins, he sat down at the right hand of the Majesty on high' (καθαρισμὸν τῶν ἁμαρτιῶν ποιησάμενος ἐκάθισεν ἐν δεξιᾷ τῆς μεγαλωσύνης ἐν ὑψηλοῖς). The Greek term used for 'purification,' καθαρισμός, is used only twice in the NT in reference to Jesus' atoning work, here and in 2 Pet 1:9, though it is used in other NT contexts for various types of cleansings: in the Synoptics in discussions about purifications involving leprosy (Mark 1:44; Luke 5:14) and childbirth (Luke 2:22); in John in a description of the water jars at Cana (2:6) and as a subject of debate between a Jew and disciples of John the Baptist (3:25). The term, which has strong cultic overtones, is used 19 times in the LXX and may translate words from five different Hebrew roots, including כפר.[31] Notable among the LXX uses of the term is its appearance in Exod 30:10 in the discussion of the Day of Atonement ceremony. Use here is particularly relevant for the author of Hebrews, who frequently alludes to this context; he understands Jesus as both the Day of Atonement sacrifice and the high priest administering it.[32]

Also significant is that Jesus' priestly act of purification is connected with his glorification as Son 'at the right hand of the Majesty on high.' As noted above, an allusion to the (royal) Ps 110:1 lies behind this assertion of Jesus' heavenly session: 'The LORD says to my lord, "Sit at my right hand until I make your enemies your footstool."' This is confirmed a few verses later in Heb 1:13, where Ps 110:1 is quoted explicitly. Of course, v. 4 of this same psalm in the LXX has a priestly motif: 'The LORD has sworn and will not change his mind, "You are a priest forever, according to the order of Melchizedek."' One finds in the discussion of purification of sins in Heb 1:3 only the faintest reflection of the 'priest according to the order of Melchizedek' language of Ps 110:4. Nevertheless a connection is warranted, because

[31] It is used in the LXX to translate אָשָׁם, טְהָר/טָהֳרָה, כִּפֻּרִים, נָקָה (D), and עָבַר (H). Nine times it is used in the LXX in texts for which there is no Semitic parallel.

[32] Attridge, *Hebrews*, 46, esp. n. 132; Friedrich Hauck, "καθαρισμός," *TDNT* 3:429-30; and "καθαρισμός," LSJ 850. The term is a later form of καθαρμός, which is much more common in both the LXX and the NT.

the author of Hebrews explicitly quotes this verse three times later in the book and bases his identification of Jesus as priest on it.[33]

After the seven statements made about the Son in Heb 1:1-4, seven quotations of Hebrew Scripture follow in the catena of Heb 1:5-14. John Meier argues that both the seven Christological designations of Heb 1:1-4 and the seven Scripture citations of Heb 1:5-14 express a general movement in theme, which he calls a 'ring-structure.' While denying a strict one-to-one relationship between the designations and citations, he nevertheless sees a common movement, graphically illustrated as counter-clockwise, from exaltation to creation, eternal pre-existence, creation/conservation of the world, purification of sins (in the designations only), creation, exaltation/enthronement, and the result of exaltation (superiority over angels, which is not expressed by a citation but rather by the author's comment in Heb 1:14 that follows the final citation).[34] Meier's observation is significant in that he recognizes that the author of Hebrews uses the first and seventh quotations to prove Jesus' exaltation. These two crucial quotations are of Ps 2:7 and Ps 110:1 (Ps 109:1 LXX). Note the words of Meier:

> The seventh and final citation brings us full circle. Having started with the naming of Christ as Son at his enthronement, as described in Ps 2,7 (Heb 1,5bc), we conclude with the Son's enthronement/exaltation as described in Ps 109,1. The two royal Davidic psalms of enthronement frame the whole catena. This inclusion is underlined by the fact that the seventh citation, like the first, begins with the rhetorical question: "For to which of the angels did he [God the Father] ever say...?" As we have seen, Ps 109,1 supplies the starting point of our author's theological reflection. By connecting Ps 109,1 with Ps 109,4 and by drawing out the implications, he grounds his basic thesis: the exalted Son (Ps 109,1) is the eternal priest like Melchizedek (Ps 109,4).[35]

The significance for this study is that in the mind of the author of Hebrews, Ps 2:7 and Ps 110:1 both speak of the Son and thus are to be interpreted together. This exegetical move sets the stage for Heb 4:14-5:10, where the author explains how Jesus, the royal Son, can also be a

[33] See the similar assertion of David M. Hay, *Glory at the Right Hand: Psalm 110 in Early Christianity* (SBLMS 18; Nashville: Abingdon, 1973), 143. The decree of Ps 110:4 is quoted in Heb 5:6 and 7:17, 21 (the last quotation cuts off before Melchizedek is mentioned). Melchizedek is discussed below in much more detail.

[34] Meier, "Symmetry," 529, in the conclusions section which draws together observations from both articles in this series, "Structure" and "Symmetry."

[35] Meier, "Symmetry," 519. Note that Meier uses chapter numbers from the LXX.

priest. The themes of Heb 4:14-5:10 also are anticipated by the presentation of Jesus' solidarity with humanity in Heb 2:5-18, to which discussion now turns.

3.2. *Hebrews 2:5-18*

Jesus' incarnation and solidarity with humanity are the major themes in Heb 2:5-18. However, it is also appropriate to recognize that the theme of the Son's superiority over the angels may also be resumed here with significant priestly discussion. Psalm 8:4-6 (5-7 LXX) receives christological interpretation whereby the Son's incarnation, temporary humiliation below the angels, solidarity with humanity through suffering, and subsequent exaltation are affirmed. Jesus is not explicitly called 'Son' here, though the Hebrew idiom 'son of man' is retained in Ps 8:5 LXX; perhaps that 'son' language influenced the author of Hebrews to understand the psalm as speaking of Jesus.[36]

Familial language is very strong in Heb 2:11-18. Jesus is not ashamed to call humans 'brothers' in Heb 2:11, and the quotation of parts of Isa 8:17-18 in Heb 2:13 shows that the author of Hebrews is thinking of Jesus as 'Son' in this discussion. In the original context of Isa 8:18, the prophet Isaiah is the speaker and he makes reference to his physical children. However, while precisely quoting the LXX, the author of Hebrews recasts the quotation in such a way that the words appear to be on Jesus' lips and 'the children' now are God's (spiritual) children. This kinship motif is further clarified in the discussion that resumes in Heb 2:14-18. Jesus shares human characteristics with the 'children' (2:14), and he has to become like his 'brothers' in every way (2:17-18).[37] More importantly, the theme of Jesus' (i.e., the Son's) superiority over the angels gets significant attention:

---

[36] As discussed below, some interpreters do not see Jesus discussed in the passage until Heb 2:9. Regardless, no 'Son of Man' Christology like that present in the Synoptic Gospels should be expected here. Instead, the 'Son' language from the previous chapter is in view.

[37] Against the interpretation presented above, Lane insists that the children of Heb 2:13 are to be understood as Jesus' children but admits the difficulty of his reading: "Although the concept of the people of God as τὰ παιδία, 'the children,' of the exalted Son is not found elsewhere in the NT, the image of the family suggests an intimacy of relationship and a tenderness that broadens the concept of solidarity" (*Hebrews*, 1:60). For an interpretation similar to that espoused above and references to other commentators, see Attridge, *Hebrews*, 91, especially n. 139.

a. Heb 2:5–'For [God] did not subject the coming world, about which we are speaking, to angels';

b. Heb 2:7, 9–'You made him for a little while lower than the angels . . . we do see Jesus, who for a little had been made lower than the angels'; and

c. Heb 2:16–'Obviously he is not helping angels, but he is helping descendants of Abraham.'

How the author of Hebrews read the quotation from Ps 8 has been understood in two primary ways. Ultimately assessments of his approach hinge on exegetical decisions about three issues in the passage: whom the author finds implied in the missing contrasting phrase (as an alternative to angels, i.e., the person[s] to whom God subjected the coming world) of Heb 2:5; the identification of the ἄνθρωπος and υἱὸς ἀνθρώπου of Heb 2:6 (in a quotation of Ps 8:4 [5 LXX]); and the antecedent of αὐτός in Heb 2:7-8 who was temporarily made lower than the angels and to whom all things were originally subjected.

Some interpreters see the quotation as speaking of humanity in general, which would seem to be the intent of the psalmist, with a subsequent shift to discussion of Jesus in Heb 2:9, whereas others argue that the author of Hebrews read the quotation prophetically as referring to Jesus.[38] The quotation is best interpreted as intentionally ambiguous: it is applied to Jesus but intended to evoke its original application to humanity in general in order to stress Jesus' solidarity with humanity.[39] Certainly the passage overall has that purpose, and the author's major point becomes clear in Heb 2:9—Jesus, now exalted, suffered on behalf of the faithful.[40]

This theme is continued in Heb 2:10-18, where one encounters the term ἀρχηγός. Jesus, 'pioneer of their salvation,' was made perfect through suffering, and this suffering also taught him empathy for his

---

[38] The latter interpretation, preferred here, is defended by Weiss (*Hebräer*, 191-202), Spicq (*Hébreux*, 2:30-32), Attridge (*Hebrews*, 69-77), and Ellingworth (*Hebrews*, 143-52). For the former view (reflected in the NRSV's translation), see Wilson, *Hebrews*, 50-52. Dunn argues that the passage reflects an Adam Christology; Jesus becomes incarnate and then receives the exaltation which was part of God's original intention for humanity. See Dunn, *Christology*, 109.

[39] Cf. the similar interpretations of Lane, *Hebrews*, 1:41-50; and Koester, *Hebrews*, 214-17.

[40] See Kevin McCruden, "Christ's Perfection in Hebrews: Divine Beneficence as an Exegetical Key to Hebrews 2:10," *BR* 47 (2002): 40-62, esp. 42-49, for a treatment that differs from the present study on the approach to the quotation of Ps 8 yet ultimately finds a very similar thrust in the broader passage.

people so that he could be 'a merciful and faithful high priest' and make atonement for them. In this context, Jesus is described as 'having been crowned with glory and honor because of the suffering of death' after having been 'for a little . . . made lower than the angels' (Heb 2:9, a striking comment in light of the emphasis in Heb 1:5-14 on the Son's superiority over angels) and having endured suffering in order to bring salvation to the faithful. These sufferings make Jesus 'perfect' (τελειῶσαι; 2:10) and enable him to relate to humans (2:11b-13), defeat the devil in his death (thereby freeing those enslaved by the fear of death; 2:14-15), and become 'a merciful and faithful high priest' who could make a sacrifice of atonement (2:17-18). Here it is stressed that suffering influences the *nature* of his priesthood.[41] Hebrews' presentation of Jesus as ἀρχηγός seems appropriate, as suffering is also an important part of Heracles mythology.[42] Thus Jesus, as ἀρχηγός of his people, suffers, and it is this suffering which is crucial to his role as priest, in which he delivers his people to salvation (2:13-15).

The priestly motif is overt in Heb 2:5-18, and for the first time Jesus explicitly is called 'high priest' in Heb 2:17. However, other priestly language is evident in Heb 2:11 with a statement which further stresses the appropriateness of Jesus' empathy with God's people. Here the NRSV renders (with significant paraphrase) ὁ τε γὰρ ἁγιάζων καὶ οἱ ἁγιαζόμενοι ἐξ ἑνὸς πάντες as: 'For the one who sanctifies and those who are sanctified all have one Father.'[43] The precise meaning of the final phrase ἐξ ἑνὸς πάντες, literally 'all from [or 'out of'] one,' is elusive. The 'one' is not defined explicitly, and suggestions include God, humanity, Adam, and Abraham.[44] Nevertheless the argument of Heb 2:10-13, where Scripture quotations are cast as statements of

[41] Perhaps this suffering includes trials associated with Jesus' incarnation, especially his passion. This is the interpretation of Ellingworth, *Hebrews*, 158. He also notes that Ps 22:22 is quoted in Heb 2:12, implying that this connection with Jesus' passion is strengthened because Mark 15:34 and Matt 27:46 record Jesus' quotation of Ps 22:1 from the cross. Similar questions arise with Heb 5:7. See Attridge, *Hebrews*, 148-50.

[42] Aune, "Heracles and Christ," 16; similarly Lane, *Hebrews*, 2:56-57.

[43] The verb ἁγιάζω is the term normally used in the LXX to translate verbs from the קדשׁ root and refers to a cultic state. The term is used several times in Hebrews (2:11; 9:13; 10:10, 14, 29; 13:12) to refer to Jesus' self-sacrificial activity in passages that clearly relate the concepts of atonement and sanctification. See Otto Procksch, "ἁγιάζω," *TDNT* 1:111-12.

[44] Koester, *Hebrews*, 229-30.

Jesus, makes it clear that it is an affirmation of the solidarity between Jesus and God's children based on a common origin, God.[45] Perhaps one might also see in Heb 2:11 an attempt to give a logical (in the mind of the author) explanation for why 'it was fitting' (ἔπρεπεν; Heb 2:10) that God qualify Jesus for his mission by means of suffering. In Heb 2:10, God is called the one 'for whom and through whom all things exist,' and God perfects Jesus through sufferings. Jesus, 'the one who sanctifies,' and the people 'who are being sanctified,' have testing and suffering in common (see 2:14-18, esp. 2:18) as well as a common origin (ἐξ ἑνὸς πάντες). Thus, because Jesus has this unity with the people, it was fitting that he suffer like them; by his sufferings he would be made perfect so that he might make them perfect.[46]

---

[45] One can sense the difficulty of translating ἐξ ἑνὸς πάντες by comparing the interpretative renderings in the NRSV ('all have one Father') and NIV ('of the same family'). Commentators display a similar variety of translations, variously seeing the common origin in God or some human ancestor, yet uniformly agree that stress is placed on the solidarity of Jesus and the people. See Attridge, *Hebrews*, 88-89; Lane, *Hebrews*, 1:58; Koester, *Hebrews*, 229-30; and Spicq, *Hébreux*, 2:40-41.

[46] The author of Hebrews seems to be playing on different meanings of the verb τελειόω in Heb 2:10. Here he uses it in reference to the purpose of Jesus' sufferings, thus it must have a meaning like that proposed by Attridge of "a vocational process by which he is made complete or fit for his office" (*Hebrews*, 86). Gerhard Delling ("τελειόω," *TDNT* 8:83) understands the term in Heb 2:10 in the sense of 'qualify.' BDAG ("τελειόω," 996) gives two options for the term in Heb 2:10. The first is "to overcome or supplant an imperfect state of things by one that is free fr[om] objection, *bring to an end, bring to its goal/accomplishment*;" the second is "consecrate, initiate." Neither of these definitions from BDAG seems totally satisfactory, though perhaps the first is to be favored with the understanding that Hebrews sees Jesus' sufferings as preparation for his service of priesthood, not as a correction of or atonement for his moral failures. Though the author of Hebrews does not specifically use the term τελειόω in this context in reference to the people of God, it does seem that he is playing on its multiple meanings. Jesus is made perfect by God, and God brings 'many sons to glory' (following Attridge, *Hebrews*, 83: "a heavenly and eschatological condition") in Heb 2:10 though him; in Heb 2:11 Jesus sanctifies (ἁγιάζων) and they are sanctified (ἁγιαζόμενοι). Numerous times in the epistle one reads that the law and Israel's sacrificial system could not perfect the people (Heb 7:19; 9:9; 10:1; cf. 7:11), but Jesus accomplishes this with his self-sacrifice (Heb 10:14; 11:40; cf. 12:2, 23). This is best seen at Heb 10:14, where the two key terms from Heb 2:10-11 are neatly brought together: 'For by a single offering he has perfected (τετελείωκεν) for all time those who are being sanctified (ἁγιαζομένους).' For a similar understanding of 'perfection' as that articulated above, see David Peterson, *Hebrews and Perfection: An Examination of the Concept of Perfection in the Epistle to the Hebrews* (SNTSMS 47; Cambridge: Cambridge University Press, 1982), 49-73.

3.3. *Hebrews 4:14-5:10*

As mentioned above in discussion of Heb 1:1-14, the author of Hebrews explains how Jesus the Son can also be Jesus the priest in Heb 4:14-5:10. In fact, high priestly designations form an *inclusio* to the passage.

Because Jesus is 'a great high priest who has passed through the heavens,' the recipients are to be emboldened in their 'confession' (4:14), which they had at some earlier time professed.[47] Jesus is a sympathetic high priest who has remained sinless despite testing (4:15), allowing his followers 'to approach the throne of grace with boldness' (4:16), presumably in their prayers.[48]

Yet again this discussion began on the assumption that Jesus is a high priest, though this is not formally demonstrated (and even then not completely explained) until the appearance of the quotations of Ps 2:7 and Ps 110:4 in Heb 5:5-6, which emphasize that Jesus holds his priestly office by God's appointment. First, however, in Heb 5:1-4 the author explains that a high priest mediates between the people and God with sacrifices; he expounds on this with three criteria for the high priest:

a. he is able to be gentle with the 'ignorant and wayward' (NRSV) because he himself is subject to weakness (Heb 5:2);

b. he must offer sacrifice for his own sins and for those of the people (Heb 5:3); and

c. he takes office by the call of God, not on his own initiative (Heb 5:4).

The author then proceeds in a chiastic manner in Heb 5:5-10 to show how Jesus meets these three criteria. In Heb 5:5-6, the author shows that God installed Jesus as high priest—thus fulfilling the third criterion—by appealing to statements of divine oath in Scripture. The author previously had read Ps 2:7 and Ps 110:1 together in Heb 1:5-14.

---

[47] The phrase 'passed through the heavens' (διεληλυθότα τοὺς οὐρανούς) likely is a reference to Jesus' exaltation, though the idea of Jesus' movement, especially in the inner sanctuary, is quite important in Hebrews. See Attridge, *Hebrews*, 139; Lane, *Hebrews*, 1:103; Aune, "Heracles and Christ," 18; Michel, *Der Brief*, 204-7; and Herbert Braun, *An die Hebräer* (HNT 14; Tübingen: Mohr, 1984), 124.

[48] Lane (*Hebrews*, 1:115-16), sees a reference to prayer in Heb 4:16 as does Attridge, though the latter (Attridge, *Hebrews*, 141) is more cautious about restricting this reference to only one particular activity: "'Approaching' God is used as a more encompassing image for entering into a covenantal relationship with God."

He now returns to Ps 2:7, interpreted in Hebrews as a statement addressed to the Son, and reads with it Ps 110:4, here understood as bestowing a priesthood on the figure addressed in Ps 110:1 and Ps 2:7.[49] Though only the words of God in Ps 110:4 are quoted, omitting the narrative remarks found in the psalm, the author of Hebrews can construe this statement as a divine appointment because it clearly is God's eternal oath in its original context. The concluding line of the passage in Heb 5:10, which serves in part to build anticipation of the fuller discussion of Jesus' relationship with Melchizedek, repeats the theme introduced here.

The second criterion is presented as fulfilled in Heb 5:9, where one reads that Jesus himself becomes 'the source of eternal salvation for all who obey him,' i.e., he offers the sacrifice of himself. As is stressed later in the book, no sacrifice need be made on his own behalf, clearly distinguishing Jesus from Levitical priests.[50]

Finally, the first criterion is affirmed for Jesus in Heb 5:8-9. Jesus is said to have learned obedience through his sufferings, echoing the assertion in Heb 4:15 (and foreshadowed in Heb 2:5-18) about the significance of his experience of the human plight. This experience has prepared him to be sympathetic toward the people, and in this way he has 'been made perfect,' or prepared, for his role of priestly intercession. Admittedly this interpretation of τελειόω in 5:9 differs from that preferred in BDAG ("this is usu[ally] understood to mean the completion and perfection of Jesus by the overcoming of earthly limitations").[51] Context demands, however, a different interpretation. As Attridge notes, "It is, at least in part, vocational, referring to the

---

[49] Another connection between these verses possibly utilized by ancient exegetes is suggested by James C. VanderKam, "Sabbatical Chronologies in the Dead Sea Scrolls and Related Literature," in *The Dead Sea Scrolls In Their Historical Context* (ed. T. H. Lim; Edinburgh: T&T Clark, 2000), 159-78, esp. 174. VanderKam (following David Flusser and James Kugel) notes that the LXX renders the Hebrew יַלְדֻתֶיךָ ('your youth') of Ps 110:3 as ἐξεγέννησά σε ('I have begotten you'). This provides a possible connection to Ps 2:7 since there one finds similar language in the LXX (γεγέννηκά σε).

[50] Some scholars understand the statement in Heb 5:7 that Jesus had 'offered up prayers and supplications, with loud cries and tears' as the functional equivalent of the sacrifices Levitical priests made for their own sins (5:3), but the ideas are not parallel. Nor, for that matter, is it clear what the author of Hebrews alludes to in this statement. See Attridge, *Hebrews*, 148-52.

[51] BDAG 996, meaning 2a.

adaptation of Christ for his intercessory offices through his educative suffering."[52]

A very important aspect of this passage is that the author finally provides exegetical support for his identification of Jesus as priest—Jesus is priest because God appointed him to the office. God also prepared him through his suffering to be the sympathetic mediator who would offer himself for the atonement of the people. Because the author describes Jesus in light of the Day of Atonement sacrifice (and does so more explicitly later in the book), Jesus must be the *high* priest, even though Melchizedek is only called a priest in Ps 110:4. (Admittedly, however, presence of the divine oath in Ps 110:4 would also imply appointment to the apex of priesthood.) The high priestly imagery also is evident in 6:19-20, where Jesus is said to have entered the Holy of Holies as a 'forerunner' (πρόδρομος) on behalf of his followers.

3.4. *Hebrews 7*

The author of Hebrews goes to great lengths to explain Jesus' role as heavenly high priest in light of Melchizedek's priesthood. Earlier in the book the author offers tantalizing hints of their relationship by commenting three times (5:6; 5:10; 6:20) that Jesus is priest 'according to the order of Melchizedek'—or even high priest, thanks to the prominence of Day of Atonement imagery in Hebrews—and, as discussed above, he lays the exegetical groundwork for this correlation by reading Ps 2:7; Ps 110:1; and Ps 110:4 together in Heb 1:5-14 and 5:5-6. It is not until Heb 7:1-10, however, that the author finally explains this relationship, then he promptly drops Melchizedek from further discussion after 7:15. Though this occurs only about midway through the 13-chapter book, the author apparently is convinced that Melchizedek has served his purpose, and he does not mention him again in the final six chapters of the book.

The author of Hebrews makes several surprising comments about Melchizedek in Heb 7:1-10, particularly in Heb 7:3.[53] The passage

[52] Attridge, *Hebrews*, 153. See also Peterson, *Hebrews and Perfection*, 96-103.

[53] These issues are addressed in Eric F. Mason, "Hebrews 7:3 and the Relationship between Melchizedek and Jesus," *BR* 50 (2005): 41-62, from which much of the current section is taken.

commonly is identified as a midrash; the Melchizedek of Ps 110:4 is already in view, and now the additional passage of Gen 14:18-20 is evoked to allow further discussion.[54] While retelling the Genesis account of the encounter between Melchizedek and Abraham, the author of Hebrews confuses certain parts of the story or else adds details absent from Genesis but paralleled elsewhere in Second Temple Jewish discussions of the encounter.[55]

The author of Hebrews grounds his discussion of Melchizedek in the account from Gen 14 about the figure's encounter with Abram, but he refers to the patriarch anachronistically as Ἀβραάμ, or Abraham, matching the Septuagint's spelling in subsequent chapters of this changed name.[56] In Heb 7:1, one reads that Melchizedek met Abraham as he was returning from war and blessed him. However, in Gen 14:17, it was the king of Sodom who went out to meet Abraham. One easily excuses the author of Hebrews for this minor error. In his defense, in Gen 14 Abraham does indeed encounter Melchizedek at some unspecified place, a blessing is pronounced, and a tithe is paid. The awkward nature of the Genesis account, in which the king of Sodom went

[54] See, for example, Lane, *Hebrews*, 1:158; and Ellingworth, *Hebrews*, 350.

[55] Particular parallels with aspects of other Second Temple interpretations are noted here, but the various Second Temple Jewish texts that mention Melchizedek are discussed much more systematically below in chapter 3.

[56] This is common in accounts of this meeting by writers in the Second Temple period, as evidenced by the similar habits of Pseudo-Eupolemus (Ἀβραάμ) and Josephus (Ἄβραμος). Philo does not call the patriarch by name in his accounts of the encounter with Melchizedek, but his normal practice is to use Ἀβραάμ. On the other hand, the authors of *Jubilees* and the *Genesis Apocryphon* preserve versions of the earlier name Abram for their retellings of this meeting. It should be noted that most extant Ethiopic manuscripts of *Jubilees* lack mention of Melchizedek and have a lacuna at 13:25 where his encounter with Abram is expected. Context, though, makes it clear that such once stood in the text, and a few minor manuscripts of *Jubilees* do have some remaining mention of the figure, even if only in marginal notes. It has sometimes been argued that that mention of Melchizedek was suppressed in the scribal tradition; for discussion of this view, see Richard Longenecker, "The Melchizedek Argument of Hebrews: A Study in the Development and Circumstantial Expression of New Testament Thought," in *Unity and Diversity in New Testament Theology: Essays in Honor of George E. Ladd* (ed. R. A. Guelich; Grand Rapids: Eerdmans, 1978), 161-85, esp. 164-65; followed by Lane, *Hebrews*, 1:160; a similar theory is implied by James L. Kugel, *Traditions of the Bible: A Guide to the Bible as It Was at the Start of the Common Era* (Cambridge, Mass.: Harvard University Press, 1998), 293. On the other hand, James VanderKam, editor of the most recent critical edition of the Ethiopic *Jubilees*, argues instead that haplography occurred in the Hebrew textual tradition of Jubilees that predated its translation into Ethiopic. See James C. VanderKam, *The Book of Jubilees* (2 vols.; CSCO 510-11; Scriptores Aethiopici 87-88; Louvain: Peeters, 1989), 1:82; 2:81-82.

out to meet Abram but Melchizedek instead encounters him first, prompted multiple explanations in the Second Temple period. The author of the *Genesis Apocryphon*, for example, sought to smooth over the disjuncture, perhaps even implying that the two kings rendezvoused first and then traveled together to meet Abraham (1QapGen ar XXII 13-14).[57]

As for the tithe, the Hebrew of Gen 14:20 actually is ambiguous about who pays whom, though most readers no doubt assume that priests are on the receiving end of tithes. The author of Hebrews, like Josephus (*Ant.* 1.181), Philo (*Congr.* 99), the author of the *Genesis Apocryphon* (1QapGen ar XXII 17), and numerous modern Bible translation committees (including those of the NRSV, NIV, and NAB), confidently asserts that Abraham pays the tithe, though Pseudo-Eupolemus (Eusebius, *Praep. ev.* 9.17.6) may preserve an alternate tradition.[58] Perhaps surprisingly, especially in light of Hebrews' emphasis on the discontinuity between the priesthood of Melchizedek and the later Levitical line, Philo and the author of *Jubilees* (13:25) use this passage to support the practice of tithing in the Levitical system, though Philo as expected allegorizes the tithe.

Melchizedek is identified in Gen 14:18 as priest of אֵל עֶלְיוֹן, and his own name literally means 'my king is Sedek.' Though assimilated into the Pentateuch as a priest of Abram's God Most High, modern scholars uniformly understand him originally as a character in the service of a Canaanite deity, either Sedek or El 'Elyon.[59] Most Second Temple period interpreters of Melchizedek followed this biblical example of assimilating Melchizedek into the priesthood of Abraham's God. Josephus (*J.W.* 6.428) and likely also Philo (*Congr.* 99) understood him to be God's first priest, and Josephus, who explicitly remarks that Melchizedek was Canaanite, nevertheless credited him—and not Solomon—as having constructed the first Temple devoted to the

---

[57] Admittedly the author does not explicitly state that the two kings traveled together, but the king of Sodom is said to travel to Salem, home of Melchizedek, and both kings subsequently encounter Abram, who was camped in the Valley of Shaveh. Michael C. Astour, "Shaveh, Valley of," *ABD* 5:1168, notes that several ancient writers located this valley near Jerusalem.

[58] Pseudo-Eupolemus states that παρὰ δὲ τοῦ Μελχισεδὲκ . . . λαβεῖν δῶρα, but the identification of these 'gifts' and their possible correlation with elements of Gen 14:18-20 are uncertain. Among major modern Bible translations, the editors of the NJPS are most cautious, printing the name of Abram as payee in brackets.

[59] See, for example, Claus Westermann, *Genesis 12-36* (CC; Minneapolis: Fortress, 1995), 203-04.

Hebrew God in Jerusalem. In book 6 of the *Jewish War*, Josephus dates the destruction of the Temple by the Babylonians as occurring 1468 years and six months after its foundation, which obviously connects it to Melchizedek rather than Solomon, especially since the time since David's reign is specified as 477 years and six months (*J.W.* 6.437-39). Hebrews alone contrasts the priesthoods of Melchizedek and the Levites.

Not content simply to identify Melchizedek by his vocations, the author of Hebrews offers etymological interpretations of the mysterious figure's name and royal title in Heb 7:2. Thus the name 'Melchizedek' is said to mean 'king of righteousness,' and as king of Salem he is 'king of peace.' These popular etymologies are similar to those of Philo (*Leg.* 3.79) and Josephus (*Ant.* 1.180), for whom Melchizedek means 'righteous king,' and as in Hebrews, Philo (*Leg.* 3.79) also sees the figure as 'king of peace.' Though not addressed by the author of Hebrews, the identity of the city of Salem was a common topic of discussion in the Second Temple period. Reference has already been made above to interpretations that credit this king of Salem as establishing the first Temple in Jerusalem. A close reading of Genesis in both the MT and LXX, however, could imply that Salem was Shechem.[60] Also, Pseudo-Eupolemus, a writer often thought to have Samaritan leanings, identified Salem with Mt. Gerizim (Eusebius, *Praep. ev.* 9.17.5).

In Heb 7:3 the author of Hebrews makes grand assertions about Melchizedek that are absent from Gen 14—he is eternal and 'remains a priest forever.' The language of Heb 7:3 is striking, and the Greek is exquisite. Attridge finds in this single verse an "elaborate rhetorical flourish, marked by isocolon, asyndeton, alliteration, assonance, and chiasm."[61] The elevated nature of Heb 7:3 has prompted numerous scholars to propose that the author of Hebrews has appropriated and redacted a pre-existing hymn, whether originally to Melchizedek himself or to Christ. As with so many hymn theories, however, the reconstructions vary widely, as do theories of what in Hebrews is indebted to the source. Some scholars would propose an underlying hymn stretching back to Heb 7:1 and as deep into the chapter as 7:26, while others find such borrowed language only in 7:3. Though such

[60] See discussion of this issue in chapter 4 below.
[61] Attridge, *Hebrews*, 189.

theories can still be found, they have fewer adherents today.[62] The sophisticated Greek style displayed by this author elsewhere in Hebrews—such as the 72-word, π-alliterated period in Heb 1:1-4—implies that he certainly was capable of composing the language in Heb 7.[63] Another troublesome point for such reconstructions is that relative pronouns, typically a marker of hymnic quotations, are absent from Heb 7:3, though a few participles are prominent.

The more important question for most contemporary interpreters concerns exactly what is being affirmed about Melchizedek in Heb 7:3. In other words, what does it mean that he lacks parentage, a genealogy, and both temporal origin and terminus? Clearly the *ultimate* purpose of this language for the author of Hebrews is to describe the Son of God by extension, yet the words here are presented as pertaining to Melchizedek. Many interpreters assert that the author seems to have based these assertions on the silence about Melchizedek's origins and death in Gen 14 along with the statement that the honoree of Ps 110:4 is a 'priest *forever* according to the order of Melchizedek,' with the assumption that the latter must also be eternal.[64] However, one should also note that Second Temple Jewish writers could come to conclusions that elevated Melchizedek's importance without citing Ps 110:4; Josephus reckoned Melchizedek as the first priest mentioned in Scripture, and Philo considered him 'self-taught.'[65]

Two major approaches are common today, each also finding a different biblical precedent for this stunning language. Fred Horton, author of the very influential volume *The Melchizedek Tradition*, is a major spokesman for the view that the author of Hebrews understood Melchizedek as a mere mortal priest.[66] Horton notes that numerous interpreters have argued that the affirmations about Melchizedek in Heb 7:3 were derived from the ancient Jewish interpretative principle *quod non in thora non in mundo*, that what is not specified in the

[62] For a recent survey of proposals for an underlying hymn, see Ellingworth, *Hebrews*, 352-53.

[63] On the period, see Aune, "Hebrews, Letter to the," 212.

[64] For example, Attridge, *Hebrews*, 190; Lane, *Hebrews*, 1:166; and Koester, *Hebrews*, 348.

[65] Josephus, *J.W.* 6.438; Philo, *Cong.* 99.

[66] Fred L. Horton, Jr., *The Melchizedek Tradition: A Critical Examination of the Sources to the Fifth Century A.D. and in the Epistle to the Hebrews* (SNTSMS 30; Cambridge: Cambridge University Press, 1976). Horton's views are generally followed in Lane, *Hebrews*.

biblical text does not exist. Most interpreters have then argued that the author of Hebrews declares Melchizedek to be without parentage, genealogy, beginning or end, etc., because no data for any of these things can be found in Genesis, hence the silence there actually speaks loudly. Horton rejects this particular exegetical move, noting that numerous figures appear in Scripture without such information being discussed yet are not regarded as otherworldly.[67] Instead, Horton uses this ancient Jewish interpretative assumption from silence in a slightly different way. Horton notes, as seen above, that both Josephus and Philo seem to derive the idea that Melchizedek was the first priest of God from the silence about any prior priests in Genesis. Horton then asserts that the author of Hebrews has done a similar thing, so the issue in Heb 7:3 is the lack of a *priestly genealogy*, not a lack of ordinary human ancestry.[68] The exalted language of this verse is in reference to Melchizedek's priestly office only and says nothing about his ontology.

So, then, for Horton, Melchizedek's priesthood is a model for understanding Jesus' priesthood because both lack the expected priestly, Levitical genealogy. Nothing implies anything other than a mortal existence for Melchizedek. The phrase 'without genealogy' can *only* mean the lack of a *priestly* genealogy. This for Horton is clear because Jesus is said to share that quality with Melchizedek, yet just a few verses later Jesus is identified by the author of Hebrews as a descendent of the tribe of Judah (7:14).[69] Jesus is not a *successor* to Melchizedek; instead "every feature of significance in Melchizedek's priesthood is recapitulated on a grander scale in Christ's priesthood."[70]

A very different approach to these verses results in the idea that the author of Hebrews was indeed talking about Melchizedek's ontology in Heb 7:3 and thus considered him to be a heavenly figure, perhaps even angelic. Such arguments have appeared in various forms, including versions presented in a classic mid-1960s article by Marinus de

---

[67] Horton, *Melchizedek Tradition*, 153-54.
[68] Horton, *Melchizedek Tradition*, 156-60.
[69] Horton, *Melchizedek Tradition*, 162-63.
[70] Horton, *Melchizedek Tradition*, 161.

Jonge and Adam S. van der Woude and more recently in Attridge's commentary.[71]

Paul Kobelski also takes up this position and opposes Horton's interpretation head-on.[72] Unlike Horton, he accepts the theory—albeit in a restrained form—that traditional hymnic language about Melchizedek has been appropriated by the author of Hebrews.[73] More significantly, Kobelski flatly rejects Horton's interpretation that Heb 7:3 addresses only Melchizedek's lack of priestly credentials. Whereas Horton asserted that both Josephus and Philo understood Melchizedek as the first priest based on the silence of Scripture about any predecessors—and thus the author of Hebrews likely did the same—Kobelski argues that Horton has misread Philo, who is more concerned with allegorical notions of Melchizedek's perfection than his supposed status as the original priest.[74] Instead of basing his interpretation of Heb 7:3 on any variant of an argument from the silence of Gen 14, Kobelski links Hebrews' talk of Melchizedek's mysterious qualities with Ps 110:4.[75] Thus the divine oath directed to the Son, 'you are a priest forever, according to the order of Melchizedek,' must also mean that Melchizedek himself is eternal.[76] In doing so, Kobelski takes a position similar to that earlier articulated by Joseph Fitzmyer, who proposed that since the author of Hebrews knows that Jesus is of the tribe of Judah (Heb 7:14) and thus has a human genealogy, the real comparison in Heb 7 must be that both have "a life which cannot end."[77] Kobelski adds that speculation on an otherworldly Melchizedek in the Second Temple period confirms and even contributes to Hebrews' thought, which already is saturated by Ps 110:4; this understanding of an eternal Melchizedek is supported internally by the statement in Heb 7:8 that Melchizedek is 'one of whom it is testified that he lives.'[78]

---

[71] M. de Jonge and A. S. van der Woude, "11Q Melchizedek and the New Testament," *NTS* 12 (1965-66): 301-26; Attridge, *Hebrews*, 192-95. The work of de Jonge and van der Woude is discussed further in chapter 4.

[72] Paul J. Kobelski, *Melchizedek and Melchireša'* (CBQMS 10; Washington: Catholic Biblical Association of America, 1981).

[73] Kobelski, *Melchizedek*, 120.

[74] Kobelski, *Melchizedek*, 116-17.

[75] Kobelski, *Melchizedek*, 123.

[76] Kobelski, *Melchizedek*, 126.

[77] Joseph A. Fitzmyer, "'Now This Melchizedek . . .' (Heb 7:1)," in *The Semitic Background of the New Testament* (Grand Rapids: Eerdmans, 1997), 221-43, esp. 238.

[78] Kobelski, *Melchizedek*, 123.

Kobelski finds himself walking the tightrope of appealing to extrabiblical traditions of a heavenly Melchizedek while rejecting the idea that the author of Hebrews drew upon particular texts like 11QMelchizedek, a Dead Sea Scroll that presents Melchizedek as an angelic, eschatological warrior figure.[79] Attridge takes a similar position, stating,

> It seems likely, then, that [the author of Hebrews'] exposition of Gen 14 is not simply an application to the figure of the Old Testament of attributes proper to Christ, but is based upon contemporary speculation about the figure of Melchizedek as a divine or heavenly being. While lack of parentage, genealogy, and temporal limits are predicated of Melchizedek to evoke the character of the true High Priest, they are qualities probably applicable to the ancient priest as the author knew him.[80]

Attridge is content to survey a variety of speculative treatments of Melchizedek—from Philo's allegorical and psychological interpretations to Qumran to *2 Enoch* to manifold rabbinic, patristic, and Gnostic treatments of the figure—without identifying *the* tradition most likely shared with Hebrews. Koester goes even further and flatly rejects *all* notions that Hebrews reflects extrabiblical traditions about Melchizedek, allowing only that Hebrews uses for Melchizedek language that would affirm true divinity in Greco-Roman contexts.[81]

This issue strikes at the heart of this study, and naturally it is addressed more fully below. For now a few observations will suffice. In light of the language used to describe Melchizedek, it seems difficult to escape the impression that the author of Hebrews construes him as more than a mere historical person. Admittedly he is never called an angel in Hebrews—something that might have been problematic in light of the argument of Heb 1-2—but he is described in language that implies a heavenly status. While not denying the presence of a Jewish argument from silence, Jerome Neyrey notes that the author of Hebrews describes Melchizedek with language portraying him as a Greco-Roman deity, though the author's real intent is to describe Jesus. This is done by describing Melchizedek according to

[79] Kobelski, *Melchizedek*, 127.
[80] Attridge, *Hebrews*, 191-92.
[81] Koester, *Hebrews*, 341. On the issue of the language implying divinity, Koester follows Neyrey, "Without Beginning."

standard Greco-Roman *topoi* for deity—ungenerated, uncreated in the past and imperishable in the future, and eternal or immortal.[82]

Note that while the previous description of Jesus in Hebrews would seem to make it obvious, Jesus never *explicitly* is said to be greater than Melchizedek, though this may be implied in Heb 7:3. Instead, the author states that Melchizedek 'was made to resemble the Son of God' (Heb 7:3), and later he says that Jesus 'resembles Melchizedek' (Heb 7:15). Exalting Jesus by associating him with this exalted figure is the point. Oddly, however, this is achieved here in a way different from that normally utilized by the author. Usually he uses the method of *synkrisis*, or comparison.[83] Forms of the Greek term translated 'better,' κρείσσον, appear 13 times in this book (including three occurrences later in Heb 7), compared to only six occurrences in the rest of the New Testament.[84] Here, however, the author of Hebrews exploits the mysterious nature of Melchizedek in order to exalt Jesus.

In Heb 7:4-10 the author develops his assertion that Melchizedek's priesthood is greater than that of the Levitical priests. He does this with a novel interpretation of Melchizedek's encounter with Abraham,

---

[82] Neyrey, "Without Beginning," 439-55. For further discussion of Hebrews' source for this language, see Kobelski, *Melchizedek and Melchireša'*, 120; and Attridge, *Hebrews,* 191-92.

[83] The method is at least as old as Aristotle, who when discussing use of the encomium as a form of epideictic rhetoric commends the use of comparisons of the subject of the praise with other esteemed and worthy persons. If the subject can be shown to surpass others of renown, then his own reputation is therefore amplified (see *Rhet.* 1.9.38/1368a). Perhaps even more relevant to Hebrews is the fact that comparison was a standard rhetorical skill taught in the *progymnasmata*, or basic handbooks used for rhetorical education in the Greco-Roman world. The earliest extant *progymnasmata* date to the first and second centuries C.E., those of Aelius Theon of Alexandria (late first-early second century C.E.) and Hermogenes of Tarsus (late second century C.E.). Christopher Forbes argues that other sources attest to the use of such texts clearly by the first century B.C.E. and perhaps as early as the third century B.C.E. Someone with the sophisticated Greek skills displayed in the book of Hebrews almost certainly would have enjoyed this sort of literary training. For further discussion of comparison, see David E. Aune, "Comparison," *WDNT* 110. On *progymnasmata*, see Ronald F. Hock, "General Introduction to Volume I," *The Chreia in Ancient Rhetoric: Volume I. The Progymnasmata* (ed. R. F. Hock and E. N. O'Neil; SBLTT 27; Graeco-Roman Religion Series 9; Atlanta: Scholars Press, 1986), 3-60; and Christopher Forbes, "Comparison, Self-praise and Irony: Paul's Boasting and the Conventions of Hellenistic Rhetoric," *NTS* 32 (1986): 1-30. See further Timothy W. Seid, "Synkrisis in Hebrews 7: The Rhetorical Structure and Strategy," in *The Rhetorical Interpretation of Scripture: Essays from the 1996 Malibu Conference* (ed. S. E. Porter and D. L. Stamps; JSNTSup 180; Sheffield: Sheffield, 1999), 322-47.

[84] Heb 1:4; 6:9; 7:7, 19, 22; 8:6 [twice]; 9:23; 10:34; 11:16, 35, 40; and 12:24; elsewhere used in 1 Cor 7:9, 38; 11:17; Phil 1:23; 1 Pet 3:17; and 2 Pet 2:21.

reading it in a way that is unprecedented in other extant treatments of their meeting. As noted above, some Second Temple period interpreters saw continuity between the tithes received by Melchizedek and the Levitical priests, but here those tithes are contrasted. Whereas the latter receive tithes from descendents of Abraham, Melchizedek received tithes from Abraham himself and blessed the patriarch. Citing proverbial wisdom that only the greater can bless the lesser and contrasting the living Melchizedek with the mortal Levitical priests, the author of Hebrews infers that Melchizedek is superior to Abraham—and thus he also is superior to Abraham's priestly descendents, who are reckoned as still being in Abraham's loins numerous generations before their appearance. The exegetical move is clever and bold. As Attridge notes concerning Heb 7:9, "The author seems to admit the artificiality of his playful exegesis with his qualifying remark, 'so to speak' (ὡς ἔπος εἰπεῖν), a common literary phrase outside the New Testament."[85] This evaluation of the author's creativity seems more likely that Lindars' assertion that the author of Hebrews is claiming only "to put things in a nutshell."[86]

Obviously the major concern here is to demonstrate the superiority of Melchizedek's priesthood over that of the Levites, the traditional Jewish priestly tribe. Spicq summarized Melchizedek's "quadruple supériorité" over the Levitical priesthood in this manner: (1) he received the tithe; (2) he blessed Abraham; (3) he was the type for a priest who does not die; and (4) he received homage from the Levites' ancestor.[87]

The author's primary critique of the Levitical priesthood is asserted in Heb 7:11—it and the law under which it served could not bring perfection. Thus a new priesthood and a corresponding new law are necessary (7:12). Jesus, as a descendant of Judah, does not fit the proper priestly paradigm of Levitical descent (7:14). Instead, he resembles Melchizedek, who has a priesthood which is not based on genealogy or a legal requirement but rather 'through the power of an indestructible life' (7:16). Unlike the Levitical priests, Jesus takes office with an oath pronounced by God in Ps 110:4, thus he is the guarantor of a better covenant (Heb 7:17-22). Furthermore, Jesus' priesthood is

---

[85] Attridge, *Hebrews*, 197.
[86] Lindars, *Theology*, 76.
[87] Spicq, *Hébreux*, 2:179-80.

shown to be superior to the Levitical system because the latter are mortal; Levitical priests keep dying, but Jesus has a permanent priesthood because he continues forever and eternally makes intercession for believers. Jesus also has no need to make sacrifices day after day for himself and for the people because he did it once for all when he offered himself (7:22-27). The passage concludes in 7:28 with a contrast between Levitical high priests, who are appointed by law and subject to weakness, and the Son, who is appointed as high priest by God's oath and who 'has been made perfect forever.' Again stress is laid on the fact that the Son was appointed priest because of these characteristics of the Levitical system.

3.5. *Hebrews 8-10*

Discussion of Jesus' role as both high priest and sacrificial offering in the Day of Atonement sacrifice takes center stage in Heb 8-10. The author, having justified Jesus' position in an alternative line of priests, no longer has need to discuss Melchizedek. Nevertheless, these chapters build on the major assertions made about Jesus in Heb 7. Though not of the Levitical family, Jesus is priest and mediator of a better covenant which was instituted because of the inadequacies of the old one (Heb 8:4-13; 9:15). He offered himself as the sacrifice to remove the sins of the people (Heb 9:12, 14; cf. 10:10, 22), and his self-sacrifice need occur only once yet has eternal effectiveness (Heb 9:11-14, 25-28; 10:10-14). As stressed in earlier chapters, Jesus is the heavenly priest now seated beside God (Heb 8:1-2; 9:24; 10:12-13).

As seen earlier, Jesus' sufferings occur on earth, and by them he is prepared for his priestly service (Heb 2:17; 5:7-10). He enters the heavenly sanctuary bearing his own blood for the atonement of the sins of his people (Heb 9:12, 25-26). Later Jesus' death is referred to as suffering 'outside the gate' (Heb 13:12). It seems to be no great stretch to understand Jesus' crucifixion as a component of his self-sacrifice, an event in the earthly realm which allowed his entrance into the heavenly sanctuary bearing his blood (see below). Indeed, the major new theme in Heb 8-10 is the discussion of *where* Jesus performs his priestly duties.

The author of Hebrews is working out of a conceptual framework in which the earthly sanctuary is modeled after the heavenly one. Support for this understanding of the relationship between the heavenly and earthly sanctuaries is drawn from various statements by the author of Hebrews. In Heb 8:5, Levitical priests serve in a sanctuary that is a 'sketchy shadow' (ὑποδείγμα καὶ σκιά) of the heavenly sanctuary since Moses was commanded to make it according to the 'pattern' (τύπος) Yahweh showed him (cf. Exod 25:40).[88] In Heb 9:23-24, the earthly sanctuary is a 'copy' (ἀντίτυπος) of the heavenly sanctuary, and its implements are 'sketches of the heavenly things.' On three occasions the author compares the heavenly and earthly sanctuaries, reminding the reader that the former, unlike the latter, is neither made by human hands (χειροποίητος; Heb 9:11, 24) nor set up by a human (Heb 8:2).

The background of the author's thought about the two sanctuaries has been much debated. Many scholars have noted the presence of Platonic vocabulary in this passage and its similarity to Platonic ontology; others have argued that the vocabulary familiar from Platonism is used differently by the author of Hebrews, that the correspondence between earthly and heavenly sanctuaries is already present in the Hebrew Scriptures, and that Hebrews is ultimately concerned more with eschatology than ontology.[89] Gregory Sterling offers a

---

[88] The phrase ὑποδείγμα καὶ σκια is best read as a hendiadys, preferable to the translations 'sketch and shadow' (NRSV) and 'copy and shadow' (NAB; NIV). The translation above follows Gregory E. Sterling, "Ontology Versus Eschatology: Tensions Between Author and Community in Hebrews," *SPhilo* 13 (2001): 190-211, esp. 194. Cf. 'shadowy copy' in Attridge, *Hebrews*, 219; 'shadowy suggestion' in Lane, *Hebrews*, 1:199, 201.

[89] Aelred Cody (*Heavenly Sanctuary and Liturgy in the Epistle to the Hebrews* [St. Meinrad, Ind.: Grail, 1960], 9-46) has demonstrated that a correspondence between heavenly and earthly sanctuaries is rather common among ancient Semitic peoples and is developed in various forms in several Second Temple Jewish texts. See also an excursus on the topic in Attridge, *Hebrews*, 222-24. Spicq argued that Hebrews' use of terminology common in the writings of Philo indicated the latter's influence on the author of Hebrews (see next chapter for further discussion of Spicq's view). However, C. K. Barrett countered that the author of Hebrews envisions the heavenly sanctuary in terms much more akin to Jewish apocalypticism than the Platonism of Philo of Alexandria, as Hebrews places great emphasis on Jesus' eschatological act in this heavenly sanctuary at a particular, epoch-changing time. See his "The Eschatology of the Epistle to the Hebrews," in *The Background of the New Testament and Its Eschatology* (ed. W. D. Davies and D. Daube; Cambridge: Cambridge University Press, 1956), 363-93. George W. MacRae took a very different approach and argued that the author and recipients have divergent understandings of the heavenly sanctuary, both of which are reflected in the book. The author, steeped in Platonism and emphasizing faith as the means of gaining insight into heavenly things, views the world as the outer court(s) of the temple and heaven as the Most Holy Place. The

helpful *via media*; he affirms Platonic influences on Hebrews' spatial description of the two sanctuaries, evidenced by the shared vocabulary and appeal to common biblical texts attractive to other Platonizing interpreters of Scripture, but notes that the temporal dimension of Hebrews' treatment of the sanctuaries is indebted to eschatological concerns.[90]

While it is stated that the earthly sanctuary is a copy of the heavenly sanctuary and thus inferior and passing away, the author says very little about the nature of the heavenly sanctuary other than that it is constructed by God and that Jesus has entered its inner veil to make atonement. As indicated above, however, several passages correlate Jesus' entrance into the sanctuary with his session, i.e. he takes his place beside God (sitting, implying completion) having performing his priestly task, which might imply that the heavenly sanctuary and the divine throne room are synonymous.[91] One certainly gets this impression from Isa 6:1-13, Isaiah's vision in which he sees God enthroned in the heavenly temple and a seraph touches his lips with a burning coal from the altar.[92] While one must be careful not to assume too much from Hebrews' relative silence, this would compare favorably to descriptions of the highest level of heaven (of either three or seven

---

recipients, who hold an apocalyptic view and stress their hope in the age to come, understand the earthly sanctuary as a copy of the heavenly one. See MacRae, "Heavenly Temple and Eschatology in the Letter to the Hebrews," *Semeia* 12 (1978): 179-99. Sterling reverses the commitments, understanding the author as the one with eschatological concerns and the recipients as the Platonizing party. See Sterling, "Ontology," 210.

[90] Sterling, "Ontology," 208-11.

[91] See Heb 1:3; 8:1-2; 10:12.

[92] Admittedly Hebrews never mentions the temple but instead discusses the tabernacle, perhaps in keeping with its journey metaphor that associated the wilderness experience of Israel with life of faith in Heb 3:7-4:13 and emphasis on the Day of Atonement ritual described in Lev 16 with reference to that portable shrine. (Much less certain are theories that seek to link Hebrews' avoidance of discussing the Jerusalem temple and the date of authorship of the epistle.) On the other hand, Craig Koester makes a sharp distinction between heavenly tabernacle and temple traditions, as does Sterling to a lesser extent. See Craig R. Koester, *The Dwelling of God: The Tabernacle in the Old Testament, Intertestamental Jewish Literature, and the New Testament* (CBQMS 2; Washington, D.C.: Catholic Biblical Association, 1989), 173; and Sterling, "Ontology," 206. Whether such a distinction must be maintained for comparative purposes is debatable. See, for example, Wis 9:8, in which Solomon is said to evoke the heavenly tabernacle as the model for his Jerusalem temple: "You have given command to build a temple (ναός) on your holy mountain, and an altar in the city of your habitation, a copy of the holy tent (μίμημα σκηνῆς ἁγίας) that you prepared from the beginning."

levels) in numerous Second Temple Jewish texts, where God dwells and receives worship from an angelic priesthood.[93] Consider, for example, *T. Levi* 3:4-6 and 5:1:

> For in the highest of all dwells the Great Glory in the holy of holies far beyond all holiness. In the (heaven) next to it there are the angels of the presence of the Lord, those who minister and make propitiation to the Lord for all the sins of ignorance of the righteous, and they offer to the Lord a pleasing odour, a reasonable and bloodless offering. . . . And the angel opened to me the gates of heaven, and I saw the holy temple and the Most High upon a throne of glory.[94]

In light of the information Hebrews does provide about the parallelism between the heavenly and earthly sanctuaries, no strong reason exists to reject the idea that the author uses Greek terms with Platonic philosophical connotations to describe a very Jewish conception of God's dwelling, thus demonstrating the author's familiarity with apocalyptic Jewish traditions and use of Greek philosophical motifs to interpret Jewish texts.[95]

4. Summary

In the course of the previous discussion the centrality of the motif of Jesus as high priest in Hebrews has been noted. The author has an understanding of Jesus as priest which has resulted from conscious, sustained theological reflection on Ps 2:7 and Ps 110:1, 4. Less clear is how the author arrived at this point and what may have influenced him in this matter.

In summary, what is affirmed about Jesus as priest? Though not of priestly lineage, he becomes priest by God's affirmation and oath because he also is the divine Son. He is prepared for this priestly service by his earthly sufferings through which—along with his common origins in God—he develops solidarity with the people. He serves as

[93] See the discussion in Carol A. Newsom, "Throne," *EDSS* 2:946-47. Some scholars see the background of Hebrews' presentation of Jesus as high priest in such discussions of an angelic priesthood serving in the heavenly sanctuary. See, for example, Attridge, *Hebrews*, 100.

[94] The translation is that of H. W. Hollander and M. de Jonge, *The Testaments of the Twelve Patriarchs: A Commentary* (SVTP 8; Leiden: Brill, 1985), 136, 143.

[95] On conceptions of a heavenly sanctuary in Second Temple Judaism and their relevance to Hebrews, see further Attridge, "Hebrews and the Scrolls," 2:320-23.

priest offering the ultimate, final sacrifice for the sins of his people and is that sacrifice himself. Modeled on the Day of Atonement ritual, Jesus' sacrificial act includes his presentation of the blood of his sacrifice for his entrance into the heavenly sanctuary. There he makes eternal intercession for his people, and he is seated in glory at the right hand of the Father.

The nature of Jesus' priesthood is very significant. His priesthood is greater than the Levitical priesthood because his is like Melchizedek's, which in turn was shown superior to the Levitical order when Abraham paid tithes to him. Furthermore, Jesus' priesthood is eternal, his atoning sacrifice is final and all-sufficient, and his sanctuary is true and abiding.

It seems likely that several of these affirmations are directly based on widespread early Christian tenets. Jesus' death is consistently understood as a willing sacrifice in numerous NT books, including the epistles of Paul, which most certainly predate Hebrews.[96] Also already mentioned is that conceptions of a multi-level heaven and a heavenly temple were common in Second Temple Judaism; similar models likely were assumed in early Christianity (as implied by texts such as 2 Cor 12:2 and the various throne scenes in Revelation). The conflation of priesthood and exaltation (enthronement) is present already in Ps 110.

However, what has influenced the author of Hebrews to describe Jesus as the heavenly high priest? This question remains at the heart of this inquiry and is discussed in the following chapters.

---

[96] Perhaps the best example is Phil 2:6-11, esp. v. 8; cf. Rom 3:24-26; 8:3; 1 Cor 5:7; 2 Cor 5:21. See also James D. G. Dunn, *The Theology of Paul the Apostle* (Grand Rapids: Eerdmans, 1998), 212-18.

CHAPTER TWO

PREVIOUS THEORIES OF THE BACKGROUND OF THE MOTIF

Numerous opinions have been offered as to the background of the motif of Jesus as priest in Hebrews. Though strict lines of demarcation are difficult to draw, the options essentially fall into the following categories: the motif was largely original to the author, has a background in early Christian thought and exegesis, is derived from Gnostic thought, or comes from some aspect of Judaism. Representative arguments for these major positions are surveyed in this chapter, followed in chapters 3 and 4 by closer examinations of possibilities that Hebrews was influenced by priestly traditions and Melchizedek speculation in Second Temple Judaism.

1. LARGELY ORIGINAL TO THE AUTHOR OF HEBREWS

Numerous scholars have argued that the creativity of the author of Hebrews is primarily responsible for the book's priestly motif, and a rigorous defense of Hebrews' originality was offered by Barnabas Lindars in his recent book *The Theology of the Letter to the Hebrews*. Following a theory proposed by Martin Hengel, Lindars posited a relationship between the recipients of Hebrews and the Hellenistic Jews in Jerusalem mentioned in Acts 6-7. He proposed that the recipients of Hebrews were members of a well-educated Jewish-Christian community in the Mediterranean dispersion that resulted from the dispersion of followers of Jesus after the martyrdom of Stephen and the ensuing evangelistic fervor.[1] Lindars argued that an anonymous author, writing between 65-70 C.E., addressed a dissident group that by that time had positioned itself against the leaders of the

[1] Lindars, *Theology*, 22. See also Martin Hengel, *Judaism and Hellenism: Studies in their Encounter in Palestine during the Early Hellenistic Period* (trans. J. Bowden; 2 vols.; Philadelphia: Fortress, 1974), 1:58-106.

community. Members of this group had difficulty dealing with their post-baptismal sins. They felt that Jewish liturgy—with its sacrificial cult—dealt with this issue much better than did the Christian liturgy, thus they were tempted to participate in synagogal meals in order to show solidarity with the temple.[2]

The challenge facing the author of Hebrews was to convince the recipients that Jesus' sacrifice, though unrepeatable, is nevertheless continually effective. Lindars asserted that such a task required creativity ("a striking and original presentation of the kerygma that 'Christ died for our sins according to the scriptures'"), because certainly the leaders of the congregation already had tried unsuccessfully to convey this same point to the dissidents.[3] Describing Jesus as a priest was particularly appropriate—while priests were associated with atonement and empathy in biblical and Second Temple Jewish traditions, the *kerygma* presented Jesus' death as a sacrifice, and his suffering was emphasized in the Gethsemane tradition (Mark 14:32-42 and parallels, which Lindars understood Heb 2:18 to evoke).[4] But above all, Jesus was to be understood as priest because Ps 110:4—first read, according to Lindars, by the author of Hebrews as a messianic statement—says the messiah is also a priest. This, according to Lindars, proved that Jesus *really* is a priest: "besides these pastoral qualifications, which need not mean anything more than the metaphor of priesthood, Jesus was actually appointed high priest by God, so that his priesthood is real."[5]

Lindars asserted, "It is my view that Hebrews arrived at this position entirely as a response to the need to find a convincing argument for the benefit of his readers."[6] Thus he understood Hebrews' description of Jesus as priest as completely original and without precedent: "It has no echo elsewhere in the New Testament."[7] Lindars also dismissed notions that the author drew on the priest-king model of the Hasmoneans or the discussions of a priestly messiah in the Dead Sea Scrolls. In particular, Lindars rejected possible influences from the *Damascus Document*. Regardless of whether this

---

[2] Lindars, *Theology*, 1-25, 59; cf. 120-21, 124.
[3] Lindars, *Theology*, 59-60.
[4] Lindars, *Theology*, 61-63.
[5] Lindars, *Theology*, 62.
[6] Lindars, *Theology*, 64.
[7] Lindars, *Theology*, 126.

document discusses one or two messiahs, he noted that one certainly is priestly yet still differs from what one finds in Hebrews. Rather, Jesus' status as priest is established by appeal to Ps 110:4.

> In fact Hebrews shows no awareness of the expectations of a priestly Messiah. He is not saying that one man combines the function of two Messiahs. But he has found a text which says that the Messiah is himself a priest, and that is what he needs for his argument.[8]

Lindars certainly has not been alone in his contention that the author of Hebrews displayed great originality. Like Lindars, F. F. Bruce rejected the idea that Hebrews' conception of Jesus as priest is dependent on the Qumran documents, where (possible readings of the *Damascus Document* aside) priesthood and kingship remain distinct offices. Instead Bruce asserted, "For aught we know to the contrary, the writer to the Hebrews was the first to identify these two eschatological personages in such a way as to provide the fulfilment of the divine oracle in Ps. 110:4."[9] Graham Hughes was more cautious, allowing that there *may* have been a prior conception of Jesus as the priestly messiah; nevertheless his conclusion was similar to that of Lindars:

> Until there is a more clear demonstration of the writer's dependence on other sources than has so far been produced we may continue in the assumption, therefore, that the conception of Jesus as eschatological priest, as he presents it in his letter, arises pretty well spontaneously out of his own theological preoccupations with the relationship between the covenants.[10]

Hughes' caution actually is more akin to that of James Moffatt, who put similar stress on the theological creativity of the author of Hebrews in his commentary on the book in 1924. Moffatt, though, was more

[8] Lindars, *Theology*, 65-66.

[9] Bruce, *Hebrews*, 125-26, cf. 29, n. 126.

[10] Graham Hughes, *Hebrews and Hermeneutics: The Epistle to the Hebrews as a New Testament Example of Biblical Interpretation* (SNTSMS 36; Cambridge: Cambridge University Press, 1979), 30. See Albert Vanhoye, *Situation du Christ: Épître aux Hébreux 1 et 2* (Paris: Cerf, 1969), 361-72, for a comparable perspective. Others include Eduard Riggenbach, *Der Brief an die Hebräer* (3rd ed.; Leipzig: Deichert, 1922), 59; Hans Windisch, *Der Hebräerbrief* (2nd ed.; HNT 14; Tübingen: Mohr, 1931), 13; Friedrich Schröger, *Der Verfasser des Hebräerbriefes als Schriftausleger* (Regensburg: Pustet, 1968), 126-27; and Eduard Lohse, *Märtyrer und Gottesknecht: Untersuchungen zur urchristlichen Verkündigung vom Sühnetod Jesu Christi* (FRLANT NF 46; Göttingen: Vandenhoeck & Ruprecht, 1955), 168.

flexible than Lindars and allowed for possible 'anticipations' of Hebrews' priestly messianism while still retaining primary stress on the author's creativity.[11]

The view of Lindars, et al., is certainly commendable because ample respect is given to the provenance of the book—the author is understood to write with great sensitivity to address the needs of the recipients. However, it seems inconceivable that *no* echoes of Second Temple Jewish thought on messianism and the priesthood would be intended by the author or understood by his recipients in the swirl of ideas that characterized the Greco-Roman world. Moffatt recognized the difficulty of this position and nuanced his statements; few have found Lindars' more austere position tenable.

2. Dependent on Early Christian Theology and Exegesis

Several scholars have proposed that the priestly motif in Hebrews is indebted to broader early Christian traditions, such as motifs present in other NT books or traditional Christian interpretation of the Hebrew Scriptures (beyond Ps 110). Generally such theories have been stated with little supporting evidence and with dependence on a highly speculative reconstruction of history. Because these suggestions have tended to be rarely embraced, only brief mention of a few proposals is necessary here.

James Schaefer, arguing against scholars who held that the recipients of Hebrews were Essenes (see further in chapter 3 below), instead asserted that the author of Hebrews drew on the Servant Songs of Second Isaiah to incorporate the idea of self-sacrifice into his concept of Jesus as priest.[12] He noted that Heb 9:28 presents Jesus' death as having "the vicariously redemptive aspect of the servant's death," and he added that Hebrews' portrayal of Jesus as priest reflects other themes associated with the Servant, including "reestablishment of the covenant, compelling innocence, merited exaltation, and the

[11] Moffatt's possible 'anticipations' included Jewish texts which discuss a heavenly sanctuary, Philo's speculation on the Logos as high priest, interpretation of Ps 110 in *Testaments of the Twelve Patriarchs*, and the Enochic conception of the Son of Man. See Moffatt, *Hebrews*, xlvii-liii.

[12] James R. Schaefer, "The Relationship between Priestly and Servant Messianism in the Epistle to the Hebrews," *CBQ* 30 (1968): 359-85.

office of prophecy," each of which he illustrated with quotations from Hebrews.[13] Schaefer's argument, however, was complicated by his insistence that the author of Hebrews did not make this connection to Isaiah independently but rather received it only through the early church's servant Christology.[14] Schaefer's contention that this theme could only have been used by the author of Hebrews as mediated through early church tradition is based on Hebrews' method of argumentation. Whereas the author is quite comfortable quoting and interpreting various passages of the Septuagint to support his points, Schaefer noted that his incorporation of Servant messianism was based on broad themes and clichés rather than direct quotations from Isaiah.[15] Schaefer added that the author of Hebrews utilized only those aspects of Servant messianism that proved beneficial to his description of Jesus as priest.[16]

Leopold Sabourin rejected Schaefer's argument that Hebrews' priestly motif is indebted to Servant messianism. Instead, he asserted that Hebrews' talk of sacrifice requires someone to play the role of priest, and he concluded that the author of Hebrews shared the idea of Jesus as both sacrifice and priest with numerous other New Testament authors, especially Paul, Paul's pseudepigraphical heirs, and the evangelists:

> What has been said till now is like the major premise in our reasoning: early and numerous formulations of Christ's death describe it, implicitly at least, as a sacrifice, and this certainly reflects a generalized conviction of the first Christian generation. Our second premise will be: if Christ freely gave his life in sacrifice for the redemption of mankind it is as priest that He did it. It should be legitimately concluded that even if Christ is not explicitly called priest outside Heb it is implied that He is in the texts that present His death as a sacrifice.[17]

Unlike the author of Hebrews, Sabourin contended that these other biblical authors stopped short of making the connection explicit out of fear of overly associating Jesus with the Levitical (and also pagan)

---

[13] Schaefer, "Relationship," 377, 380.
[14] Schaefer, "Relationship," 377.
[15] Schaefer, "Relationship," 378.
[16] Schaefer," Relationship," 385. For a differing evaluation of the impact of Servant messianism on Hebrews' thought, see Morna Hooker, *Jesus and the Servant: The Influence of the Servant Concept of Deutero-Isaiah in the New Testament* (London: SPCK, 1959).
[17] Sabourin, *Priesthood*, 214-15.

priesthoods.[18] Sabourin was familiar with numerous Qumran texts that have often been discussed in conjunction with priestly traditions in that corpus (including 1QS, 1QSa, CD, 1QapGen ar, and 11QMelchizeek), but he dismissed them as irrelevant to his interpretation of Hebrews.[19]

Several other scholars also have argued that Hebrews' presentation of Jesus as priest was derived from presentations of Jesus in various gospels.[20] Oscar Cullmann went a step further, however, arguing that the author of Hebrews expounded this idea because Jesus consciously saw himself as the messianic priest expected in Second Temple Judaism.[21] As is discussed below in chapter 3, the expectation of a priestly figure deemed messianic indeed is attested in several of the Qumran scrolls, including 1QS, 1QSa, and CD. However, one should not overestimate Cullmann's appraisal of the value of the Dead Sea Scrolls for understanding Hebrews since he also cited Ernst Käsemann's theory of the Jewish appropriation of the Gnostic myth as supporting this priestly expectation.[22]

According to Cullmann, Jesus tapped into this priestly expectation by associating himself with Ps 110 and by standing in opposition to his priestly contemporaries in Jerusalem. He argued that various streams of thought in Second Temple Judaism contributed to the expectation of an ideal priestly figure. Chief among these streams was Ps 110 itself. According to Cullman, this psalm clearly was intended for the enthronement ceremony of a king yet also invested him with an eternal priestly status. As such, it set the Melchizedekian priest in opposition to the present Levitical priestly figure.[23] This psalm engendered extrabiblical speculation associating Melchizedek with the messiah or

---

[18] Sabourin, *Priesthood,* 208-9, 212-16.

[19] As is evident in Sabourin, *Priesthood*, 168-77.

[20] For the Synoptics, see Gerhard Friedrich, "Beobachtungen zur messianischen Hohenpriestererwartung in den Synoptikern," *ZTK* 53 (1956): 265-311; and Olaf Moe, "Der Gedanke des allgemeinen Priestertums im Hebräerbrief," *TZ* 5 (1949): 161-69. Against Friedrich's thesis, see Ferdinand Hahn, *Christologische Hoheitstitel: Ihre Geschichte im frühen Christentum* (5th ed.; Göttingen: Vandenhoeck & Ruprecht, 1995), 231-41. For John, see Ceslas Spicq, "L'origine Johannique de la conception du Christ-Prêtre dans l'Épître aux Hébreux," in *Aux sources de la tradition chrétienne: Mélanges offerts à Maurice Goguel* (Neuchâtel: Delachaux et Niestlé, 1950), 258-69; and A. J. B. Higgins, "The Priestly Messiah," *NTS* 13 (1966-67): 211-39.

[21] Oscar Cullmann, *The Christology of the New Testament* (rev. ed.; New Testament Library; Philadelphia: Westminster, 1964), 83.

[22] Cullmann, *Christology*, 85-86. See the discussion below of Ernst Käsemann's theory.

[23] Cullmann, *Christology*, 84.

other eschatological figures and, Cullman proposed, may also have been merged with Gnostic-Christian speculation of this shadowy figure.[24]

According to Cullmann, Jesus was certainly aware of this speculation and associated himself with it. He did so by interpreting Ps 110 as speaking of himself and by expressing opposition to the Jerusalem temple and its priesthood. In Mark 12:35-37 (and parallels) Jesus used the passage in the discussion of the relationship between the Messiah and David:

> While Jesus was teaching in the temple, he said, "How can the scribes say that the Messiah is the son of David? David himself, by the Holy Spirit, declared, 'The Lord said to my Lord, "Sit at my right hand, until I put your enemies under your feet."' David himself calls him Lord; so how can he be his son?" And the large crowd was listening to him with delight.

Cullmann argued that Jesus clearly associated himself with the figure of Ps 110:1 by quoting the verse in this conflict story. He assumed that Jesus thereby understood himself to fulfill the entire psalm, thus he implicitly claimed also to be the 'priest in the order of Melchizedek' of Ps 110:4. Cullmann argued that a similar situation occurs in Mark 14:62. When asked during his trial before the high priest if he is the messiah, Jesus responds with a conflation of Ps 110:1 and Dan 7:13—"I am; and 'you will see the Son of Man seated at the right hand of the Power,' and 'coming with the clouds of heaven.'" Cullmann asserted that the notion of the session clearly comes from Ps 110:1, and this exchange was particularly significant because Jesus speaks these words to the earthly high priest. This fit Jesus' pattern of questioning the authority of the temple and its cult (Matt 12:6; Mark 14:57 and parallels; John 2:19) and offering himself as its replacement (John 2:21). Since Jesus spoke in such a manner about the temple, it seemed to Cullmann no stretch to imagine that he saw himself as the true priest as well.[25]

---

[24] The possibility that Gnostic thought lies behind Hebrews is addressed later in this chapter, and Melchizedek speculation receives significant attention in chapter 4 below.

[25] Cullmann, *Christology*, 84, 87-89.

In the words of Cullmann:

> We conclude, then, that Jesus considered it his task to fulfill the priestly office. This opens perspectives which are of far-reaching importance for the self-consciousness of Jesus. It is in any case important that a later Christological interpretation such as that of the Epistle to the Hebrews could find a point of contact in these two citations of Ps. 110 by Jesus himself.[26]

Numerous other suggestions have been offered that posit the background of Hebrews' thought elsewhere in early Christian thought or exegesis, but only one more needs attention here.[27] F. C. Synge argued that the background of Hebrews' priestly discussion was to be found in the author's correlation of Jesus with Joshua son of Nun and the high priest Joshua son of Jehozadak (both called Ἰησοῦς in the LXX), thus explaining how Jesus could be deemed 'apostle' and 'high priest' in Heb 3:1.[28] According to Synge, the recipients would have understood the two earlier figures as types of Jesus because they shared the same Greek name.[29]

After correlating Jesus with the earlier Joshua, Synge related Jesus with Joshua the priest by means of the assertion in Heb 3:3 that Jesus is the builder of a house. This for Synge evoked Zech 6:12, which says that Joshua "shall build the temple of the Lord."[30] Synge saw other connections between the two figures: "What do we know about him

---

[26] Cullmann, *Christology*, 89.

[27] Straining credulity are the proposals of Mary E. Clarkson, "The Antecedents of the High-Priest Theme in Hebrews," *ATR* 29 (1947): 89-95; Cameron MacKay, "Why Study Ezekiel 40-48?" *EvQ* 37 (1965): 155-67; and MacKay, "The Argument of Hebrews," *CQR* 168 (1967): 325-38. Clarkson explained Jesus' priesthood like Melchizedek's in Hebrews as an attempt to comfort heartbroken former Levitical priests who had converted to Christianity and joined a community of former disciples of John the Baptist in Ephesus. These former priests were distraught that their friend Caiaphas had played a leading role in Jesus' crucifixion and could not have handled discussion of Jesus' heavenly priesthood in Levitical terms. MacKay, on the other hand, finds the heavenly temple of Ezek 40-48 lurking under the surface of Hebrews along with a complex historical setting in which Hebrews was written to assuage hard feelings resulting from previous conflicts between the author and recipients. The recipients supposedly had earlier been offended by the author's suggestion that Jesus be understood in light of a Canaanite figure. MacKay chides his own readers who might question the legitimacy of his argument, which seems more inspired by 2 Corinthians than Hebrews.

[28] F. C. Synge, *Hebrews and the Scriptures* (London: SPCK, 1959).

[29] Synge, *Hebrews*, 19.

[30] Synge did not address the likely possibility that Zech 6:12 reflects a textual emendation.

[Joshua son of Jehozadak] that is relevant? He was high priest; he built the temple; he was put to shame, Zech. 3, and then given honour by God. In these matters he foreshadows Jesus the Christ."[31]

Having argued that the readers would understand the correspondences to these two Jesuses from Israel's past, Synge then sought to relate Jesus as a high priest like Joshua to Hebrews' discussion of Jesus as priest in the order of Melchizedek, the motif so prominent in Hebrews.[32] Synge did this by noting that Ps 110:4—like many quotations of Scripture in Hebrews—is quoted as if God is speaking directly to a 'Heavenly Companion,' whom Synge understood as Jesus.[33] Since Jesus is high priest because of his association with Joshua son of Jehozadak and clearly is the Heavenly Companion addressed elsewhere as Son, Synge argued that this allowed the author of Hebrews to declare that Jesus must also be the priest addressed in the psalm.[34]

Though unusual, Synge's argument does have the advantage of drawing on patristic readings of Hebrews, as he frequently cited Justin Martyr in support of his reading. Also, others have found the Jesus/Joshua pun intriguing. Yet Synges' approach remains problematic. Synge argued that the author of Hebrews related Jesus to Joshua in order to establish Jesus' status as high priest, then he connected Jesus to Melchizedek in order to legitimize Jesus' priestly lineage. It was observed in chapter 1 above, however, that in Heb 5:5-6 Jesus' priesthood is grounded in God's declarations (Ps 2:7; Ps 110:1, 4), and in Heb 7 the author begins differentiating Jesus' priesthood from that of the Levitical line by means of Jesus' correspondences to Melchizedek. As also seen in the discussion above, ultimately the author of Hebrews assumes Jesus must be high priest because his sacrificial death corresponds to the Day of Atonement sacrifice. Thus the argument of Hebrews does not demand the tie between Jesus and

---

[31] Synge, *Hebrews*, 21. He saw another tie in that Heb 8:1, which says Jesus 'is seated at the right hand of the Majesty in the heavens,' may be an allusion to Zech 6:13 LXX (*Hebrews*, 25).

[32] Synge (*Hebrews*, 21) found a parallel for this identification in Justin, citing *Dialogue* 115: "The revelation of the Jesus who was a priest of your nation was a foreshadowing of the things which were to be done hereafter by our Priest and God and Christ, the Son."

[33] Synge, *Hebrews*, 22. For more on the Heavenly Companion, see his earlier discussion at 1-9.

[34] Synge, *Hebrews*, 22.

Joshua the priest that Synge proposes. Even if the author of Hebrews had intended it, it seems too obscure to have been understood by the readers; there are no explicit references to Joshua the priest that might induce them to recognize the proposed allusion.

3. Dependent on Gnostic Mythology

In *The Wandering People of God*, Ernst Käsemann located the background of Hebrews' high priestly motif in Gnostic discussion of the *Urmensch*.[35] His proposal has been much more influential in the history of scholarship on Hebrews than those previously surveyed. The history behind Käsemann's book is very interesting in its own right. Käsemann, who wrote the first draft of the work in 1937, observed that he had penned it "in the leisure of a prison cell" due to his opposition to the Nazis. Scholarly response to his thesis at that time was limited because of the prevailing situation, yet he decided not to rework his manuscript for the 1957 second edition; he felt it would require more work to revise it than to rewrite it totally, and he noted that the political situation had impeded discussion of his original manuscript regardless.[36] As a result, neither edition of his book took into account the discoveries at Qumran or Nag Hammadi even though his second edition appeared a decade after these texts began coming to light.

Though mostly rejected by American and British scholars—and, as noted below, ultimately by Käsemann himself—his thesis has been incorporated in a variety of ways by several prominent German scholars, including Rudolf Bultmann, Erich Grässer, Helmut Koester, Franz Laub, Walter Schmithals, and Gerd Theißen.[37] On the other

---

[35] Ernst Käsemann, *The Wandering People of God* (trans. R. A. Harrisville and I. L. Sandberg; Minneapolis: Augsburg, 1984); trans. of *Das wandernde Gottesvolk: Eine Untersuchung zum Hebräerbrief* (2nd ed.; Göttingen: Vandenhoeck & Ruprecht, 1957).

[36] Käsemann, *Wandering*, 15-16.

[37] Rudolf Bultmann, *Theology of the New Testament* (trans. K. Grobel; 2 vols.; New York, Scribner's, 1951-55), 1.176-78; Erich Grässer, *Der Glaube im Hebräerbrief* (MThSt 2; Marburg: Elwert, 1965) and more recently *An die Hebräer* (3 vols.; EKKNT VII.1-3; Zürich: Benzinger; Neukirchen-Vluyn: Neukirchener Verlag, 1990-97); Helmut Koester, *History and Literature of Early Christianity* (2nd ed.; vol. 2 of *Introduction to the New Testament*; New York: de Gruyter, 2000), 275-80; Franz Laub, *Bekenntnis und Auslegung: Die paränetische Funktion der Christologie im Hebräerbrief* (BU 15; Regensburg: Pustet, 1980); Walter Schmithals, *Neues Testament*

hand, relatively few English-speaking scholars have followed this line of thought.[38]

Käsemann finds the background of the priestly motif—as well as that of two other themes in Hebrews, the 'wandering' of the people of God and the relationship between the 'Son' and the 'sons' of God—in the Gnostic *Urmensch* salvation myth. Käsemann asserted that the author of Hebrews drew on the Gnostic myth for motifs which he adapted to proclaim the Christian message, but he argued that the author did not endorse Gnostic tenets such as naturalism, the preexistence of souls, and the innate human capacity for redemption.[39] This borrowing occurred, he argued, as a practical matter when Christianity spread to the Hellenistic world:

> *Accordingly, the primitive Christian message must have been able to use the myth and its forms of expression in a certain way.* To what extent could it do so? We must note first that with its penetration of the Hellenistic world it left the influence of Palestinian soil and inner-Jewish history. It was thus compelled to think through and form its content in a new way, so as to make the gospel accessible to new hearers originating in other contexts. And it could do so only by becoming contemporary with these hearers and speaking to their concrete situation. Today it is clearer than ever that the concrete situation of the Hellenistic world into which Christianity made its way was in essence characterized by the Gnostic myth of the redeemed Redeemer and faith in this myth. . . . *If*

---

und Gnosis (EdF 208; Darmstadt: Wissenschaftliche Buchgesellschaft, 1984), 138-44, and *The Theology of the First Christians* (trans. O. C. Dean, Jr.; Louisville: Westminster John Knox, 1997), 65; and Gerd Theißen, *Untersuchungen zum Hebräerbrief* (StNT 2; Gütersloh: Mohn, 1969). For further discussion of the reception of Käsemann's theory in German scholarship, see Otfried Hofius, *Katapausis: Die Vorstellung vom endzeitlichen Ruheort im Hebräerbrief* (WUNT 11; Tübingen: Mohr, 1970), 5-12.

[38] An American scholar holding to a form of the Gnostic thesis is Kenneth L. Maxwell, "Doctrine and Parenesis in the Epistle to the Hebrews, with Special Reference to Pre-Christian Gnosticism" (Ph.D. diss., Yale University, 1953). James Thompson notes several parallels between Gnostic thought and Hebrews but instead emphasizes the latter as an early step toward 'Christian Platonism,' under the influence of Alexandrian Jewish thought. See James W. Thompson, *The Beginnings of Christian Philosophy: The Epistle to the Hebrews* (CBQMS 13; Washington: Catholic Biblical Association of America, 1982). The relative lack of interest in the Gnostic hypothesis among American scholars is typified by the silence on the issue by Philip Edgcumbe Hughes in his article surveying post-World War II scholarship on Hebrews ("The Epistle to the Hebrews," in *The New Testament and Its Modern Interpreters* [ed. E. J. Epp and G. W. MacRae; Atlanta: Scholars Press, 1989], 351-70).

[39] Käsemann, *Wandering*, 150-52, 176-78.

> *there ever were specific centuries determined by the myth, then the first post-Christian centuries certainly take priority.*[40]

A result of this adaptation was that importance shifted away from the historical Jesus toward the significance of Christ as Redeemer.[41]

The opening section of the book concerned the "wandering" motif. Käsemann noted that the λόγος τῆς ἀκοῆς in Hebrews took on an almost personal nature and called God's people—demanding a decision—to journey in union with it toward God's promise, attainment of a spatial heavenly homeland.[42] Such a journey is undertaken in community, not individually.[43] Käsemann opposed notions that the epistle addresses a temptation to apostatize to Judaism or a Judaizing threat.[44] Apostasy indeed is presented as a real danger, but it is understood as a turn toward wanton sin, not toward Judaism.[45] The temptation toward apostasy arose from suffering:

> On the other hand, what danger actually threatens the community is perfectly clear: Behind it lies a struggle for faith, and, like the Christian struggle of faith in every age, it has been waged in suffering. If that struggle first summoned to joyfulness in endurance, fellowship in love, and growth in knowledge, then its further progress suffered a setback manifest in *the weariness and weakness of faith*. One wishes an end to the time of distress, neglects the admonition to faithfulness in worship, and in practice more and more neglects the ὁμολογία τῆς ἐλπίδος (10:23). If in the beginning the certainty of a better and abiding good in heaven following the loss of earthly possessions (10:34) was a comfort and spur to perseverance, now this very certainty gradually retreats in face of present tribulation. This creates a situation that renders intelligible a comparison with the Old Testament wilderness generation and calls faith a παράκλησις (13:22). But in what should such "admonition" consist than in the renewed unfolding of just that wavering homology of hope, and in a summons to complete the wandering of faith?[46]

Käsemann asserted that this "wandering" motif was borrowed from the Christian Gnosticism of Alexandria, Egypt, and that its gnostic origin was evidenced by a parallel trajectory of development in

---

[40] Käsemann, *Wandering*, 175 (emphasis his).
[41] Käsemann, *Wandering*, 178-79.
[42] Käsemann, *Wandering*, 18-19, 36.
[43] Käsemann, *Wandering*, 22.
[44] Käsemann, *Wandering*, 24.
[45] Käsemann, *Wandering*, 46-48.
[46] Käsemann, *Wandering*, 25.

Mandaean Gnosticism.[47] (That Käsemann would propose such a relationship with Egyptian Gnostic thought is all the more striking when one remembers that he formulated his thesis a decade before the discovery of the Nag Hammadi texts.)

This Gnostic wandering motif, according to Käsemann, also explained the relationship between the 'Son' and the 'sons.' The 'Son,' the preexistent Christ, served as archetype for his followers and leads them on their heavenly journey.[48] Interpreting Hebrews alongside assertions about Christ in Col 1 and Phil 2, Käsemann argued that Christ, as a divine-man like the Gnostic *Anthropos*, descended to earth in order to lead his followers to their heavenly homeland.[49] This was drawn from the Gnostic myth in which "the *Urmensch* and his parts are reminded of their divine origin and are induced to detach from the material world as well as to return to their heavenly homeland."[50] The concept of τελειοῦν, usually understood as 'perfection' or 'completion' and very important in Hebrews, referred to attainment of the goal—in this case, entrance into the heavenly sphere—rather than moral or ethical development.[51] Thus,

> Completion of the righteous, as well as of the Old Testament witness of faith, occurs through entry into heaven or through membership in the divine festal gathering. *Perfection and completion are thus allotted only to the heavenly creature.* For this reason, in 7:11 and 18 the possibility of creating τελείωσις must then be denied the Levitical priesthood of the Old Testament *nomos*. Yet the latter passages still deserve special attention because they give notice of a new element for the investigation of our concept, which is then more clearly marked in 9:9; 10:1; and 14. *The cultic act of Christ's self-sacrifice effects the completion of his people* which the cultus of the first testament was unable to do. Cultus and perfection are thus connected here.[52]

Käsemann saw the background of Hebrews' presentation of Jesus as priest in this Gnostic realm as well, as mediated through early Christian liturgy. He asserted that the early church was drawn to Gnostic documents as fertile sources of liturgical texts and themes:

---

47 Käsemann, *Wandering*, 74, 88-96.

48 Käsemann, *Wandering*, 105. He notes, however, that the author of Hebrews rejects the Gnostic notion of the preexistence of human souls (151).

49 Käsemann, *Wandering*, 101-11, 130.

50 Käsemann, *Wandering*, 87.

51 Käsemann, *Wandering*, 133-44.

52 Käsemann, *Wandering*, 141 (italics his).

> All liturgy relies on an already fixed store of ideas, and in doing so prefers especially peculiar ideas, though arisen on strange soil. Gnosticism, with its wealth of hymnic pieces, had to attract the formation of primitive Christian worship. That it actually did so, is proved not only by the odes of Revelation, but above all by Phil. 2:5ff., and 1 Tim. 3:16, and perhaps also by the prologue of John's gospel.[53]

For Käsemann, the book of Hebrews—with its stress on the importance of holding fast to the community's ὁμολογία—actually is a commentary on that very confession:

> Thus a high degree of probability attaches to our assumption that the ὁμολογία of Hebrews not only denotes the primitive Christian liturgy of the community, *but that in addition the Christology of Hebrews represents a detailed exposition and interpretation of the community's liturgical ὁμολογία.* In fact, we could simply regard Phil. 2:5ff.; 1 Tim. 3:16; and *1 Clement* 36 as fragments of the liturgical tradition on which the Christology of Hebrews is based.[54]

According to Käsemann, the motif of a high priestly messiah was then imported by early Christianity from its Gnostic source texts. That it came via the liturgy, he argued, is certified by use of the high priestly motif in liturgical contexts in *1 Clement*, Hebrews, Ignatius, and Polycarp.[55] Käsemann dodged the difficulty of the literary relationship of Hebrews and *1 Clement* by asserting that the author of the latter, "naturally . . . already aware of Hebrews," also uses the high priestly language in formulations not found in the former.[56] Thus he assumed that this made *1 Clement* an independent witness for his liturgical theory.

Käsemann saw a Gnostic background as the only logical explanation for the motif of the Jesus as priest in Hebrews.

> Actually, the religious-historical derivation of the idea of high priest in Hebrews is the most difficult problem of the letter as such. Here all exegesis which sees itself forced at this point to fall back on exclusively Old Testament roots becomes conflicting and unclear, while elsewhere it cannot deny Hellenistic influences on Hebrews.[57]

---

[53] Käsemann, *Wandering*, 171.
[54] Käsemann, *Wandering*, 171 (emphasis his).
[55] Käsemann, *Wandering*, 170.
[56] Käsemann, *Wandering*, 170.
[57] Käsemann, *Wandering*, 183.

Käsemann rejected notions that the author of Hebrews borrowed this motif from the Gnostic Melchizedek sect or Philo. That Gnostic sect, he countered, is more informative about Melchizedek speculation than high priestly speculation, and Philo's discussion of the λόγος as ἀρχιερεύς differs much from the discussion in Hebrews because Philo's portrayal "bears only very pallid soteriological, and in essence cosmological, features."[58] Nevertheless, Käsemann did find Philo's discussion enlightening, as he proposed that Philo gives evidence of a Jewish appropriation of the Gnostic *Urmensch* myth that fostered Christian usage of the motif. In his terms, "Philo and Hebrews may be pursuing a common underlying tradition, though on divergent paths."[59]

Käsemann asserted that discussions of the archangel Michael in Jewish apocalyptic literature (including *1 Enoch* and *Testaments of the Twelve Patriarchs*) and speculations about Elijah and Adam in rabbinic literature also reflect appropriation of the *Urmensch* myth. These documents, while postdating the New Testament texts in their extant forms, nevertheless must reflect pre-Christian Jewish thought because "these sources reveal a mythical scheme in which the motifs of Messiah and high priest are fused in an original and logically inseparable unity." In addition, they lack the polemical tone one would expect if they were written in reaction to Christian claims, counter only one of the numerous Christian messianic claims, and reveal a more primitive use of the *Urmensch* myth.[60] This last assertion is based on Käsemann's observation that various Jewish high priestly figures are discussed in manners transparently dependent on the *Urmensch* myth: "this coheres with the idea current in Gnosticism that in various generations various envoys appear as incarnations of the one *Urmensch*-Redeemer."[61] Käsemann explained,

> *Further, from the perspective of content, this late Jewish view represents a more original stage than does Hebrews.* Whereas the only outcome in Hebrews is that Christ is high priest, the late Jewish texts also explain why Moses, Elijah, Metatron, Melchizedek, and Michael can be high priests: They are incarnations of Adam, who on the basis of a divine decree as firstborn of the world was likewise high priest.[62]

---

[58] Käsemann, *Wandering*, 196.
[59] Käsemann, *Wandering*, 196.
[60] Käsemann, *Wandering*, 195-217.
[61] Käsemann, *Wandering*, 201.
[62] Käsemann, *Wandering*, 206 (emphasis his).

Thus according to Käsemann, Hebrews drew on the motif of Jesus as priest that was common in the Christian liturgy. These liturgical materials were in turn drawn from Gnostic *Urmensch* mythology, from which contemporary Judaism was also borrowing themes. Hebrews presents Christ as the self-sacrificing *Urmensch*; the body which he assumes and sacrifices is actually that of Adam, the first-born or *Anthropos*.[63] In summary,

> Though expectation of the messianic high priest may have emerged in the days of the Hasmoneans, only when Jewish expectation of the Messiah was linked to the Gnostic Anthropos myth did the idea appear of the Urmensch-high priest who in sacrificing himself atones for the people's sins. Philo and Hebrews are the first witnesses to this synthesis developed clearly and in entirely fixed written form only in late Judaism.[64]

Though intriguing, Käsemann's thesis is fraught with difficulties. Perhaps the most frequent criticism of his theory is that it is grounded on the assumption that there was such a thing as pre-Christian Gnosticism.[65] Similarly glaring is Käsemann's confidence that he can base his argument on texts which in their extant forms are much later than the first century C.E. and Hebrews. In the present generation, scholars are particularly cautious about attempts to use rabbinic sources in New Testament interpretation because of the uncertainty of dating even those sayings attributed to Tannaitic rabbis of the first century. While one might excuse Käsemann in this area since he clearly assumes that the rabbinic sources contain developments along a continuum, he does face an opposite problem—some of his texts may actually be more ancient than he supposed. For example, discoveries of pre-Christian portions of *1 Enoch* and *Aramaic Levi* (the relation of which to the Greek *Testament of Levi* is much debated, as discussed below in chapter 3) at Qumran could derail his developmental thesis.

Käsemann clearly asserted that Hellenistic Christianity adapted and sanitized the *Urmensch* myth for its theological use. However, one must ask how necessary this might have been. He drew a stark

---

[63] Käsemann, *Wandering*, 216.

[64] Käsemann, *Wandering*, 217 (emphasis his).

[65] For example, see the discussions in L. D. Hurst, *The Epistle to the Hebrews: Its Background of Thought* (SNTSMS 65; Cambridge: Cambridge University Press, 1990), 74; Ellingworth, *Hebrews*, 42-44; and Feld, *Hebräerbrief*, 49-51; and Helmut Feld, "Der Hebräerbrief: Literarische Form, religionsgeschichtlicher Hintergrund, theologische Fragen," *ANRW* 25.4: 3558-60.

distinction between Palestinian and Hellenistic Christianity, a distinction hard to maintain since Martin Hengel's *Judaism and Hellenism* demonstrated that such cannot be supported for Christianity's mother faith. The major motifs that Christianity borrowed from the myth were those of the journey of the divine Redeemer, the relationship between this figure and his followers, and the sacrifice of this figure's body. Scholars of the historical Jesus will continue to debate whether Jesus considered himself divine, but few would doubt that the ideas that Jesus was sent by the Father and died on behalf of his followers come from earliest Christianity. Likewise, the journey motif in Hebrews seems most strongly drawn from the author's interpretation of Ps 95 and the Exodus event in Heb 3:7-4:13, where he emphasizes Israel's disobedience under Moses and lack of rest despite conquest under Joshua.[66] So while the author of Hebrews may well have been a Diaspora Jew who converted as part of the second Christian generation, there is no need to think these major motifs could not have been received from earliest Christianity in its Semitic locale. Similarly, Käsemann asserts that Jewish use of the myth is shown by the recurrence of priestly figures, but these figures are already prominent priests in the Hebrew Bible. In short, one might question what Käsemann's theory actually contributes.

Finally, while the canonicity of Hebrews was hotly debated in the early church, the concerns were authorship and its teaching on repentance, not its Gnostic background. The latter almost certainly would have been a major issue had the early church detected such thought in the book.[67] Likewise, one might legitimately question whether an author willing to adapt a Gnostic myth would approach the Hebrew Scriptures (albeit in Greek translation) so positively.

Käsemann wrote in an era when Paul was viewed as the inventor of Christianity, sharp divides were assumed between Palestine and the Hellenistic world, and the *Kyrios Christos* theology was viewed as foreign to Christianity's Jewish roots. It is easy in our era of appreciation for the Jewish roots of Christianity to reject Käsemann's theory in hindsight, and his own unwillingness to revise his work after the discovery of the Qumran documents testifies to his conviction that

---

[66] Brown, *Introduction*, 692.
[67] See, for example, the discussion in Lane, *Hebrews*, 1:cl-clv.

those texts exposed his thesis as lacking.[68] In Käsemann's later work he left aside his Gnostic thesis and instead developed the theme of the people of God as a pilgrim people called to faithfulness. Though his Gnostic thesis certainly has been much discussed, most scholars of Hebrews likely would agree that his later emphasis provided his "abiding contribution" to study of Hebrews.[69]

4. DEPENDENT ON THE THOUGHT OF PHILO OF ALEXANDRIA

As noted at the beginning of the chapter, many scholars have seen the background of Hebrews' presentation of Jesus as priest in contemporary Jewish thought.[70] Suggestions that Hebrews' priestly messianism is rooted in discussions of messianic priests and Melchizedek in Second Temple Jewish texts are discussed in the next two chapters. Here, however, attention is given to the theory that Hebrews' priestly motif has its background in the philosophical approach of Philo of Alexandria.

Virtually all scholars agree that the author of Hebrews was a Greek-speaking (or, less precisely, a 'Hellenistic') Jew. Others, however, go further and assert that his familiarity with Greek thought strongly influenced his Christology. Perhaps the most venerable tradition concerning the background of thought in Hebrews locates it in Jewish appropriation of Middle Platonism as mediated though the philosophical tradition of Philo of Alexandria. Obviously Philo's influence on later Christian thought is beyond dispute and need not be addressed

[68] He admits as much in the preface (Käsemann, *Wandering*, 15).

[69] So notes Koester, *Hebrews*, 61, commenting on Käsemann's *Jesus Means Freedom* (Philadelphia: Fortress: 1970), 101-19.

[70] A different attempt to find the background in Jewish thought is that of George Wesley Buchanan. He argued that the author of Hebrews was steeped in the theology of 1-4 Maccabees and modeled his presentation of Jesus on Simon the Hasmonean ruler, called 'the great high priest, general, and ruler of the Jews' in 1 Macc 13:42. Buchanan partially bases his theory on the idea that both Hebrews and those seeking to legitimate the Hasmonean dynasty drew on Ps 110:4. Buchanan surmises that Hebrews is a homily which the author composed and delivered sometime before the destruction of the Jerusalem temple to a group of Jewish Christian migrants who had huddled in a monastery in Jerusalem to live out the days until the coming of the kingdom. The author wrote because they had become discouraged and inclined to return to their homes or participate in the Day of Atonement observances. Buchanan's theory has been widely rejected. See George Wesley Buchanan, *To the Hebrews* (AB 36; Garden City, N.Y.: Doubleday, 1972).

here. As early as 1646, though, Grotius suggested Philonic influence on Hebrews, and the first full-scale defense of this view was presented by E. Ménégoz in his *La Théologie de l'Epître aux Hébreux* in 1894.[71] Discussion of this view dominated scholarship of Hebrews through the mid-20th century, and it reached its apex with the publication of Ceslas Spicq's masterful two-volume *L'Epître aux Hébreux* in 1952-53.[72] Considered the classic defense of Philonic influence on Hebrews, it is widely known for Spicq's bold assertion that the author of Hebrews was a student of Philo who later converted to Christianity but retained much of the influence of his *professeur*.[73] Spicq later adapted his approach to Hebrews in light of the publication of 1QS and CD, as discussed below in chapter 3.

---

[71] Hurst, *Hebrews*, 7, 134, n. 1.

[72] For surveys demonstrating the dominance of this view, especially in English-speaking scholarship, see Ronald Williamson, *Philo and the Epistle to the Hebrews* (ALGHJ 4; Leiden: Brill, 1970), 1-6 (a work itself recently critiqued as overstating the case against Philonic ties with Hebrews by Kenneth L. Schenck, "Philo and the Epistle to the Hebrews: Ronald Williamson's Study after Thirty Years," *SPhilo* 14 [2002]: 112-35); Schnelle, *History*, 378; and Hurst, *Hebrews*, 7-11. Scholars who have written in support of a Philonic background for Hebrews in the last century include E. C. Blackman, *Biblical Interpretation* (London: Independent Press, 1957); H. Chadwick, "St. Paul and Philo of Alexandria," *BJRL* 48 (1965-66): 286-307; Cody, *Heavenly*; Lala K. K. Dey, *The Intermediary World and Patterns of Perfection in Philo and Hebrews* (SBLDS 25; Missoula, Mont.: Scholars Press, 1975); C. H. Dodd, *The Authority of the Bible* (London: Collins, 1978); A. Eager, "The Hellenistic Elements in the Epistle to the Hebrews," *Herm* 11 (1901): 263-87; Floyd Filson, "The Epistle to the Hebrews," *JBR* 22 (1954): 20-26; G. H. Gilbert, "The Greek Element in the Epistle to the Hebrews," *AJT* 14 (1910): 521-32; R. M. Grant, *The Letter and the Spirit* (London: SPCK, 1957); Harald Hegermann, *Der Brief an die Hebräer* (THKNT 16; Berlin: Evangelische Verlagsanstalt, 1988); Jean Héring, *The Epistle to the Hebrews* (London: Epworth, 1970); W. F. Howard, *The Fourth Gospel in Recent Criticism and Interpretation* (4th ed; London: Epworth, 1955); H. A. A. Kennedy, *The Theology of the Epistles* (London: Duckworth, 1919); Otto Kuss, *Der Brief an die Hebräer* (Regensburg: Friedrich Pustet, 1966); A. H. McNeile, *New Testament Teaching in the Light of St. Paul's* (Cambridge: Cambridge University Press, 1923); Moffatt, *Hebrews*; Hugh Montefiore, *The Epistle to the Hebrews* (BNTC; London: A. &. C. Black, 1964); C. F. D. Moule, "Commentaries on the Epistle to the Hebrews," *Theology* 61 (1958): 228-32; Alexander Nairne, *The Epistle to the Hebrews* (Cambridge: Cambridge University Press, 1917); A. E. J. Rawlinson, *The New Testament Doctrine of Christ* (London: Longmans, Green, & Co., 1926); August Strobel, *Der Brief an die Hebräer* (4th ed; NTD 9; Göttingen: Vandenhoeck & Ruprecht, 1991); T. H. Robinson, *The Epistle to the Hebrews* (London: Harper, 1933); Sidney G. Stowers, *The Hermeneutics of Philo and Hebrews: A Comparison of the Interpretation of the Old Testament in Philo Judaeus and the Epistle to the Hebrews* (Zürich: EVZ-Verlag, 1965); Thompson, *Beginning*; and Windisch, *Hebräerbrief*.

[73] Spicq, *Hébreux*, 1:87-91.

Spicq's view of the background of Hebrews' priestly motif is inseparable from his thesis on the Philonic influences on the book's thought as a whole. The latter is systematically expressed in an introductory chapter titled "Le Philonisme de l'Épitre aux Hébreux," in which Spicq laid out numerous categories of contact between Philo and Hebrews which, in his opinion, demand a Philonic background for the biblical author and his thought. These correspondences include shared vocabulary; phrases and metaphors; arguments and exegesis; themes and schemes of thought; numerous aspects of Heb 11; and *psychologie* (intellectual and religious thought).[74] In light of this massive collection of similarities, Spicq concluded that the influence of Philo on the author of Hebrews must have been direct, with the latter himself a student of Philo:

> On conçoit aisément l'influence qu'il a pu exercer par ses ouvrages–au nombre d'une quarantaine–sur ses contemporains et par suite sur l'auteur de l'Épître aux Hébreux; mais elle s'expliquerait au mieux si ce dernier était l'un de ses compatriotes et s'il avait suivi son enseignement personnel.[75]

Spicq recognized that Hebrews does on occasion depart from Philonic tenets, though even here the influence of Philo is perceptible. This is to be expected because its author, while highly influenced by his mentor, was nevertheless writing as a Christian.[76] Spicq proposed that Apollos wrote the book in 67 C.E. to a large community of Jewish priests living on the coast of Palestine or Syria, perhaps in Caesarea or Antioch. These priests, he argued, had been converted to Christianity by Stephen in Jerusalem and fled the city after his martyrdom.[77]

Spicq noted that the author of Hebrews found fertile material for his discussion of Jesus as priest in various sources, including the presence and function of the Jewish priesthood, the connection Ps 110 makes between king and priest, statements attributed to Jesus in the gospels, and reflections on Jesus' significance in Romans and 1 Peter.[78]

---

[74] Spicq, *Hébreux*, 1:39-91.

[75] Spicq, *Hébreux*, 1:87.

[76] Spicq, *Hébreux*, 1:89.

[77] Spicq, *Hébreux*, 1:252, 261. As noted above and discussed further in chapter 3, Spicq adapted his view of the recipients after the discovery of the Dead Sea Scrolls, preferring to understand these converted priests as "Esseno-Christians" and former members of the Qumran community. See Spicq, "L'Épître aux Hébreux: Apollos, Jean-Baptiste, les Hellénistes et Qumrân," *RevQ* 1 (1958-59): 365-90.

[78] Spicq, *Hébreux*, 2:121-23.

However, Spicq found the primary background of Hebrews' motif in two aspects of Philo's thought—discussion of the Logos as mediator between God and the world, and his view that the priesthood and kingship (especially as represented by Moses; see below) operated as mediators of the old covenant. He noted,

> Dans sa réflexion sur la médiation du Christ comme souverain prêtre, *Hébr.* a été influencé peut-être par la *conception alexandrine* du Logos intermédiaire entre Dieu et le monde, et son rôle d'intercesseur; mais certainement par l'attribution du sacerdoce et de la royauté faite par Philon au médiateur de l'ancienne Alliance. *Hébr.* a emprunté ce thème à son devancier et l'a exploité au profit du médiateur de la nouvelle Alliance.[79]

Spicq added that Christ fills the role of mediator for the new covenant, and all of this priestly talk would be extremely appropriate given the priestly heritage of the recipients.

Clearly Spicq's assumption that Philo's discussion of the Logos lay behind Hebrews' priestly motif has been the more controversial of his two proposals. This has been addressed so thoroughly by Ronald Williamson that here a cursory discussion of Spicq's view should suffice.[80]

Spicq found the theme of intercession as the primary contact point between Philo's doctrine of the Logos and Hebrews' portrayal of Jesus as priest. Spicq argued that intercession is the chief priestly function for Philo, and the Jewish people were to serve along with their high priest as intercessors for all humanity. In addition, kings under the old covenant had a priestly role as intercessor for their people which continued even after their deaths. Spicq saw a connection between Philo's discussion of both Moses and the Logos with Hebrews' discussion of Jesus. Moses, essentially the 'king' of Israel who also served in the priestly role during the Exodus, was viewed by Philo "comme le pasteur idéal." Philo also sees the Logos as holding both offices, and Hebrews ascribes both to Jesus.[81]

Spicq argued that the author of Hebrews incorporated into his description of Jesus several themes Philo used to describe both Moses and the Logos. All three are seen as leaders of their people and

---

[79] Spicq, *Hébreux*, 2:123.

[80] Williamson's critique has since been supplemented by Hurst, *Hebrews*, 7-42.

[81] Spicq, *Hébreux*, 1:69. Citations of the relevant passages from Philo are given. Jesus is called 'the great shepherd of the sheep' in Heb 13:20.

mediators between God and their followers (therefore as priests). Philo actually uses the phrase ὁ ἀρχιερεὺς λόγος in *De gig.* 52 and *De fuga et inv.* 108. Philo's Logos intercedes for the world before God, and the universe is his temple. While lacking a soteriological function, the Logos nevertheless intercedes between God and creation and serves as mediator of a personal covenant. Thus Philo can correlate the high priest and the Logos in *De vit. Mos.* 2.117-35 and *De fuga et inv.* 109-18.

> Voilà pourquoi le grand Prêtre mosaïque pouvait être considéré comme une image du logos. Il est difficile de douter que ces spéculations aient attiré l'attention de Hébr. sur l'intérêt d'une médiation sacerdotale et qu'elles l'aient aidé à en préciser tel ou tel aspect dans son élaboration du sacerdoce du Christ.[82]

As mentioned above, Williamson offered the major critique of Spicq's position. Williamson asked what fundamental question Philo and the author of Hebrews were attempting to answer with their formulations. Williamson asserted that Philo, as a philosopher, was concerned with "the problem of the relationship of God to the world," specifically how to reconcile the immanence and transcendence of God in light of such questions as how a transcendent God could create the world and be known by creatures. Philo's response is that the Logos, stamped with the image of the unknowable God, mediates and (like Wisdom in other Jewish traditions) was God's instrument in creation. Personal language, such as the term 'Son,' is occasionally used in reference to the Logos, yet the Logos is not a person—it is the world of ideas which one seeks to grasp in order to understand God and the universe. Philo can associate the Logos with the high priest, but he does so in an effort to interpret aspects of the Hebrew priesthood and cult allegorically in support of his philosophical tenets.[83] Philo's interest in the Logos is purely philosophical; there are no hints, according to Williamson, that he held an 'orthodox Jewish' hope for a personal messiah.[84]

---

[82] Spicq, *Hébreux*, 1:68, 70.

[83] Williamson, *Hebrews*, 413-19.

[84] Williamson, *Hebrews*, 423. Schenck, "Philo," 123, notes that Philo did have a messianic conception as evidenced by his interpretation of Num 24:7 LXX in *Praem.* 95. See also Peder Borgen, "'There Shall Come Forth a Man': Reflections on Messianic Ideas in Philo," in *The Messiah: Developments in Earliest Judaism and Christianity* (ed. J. H. Charlesworth; Minneapolis: Fortress, 1992), 341-61.

> Put philosophically, what Philo is saying is that by contemplation of the noumenal world, the world of Ideas, the mind of man can know God. But, if he was to remain a true Jew, loyal to his national scriptures, and at the same time integrate with his Jewish scriptural theology his Greek metaphysical ideas, it seemed to him necessary to derive those ideas somehow from the Jewish scriptures. What I have just written may sound as if I am suggesting that Philo engaged in a deliberate act of scriptural falsification. That I am sure was not the case; it was simply that, being what he was—a devout Jew and an ardent convert to Greek metaphysics—and living when and where he did, his construction of a philosophy on the basis of his people's scriptures was the most natural thing in the world for him to attempt. The method of allegorical exegesis offered, of course, a perfect tool for such an assignment. Without it Philo would have perhaps been unable to retain as objects of his intense loyalty both the Jewish scriptures and the precepts of Plato and the other Greek philosophers who influenced him. So, whatever may have been his feeling and convictions about the literal meaning of the O.T. passages referring to the Levitical high priests, e.g., in Exodus, he sees in the figure of the high priest entering the Holy of Holies a symbol of the Logos as a means of access for the human mind into the world of Ideas.[85]

Williamson countered that the author of Hebrews had very different concerns. Unlike Philo, the author of Hebrews *is* concerned with messianism, and he presents Jesus as the incarnate Son of God rather than as a world of ideas. Hebrews, according to Williamson, evidences no philosophical interests; rather, its interests are soteriological.[86] While they may share similar language, the meaning is quite different. This, however, does not rule out the possibility that the author of Hebrews may have been familiar with the works of Philo.

Discovery of the Dead Sea Scrolls dealt a blow to Spicq's theory of the Philonic influences on Hebrews; even Spicq himself offered modifications of his theory in light of the Qumran texts. Few scholars today would read Hebrews as such a thoroughly Philonic text as Spicq formerly did, though this most certainly should not be taken as a denial that the author of Hebrews drew upon Middle Platonic thought or ideas paralleled in the thought of Philo for certain aspects of his presentation.[87] It is unlikely, however, that Hebrews' presentation of

---

[85] Williamson, *Hebrews*, 419.

[86] Williamson, *Hebrews*, 430-31.

[87] As only one example, the philosophical roots of the language used by the author of Hebrews to describe the relationship between the heavenly and earthly sanctuaries was noted above in chapter 1.

Jesus as priest had its roots in Middle Platonism and Philo of Alexandria.

By this point it is clear that no strong consensus exists concerning the background of Hebrews' priestly messiah motif. Two other major suggestions for the background of Hebrews' motif of the priestly messiah remain—priestly traditions in Second Temple Judaism and Melchizedek speculation. Detailed examinations of texts relevant to each of these proposals follow in the next two chapters.

CHAPTER THREE

MESSIANIC PRIEST TRADITIONS IN SECOND TEMPLE JUDAISM

Various proposals for the background of Hebrews' presentation of Jesus as the heavenly high priest were surveyed in the previous chapter and found lacking. Attention turns now in this and the following chapter to two other potential antecedents for this Christological thought, eschatological priestly and Melchizedek traditions. Though these discussions are divided over two chapters for practical purposes, in truth it is appropriate to consider them together because of the obvious overlap in their ancient milieu and modern scholarly investigations. Indeed, as will be evident below, it was the discovery of the Dead Sea Scrolls in the mid-20th century that for a time brought even the eschatological priestly and Melchizedek traditions from sources other than Qumran to the forefront vis-à-vis Hebrews.

Already in the mid-1950s, several scholars—including Otto Michel, Yigael Yadin, David Flusser, Jean Daniélou, Ceslas Spicq, and Hans Kosmala—were proposing numerous similarities of thought between the Dead Sea Scrolls and Hebrews, some even identifying the recipients of the epistle as Essenes.[1] Yadin, for example, in 1957

---

[1] Amazingly, Jean Carmignac notes that a similar position actually had been articulated as early as 1818 by David Schulz, who noted similarities between tenets of the Essenes, Therapeutae, and Hebrews. See David Schulz, *Der Brief an die Hebräer* (Breslau: Holäufer, 1818), 67-68; and Jean Carmignac, "Le document de Qumrân sur Melkisédeq," *RevQ* 7 (1970): 343-78, esp. 373. See also Michel, *Der Brief*, 557-58 (this excursus first appeared in the 10th ed. of 1957 on pp. 376-78); Yigael Yadin, "The Dead Sea Scrolls and the Epistle to the Hebrews," *ScrHier* 4 (1958), 36-55 (based on a 1957 lecture in Jerusalem); David Flusser, "The Dead Sea Sect and Pre-Pauline Christianity," *ScrHier* 4 (1958), 215-66; Jean Daniélou, *Les manuscrits de la Mer Morte et les origins du Christianisme* (Paris: Editions de l'Orante, 1957); Spicq "L'Épître," 365-90; and Hans Kosmala, *Hebräer-Essener-Christen* (StPB 1; Leiden: Brill, 1959), who proposed that the recipients held views midway on a continuum between Essenism and Christianity and hailed from the community responsible for the *Testaments of the Twelve Patriarchs*. Joseph Coppens, *Les affinités qumrâniennes de l'Épître aux Hébreux* (ALBO 6/1; Louvain: Publications Universitaires, 1962), 6-14, provides a survey of early research on the topic (and ultimately rejects the position), as

boldly called the Dead Sea Scrolls sect "the missing link" for understanding the issues addressed in Hebrews, proposing that the recipients were Christian converts who had left the Qumran community but retained some of their sectarian tenets.[2] He surveyed Hebrews' comparisons of Jesus with the prophets, angels, Moses, and Levitical priesthood before concluding the following about the significance of Hebrews' presentation of Jesus as high priest:

> In summing up the discussion of this theme in the Epistle, it seems quite obvious that this subject is forced upon the author only because his readers' conceptions regarding the Aaronic priestly Messiah make it impossible for them to accept Jesus' unique authority. Moreover, the very necessity for the writer to ascribe to Jesus priestly qualities implies that, according to the belief of the addressees, the priestly Messiah was to be superior to the royal (*i.e.* lay) Messiah. . . . It is quite clear that by repeating and stressing the onetime sacrifice of Jesus in offering up himself, the writer is aiming—*inter alia*—at the addressees' firm belief that even at the era of the End of the Days the full and continuous ritual of the sacrifices—as prescribed by Mosaic law—would have to be resumed and continued for ever under the direction of the Aaronid high priest.[3]

Yadin then turned to examine discussions in the scrolls of angels, the priestly messiah, Moses, and the eschatological prophet of Qumran. On the basis of these and the mutually heavy dependence of Hebrews and the Scrolls on the Pentateuch, he concluded, "There could be no stronger appeal to the hearts and minds of people descending from the DSS Sect than in those metaphors which are abundant and characteristic in the Epistle to the Hebrew [*sic*]."[4]

Spicq, better known for his theory of Philonic influence on the author of Hebrews, reached a similar conclusion:

> L'Épître aux Hébreux, qui est—pour le style, sinon pour le vocabulaire—l'écrit le plus grec du Nouveau Testament—, est aussi l'un de ceux qui ont le plus de contacts avec le judaïsme palestinien. D'une part, la culture alexandrine de l'auteur et sa dependance par rapport à Philon sont certaines, d'autre part, ses centres d'intérêts, son orientation

---

do F. F. Bruce, "'To the Hebrews' or 'To the Essenes'?" *NTS* 9 (1962-63): 217-32, esp. 217-18; and Higgins, "Priestly Messiah," 231-32.

[2] Yadin, "Scrolls," 38. A similar theory was expressed as late as 1972 in Charles A. Trentham, "Hebrews," in *The Broadman Bible Commentary* (12 vols.; ed. C. J. Allen; Nashville: Broadman, 1972), 12:1-99, esp. 1.

[3] Yadin, "Scrolls," 44-45.

[4] Yadin, "Scrolls," 55.

> apologétique, ses exégèses surtout, tel ou tel point de morale présentent des affinités notables avec ceux des ‹‹ exiles ›› de Damas ou de Qumrân. On ne peut relever que des indices, et il s'agit d'un arrière-plan doctrinal ou de psychologie religieuse plus que de parallèles textuels. Tout s'expliquerait au mieux si Apollos s'adressait à des esséno-chrétiens, à des prêtres juifs—parmi lesquels pouvait se trouver un certain nombre d'ex-qumrâniens—et dont il connaît la formation doctrinale et biblique, les préoccupations spirituelles, les ‹‹ préjugés ›› religieux.[5]

Such views fell out of favor, however, in the 1960s under criticism from scholars including F. F. Bruce and Herbert Braun, both of whom questioned the nature of the proposed parallels between the scrolls and Hebrews.[6] Whereas Yadin, for example, argued that the author of Hebrews went to great lengths to present Jesus as a priestly messiah (and not just an inferior lay messiah, as at Qumran) greater than that of Aaron and the Levites because the recipients expected an eschatological priest from the Levitical tribe, Bruce retorted that the comparison of Jesus and Melchizedek using Ps 110:4 is evoked to justify how a king from the tribe of Judah could also be a priest.[7]

Another wave of enthusiasm about a Qumran text's implications for Hebrews accompanied the publication of 11QMelchizedek. Indeed, interest in the possible significance of this text for understanding the presentation of Melchizedek by the author of Hebrews was present at the fragments' initial publication. Adam S. van der Woude hinted in his *editio princeps* of 11QMelchizedek in 1965 that it provided the background for the interpretation of Jesus as priest in Hebrews, and this claim was made more explicitly in another article just months later, this time coauthored with Marinus de Jonge. In his first publication, van der Woude chiefly was concerned with presenting a critical edition of the text, giving relatively little attention to the document's significance for the interpretation of other texts.[8] He did, though, briefly assert that 11QMelchizedek was extremely relevant for interpretation of Hebrews:

---

[5] Spicq, "L'Épître," 389-90.

[6] Bruce, "'To the Hebrews' or "To the Essenes'"; Herbert Braun, *Qumran und das Neue Testamant* (2 vols.; Tübingen: Mohr Siebeck, 1966).

[7] Yadin, "Scrolls," 41-45; Bruce, "'To the Hebrews' or 'To the Essenes,'" 222-23.

[8] A. S. van der Woude, "Melchisedek als himmlische Erlösergestalt in den neugefundenen eschatologischen Midraschim aus Qumran Höhle XI," *OtSt* 14 (1965): 354-73.

> Dürfen wir somit die in 11Q Melch erwähnte Gestalt des Priesterfürsten Melchisedek als himmlischen Erlöser deuten, so fällt einerseits ein neues Licht auf die Christologie des Hebräerbriefes, andererseits auf die späteren jüdischen und christlichen Melchisedek-Spekulationen. Bei Zugrundelegung von Psalm cx 4 hat der Verfasser des Hebräerbriefes die Anschauung von Jesu Hohepriesteramt offenbar mit Hilfe der auch in 11 Q Melch bezeugten jüdischen Melchisedek-tradition dargestellt. So konnte er die unvergleichliche Überlegenheit des Hohenpriesters nach der Beschaffenheit Melchisedeks gegenüber den levitischen Priestern nachweisen.[9]

Van der Woude and de Jonge resumed this discussion, arguing that 11QMelchizedek was essential for interpretation of both John and Hebrews. Concerning the latter, they proposed that two major themes in Hebrews are explicable only in light of the Melchizedek text. They first turned to Heb 1-2, where the author of Hebrews affirms Jesus' superiority to the angels. A key phrase here is the reference to πάντες ἄγγελοι θεοῦ in Heb 1:6, whereas the presumed source of this quotation, Deut 32:43 LXX, reads πάντες υἱοὶ θεοῦ.[10] De Jonge and van der Woude argued that this variation from the LXX was intentional—the author of Hebrews deliberately avoided any language that might imply that angels were God's sons, thus preserving the clear superiority of the Jesus the Son over them and developed at various points in Heb 1-2.[11] De Jonge and van der Woude saw a sharp distinction between Hebrews' presentation of Jesus as high priest, prepared for his service by suffering and death, and 11QMelchizedek's "angelic warrior-soteriology."[12] They were careful to note, however, that they did not read Hebrews as written to members of the Qumran community or to recipients who were worshipping angels.[13]

De Jonge and van der Woude then turned to Heb 7, paying special attention to the assertions in Heb 7:3 that Melchizedek is without parentage, beginning, or an end. They rejected the idea that the author of Hebrews was merely exploiting the silence of Scripture about Melchizedek's origins and destiny in a playful, creative way in order to advance his argument about Jesus' priestly status. Instead, they

---

[9] van der Woude, "Melchisedek," 372.

[10] The extant Qumran version of the verse in 4QDeut[q] (4Q44) has the unusual spelling כל אלהים. See Patrick W. Skehan and Eugene Ulrich, DJD IX, 141-42. Compare Ps 96:7 LXX and Odes 2:43.

[11] de Jonge and van der Woude, "11Q Melchizedek," 315.

[12] de Jonge and van der Woude, "11Q Melchizedek," 317-18.

[13] de Jonge and van der Woude, "11Q Melchizedek," 318.

insisted that the author of Hebrews actually did conceive of and present Melchizedek as an eternal, heavenly figure, and that he understood Melchizedek's encounter with Abraham as a meeting between the patriarch and the archangel.[14] Nevertheless Melchizedek is subordinate and inferior to Jesus; the description of him as ἀφωμοιωμένος δὲ τῷ υἱῷ τοῦ θεοῦ means that Melchizedek is a copy of Jesus and thus inferior, especially since Heb 1-2 places such stress on Jesus' superiority over angels.[15] Though asserting his inferiority to Jesus, the author of Hebrews understands Melchizedek in a manner much influenced by 11QMelchizedek. De Jonge and van der Woude further questioned if Melchizedek might also be the messianic priestly figure of 1QM and 1QSb and Levi's angelic guide (and arms supplier) in *Testament of Levi* (all texts discussed below), but they did not pursue these possibilities.[16]

Other scholars wrote in support of the significance of 11Q-Melchizedek for interpretation of Hebrews. Among them was Yadin, who asserted that this text answered the one remaining problem for the thesis that Hebrews was written to Essenes, chiefly that of why Melchizedek was so significant in the argument of Hebrews.[17]

Horton offered a major rebuttal of de Jonge and van der Woude's thesis, questioning the very foundations on which all enthusiasm about 11QMelchizedek's relationship to Hebrews was based. Whereas most scholars had understood Melchizedek in Hebrews as a heavenly figure and thus were stirred by the discovery of another celestial presentation in 11QMelchizedek, Horton demanded that Melchizedek in Hebrews be understood as the mortal antitype to Jesus' heavenly type.[18] He did note several similarities between Hebrews' presentation of Jesus and the portrait of Melchizedek in the scrolls; he further discounted the value of such parallels, however, by asserting that the argument of Heb

---

[14] de Jonge and van der Woude, "11Q Melchizedek," 320-21.

[15] de Jonge and van der Woude, "11Q Melchizedek," 321.

[16] de Jonge and van der Woude, "11Q Melchizedek," 322 n. 4.

[17] Yigael Yadin, "A Note on Melchizedek and Qumran," *IEJ* 15 (1965): 152-54. See also, for example, the cautious appraisals by Joseph A. Fitzmyer, "Further Light on Melchizedek from Qumran Cave 11," in *The Semitic Background of the New Testament* (Grand Rapids: Eerdmans, 1997), 245-67, esp. 253-54; and Higgins, "Priestly Messiah," 239; *pace* Hay, *Glory*, 152-53; and Irvin W. Batdorf, "Hebrews and Qumran: Old Methods and New Directions," in *Festschrift to Honor F. Wilbur Gingrich* (ed. E. H. Barth and R. E. Cocroft; Leiden: Brill, 1972), 16-35, esp. 28-30. See also the survey of Kobelski, *Melchizedek*, 115-16.

[18] Horton, *Melchizedek Tradition*, 160-64.

1 would make it extremely unlikely that the author of the epistle then drew on 11QMelchizedek's angelic presentation of its protagonist. Indeed, Horton opined that Hebrews' use of Melchizedek in such a crucial capacity could only indicate that the author *did not* know the scroll's angelic description of the priest-king.[19]

Kobelski in turn responded to Horton, viewing Melchizedek in Hebrews as a "historical/heavenly" figure—one who met Abraham (perhaps in an angelophany) yet also an *elohim* (but not necessarily an angel).[20] Nevertheless, like Horton he saw parallels between 11Q-Melchizedek and Hebrews, chiefly on the former's presentation of its namesake and Hebrews' portrayal of Jesus. Rejecting the idea that the author of Hebrews may have relied on 11QMelchizedek, Kobelski argued that the Melchizedek of the Qumran scroll would be a complicating rival to Jesus in Hebrews if the author of the later embraced the Qumran portrait of Melchizedek. Kobelski did allow, though, that familiarity with some other heavenly redeemer figure may have influenced Hebrews' description of Jesus.[21]

Like Horton, Franco Manzi sees a contrast between the understanding of Melchizedek's nature in 11QMelchizedek and Hebrews, but his distinctive idea is that Melchizedek is simply another name for Yahweh in the scroll rather than that of an agent of God. As for Hebrews, Manzi argues that the author of the epistle understands Melchizedek as a prefiguration of Christ, a conclusion reached by reading backwards from Ps 110 to Gen 14.[22] Anders Aschim reached more traditional conclusions about Melchizedek's identity in the scroll ("a heavenly being of particularly elevated status," likely to be identi-

---

[19] Horton, *Melchizedek Tradition*, 167-70.

[20] Kobelski, *Melchizedek*, 126. The complexity of the topic is indicated by Kobelski's seemingly contradictory statements.

[21] Kobelski, *Melchizedek*, 127-29.

[22] Franco Manzi, *Melchisedek e l'angelologia nell'Epistola agli Ebrei e a Qumran* (AnBib 136; Rome: Editrice Pontifico Istituto Biblico, 1997). Manzi's thesis about Melchizedek in 11QMelchizedek is discussed more fully in the following chapter. See the analysis of Manzi's argument in Casimir Bernas, review of F. Manzi, *Melchisedek e l'angelologia nell'Epistola agli Ebrei e a Qumran*, *RBL* 2/15/1999: n.p. [cited 2 Feb 2005]. Online: http://www.bookreviews.org/pdf/2724_1918.pdf. See also discussion of Manzi's view in Anders Aschim, "Melchizedek and Jesus: 11QMelchizedek and the Epistle to the Hebrews," in *The Jewish Roots of Christological Monotheism: Papers from the St. Andrews Conference on the Historical Origins of the Worship of Jesus* (ed. C. C. Newman, J. R. Davila, and G. S. Lewis; JSJSup 63; Leiden: Brill, 1999), 129-47, esp. 134-35.

fied with the archangel Michael) and in Hebrews (here he is an eternal figure).[23] As for the relationship between the two texts:

> The abundance of only partly successful attempts to determine the religio-historical background of the Epistle at least teaches us that the author drew upon an astonishingly wide field of learning and tradition... One of his building blocks was a tradition about Melchizedek as heavenly warrior and high priest, very similar to that represented in 11QMelch and some other documents from the Qumran library.[24]

Aschim is not so bold as to argue for direct dependence of Hebrews on 11QMelchizedek, but he does find possible parallels in their use of Day of Atonement and holy warrior imagery.[25]

Having surveyed previous proposals of the significance of Qumran's priestly messianism and portrayal of Melchizedek for interpretation of Jesus as priest in Hebrews, attention turns now to examination of the primary texts themselves. Texts discussing the expectation of a messianic priest at Qumran are addressed in this chapter. Chapter 4 is devoted to discussion of Melchizedek in various Second Temple Jewish traditions, with emphasis on appearances of the figure in Qumran texts.

1. Messianic Expectations at Qumran

For scholars of the New Testament, the abundant evidence in the Dead Sea Scrolls of messianic beliefs in a Jewish community roughly contemporary with and in close geographical proximity to earliest Christianity has been an issue of significant interest for decades. This interest is heightened for interpreters of Hebrews because various scrolls seem to describe a messianic priest, which naturally has beckoned questions of a possible relationship between the priestly messianism of the Qumran community and the priestly Christology of the author of Hebrews.[26] Less emphasized in this context, but also potentially significant because of Hebrews' stress on Jesus as both

---

[23] Aschim, "Melchizedek and Jesus," 132-33, 138-39.
[24] Aschim, "Melchizedek and Jesus," 146.
[25] Aschim, "Melchizedek and Jesus," 139-43.
[26] For a survey of the titles and roles of priests mentioned in the Qumran texts, see Robert A. Kugler, "Priesthood at Qumran," in *The Dead Sea Scrolls after Fifty Years* (2 vols.; eds. P. W. Flint and J. C. VanderKam; Leiden: Brill, 1999), 2:93-116.

priest and the Son with Davidic overtones, is that the Dead Sea Scrolls also discuss a royal messiah. Qumran texts describing priestly messianic figures are discussed below, but first attention must be given to two important prefatory issues for understanding messianism at Qumran—defining what figures may be considered 'messianic' at Qumran, and determining whether the Dead Sea Scrolls give evidence of static or evolutionary messianic conceptions.

1.1. *Identification of 'Messianic' Figures at Qumran*

In contrast to the Christian tenet of *one* messianic figure encompassing numerous roles, as expressed in Hebrews and discussed in the first chapter of this study, most Qumran scholars have long affirmed that at least two messianic figures were anticipated in the Qumran texts, a priestly figure and a royal (often Davidic) figure.[27] So, for example, VanderKam concluded after surveying the Qumran messianic texts that "at Qumran there was a dual messianism, with one messiah being priestly and the other davidic."[28] Of these two, the royal figure receives significantly more attention in the Qumran texts, though often he is understood as deferential to the priestly figure if they appear in a text together. In addition, other eschatological figures are mentioned in the Dead Sea Scrolls, including a prophet and heavenly figures such as the archangel Michael, the enigmatic Melchizedek, the 'Son of Man,' and perhaps an 'Elect of God.'[29] More is said about these various conceptions below.

---

[27] Early studies affirming the presence of two messiahs at Qumran include Karl Georg Kuhn, "The Two Messiahs of Aaron and Israel," *NTS* 1 (1954/55): 168-80; J. Liver, "The Doctrine of the Two Messiahs in Sectarian Literature in the Time of the Second Commonwealth," *HTR* 52 (1959): 149-85; and Joachim Gnilka, "Die Erwartung des messianischen Hohenpriesters in den Schriften von Qumran und im Neuen Testament," *RevQ* 2 (1960): 395-426.

[28] James C. VanderKam, "Messianism in the Scrolls," in *The Community of the Renewed Covenant: The Notre Dame Symposium on the Dead Sea Scrolls* (ed. E. Ulrich and J. VanderKam; Notre Dame, Ind.: University of Notre Dame Press, 1994), 211-34, esp. 234.

[29] John J. Collins cautiously affirms that figures like Michael, Melchizedek, and the Prince of Light in the Dead Sea Scrolls are heavenly figures modeled on the 'son of man' of Dan 7, though he hesitates to deem them messianic because they are otherworldly and not 'anointed' human figures. See Collins, *The Scepter and the Star: The Messiahs of the Dead Sea Scrolls and Other Ancient Literature* (ABRL; New York: Doubleday, 1995), 173-94, esp. 176. For the argument that a figure called the

This standard interpretation of Qumran as a community expecting two messiahs is not without its critics. Perhaps the most prominent representative of this minority position in recent years has been Martin G. Abegg, Jr., who asserts that, messianism actually is not a paramount theme in the Qumran texts:

> It is worthy of note, lest we conclude that messianism was pervasive in a large percentage of manuscripts, that the word "messiah" itself is found in only 17 (four beings [*sic*] MSS of CD) of the nearly 700 sectarian manuscripts. . . . Messianism is an eminent, but not a preeminent topic in the scrolls.[30]

Abegg's thesis is that the common presupposition of multiple messianic figures at Qumran predetermines how most scholars approach difficult passages that most naturally speak of one messianic figure. Much attention is devoted to contested passages in 1QS and CD (which are discussed further below), but he also surveys several other texts normally touted as evidence for multiple messianic expectations. While he does not conclude that all of the Qumran texts posit a uniform expectation of a single messianic figure, he does issue a call for restraint: "the dual messiah that we have come to accept as dogma in discussions of the DSS must be tempered" because "the overriding theme is one of royal messianic expectation."[31] Consistent with this call, his own conclusions evidence a similar restraint:

> There are, however, clear signs that the messianic picture was not so focused as to conclude that messianic hopes were only or always singular. The title in CD, "messiah of Aaron and Israel," reveals at the very least a dual nature. There are also indications beyond the clearly dual "messiahs of Aaron and Israel" (1QS 9:11), of a priestly consort to the royal messiah.[32]

Abegg also allows for priestly figures in texts including 1QSa, 1QSb, and 1QM, and for other eschatological figures including a messianic prophet in 11QMelchizedek.[33]

'Elect of God' in 4Q534 is to be considered messianic, see Johannes Zimmermann, *Messianische Texte aus Qumran: Königliche, priesterliche und prophetische Messiasvorstellungen in den Schriftfunden von Qumran* (WUNT 2/104; Tübingen: Mohr Siebeck, 1998), 170-204.

[30] Martin G. Abegg, Jr., "The Messiah at Qumran: Are We Still Seeing Double?" *DSD* 2 (1995): 125-44, esp. 143.

[31] Abegg, "Messiah at Qumran," 143.

[32] Abegg, "Messiah at Qumran," 143.

[33] Abegg, "Messiah at Qumran," 143.

Abegg's note of caution is an important one to heed. While most scholars admittedly have not abandoned theories of multiple messianic expectations at Qumran in the wake of his arguments, still his point is valid that the texts must be read as honestly as possible, without the conclusions being determined by ironclad presuppositions about Qumran's messianic thought. As such, the textual evidence for messianic conceptions at Qumran must be carefully considered, and the resulting theories must always be recognized as provisional. This tentative approach is all the more necessary in light of the fragmentary nature of the textual evidence itself.

Beyond this, an even more basic question concerns the definition of a 'messiah' in the Qumran texts. In other words, must a figure be explicitly called 'messiah,' or is activity in a heavenly or eschatological context on behalf of God's people sufficient to merit such a title?

The term 'messiah' is derived from the Hebrew משיח, 'anointed one.' In the Hebrew Bible, priests, prophets, and especially kings literally were anointed with oil as a sign of initiation into their offices. Scholars commonly speak of 'messianism' in the exilic and post-exilic periods despite the fact that—unlike in the Dead Sea Scrolls—the term משיח is never used in the Hebrew Bible to describe such a figure.[34] Instead, extension of the term 'messiah' to discuss a future—presumably eschatological—Davidic figure expected to be sent by God to vindicate and restore the fortunes of the Jewish people is a later development.[35]

Craig Evans calls for further caution, arguing that the yearnings for Davidic (and priestly) figures evident in various texts of the Hebrew prophets (including Hosea, Micah, Isaiah, Ezekiel, Haggai, Jeremiah, and Zechariah) are more properly understood as expectations for a *restoration* of the Davidic kingship, not evidence of 'messianism' that involves "expectation of the coming of a divinely anointed and empowered figure who inaugurates something dramatically new, something that even exceeds the idealized reigns of David and son

[34] The phrase "two sons of oil" (שְׁנֵי בְנֵי־הַיִּצְהָר) is used in Zech 4:14 to describe Zerubbabel and Jeshua, but in context this addresses present and not future figures. See below for further discussion of this verse.

[35] For fuller discussion of these issues, see Marinus de Jonge, "Messiah," *ABD* 4:777-88; and Craig A. Evans, "Messiahs," *EDSS* 1:537-42.

Solomon."[36] For Evans, a 'messiah' is a figure after whom "no successor is expected" because "everything will forever be changed."[37] While the restorationist hopes evident in the Hebrew Scriptures certainly provided fertile soil for the rise of messianism, Evans finds the first hints of messianism in the LXX and the first clear evidence of such in *Psalms of Solomon* 17.[38] Though most scholars agree that no *uniform* messianic expectation existed in Second Temple Judaism, authors of the NT gospels presuppose that Jesus' identity as the messiah, or χριστός, must be explained in light of expectations that include both militaristic and miraculous elements.[39]

While multiple eschatological figures appear in the Dead Sea Scrolls, usually only the royal and priestly figures are explicitly deemed 'messiahs.' Some scholars consider the prophet to be a messiah; most, though, recognize his eschatological role but understand him as a complementary figure of a different sort than the king or priest. Likewise, many scholars exclude the heavenly figures from consideration as 'messiahs,' preferring to reserve this specific title for a future human king or priest—not a divine or celestial figure—anointed by God to bring salvation in the last days. Note, for example, the words of Andre Caquot:

> Et un messie n'est pas un sauveur quelconque. Le messie est bien le signe visible d'un salut collectif accordé par Dieu dans un avenir dont l'homme ne peut prévoir ni prévoir seul le moment, mais le messie est en meme temps le restaurateur ou continuateur d'une institution historique, le détenteur d'un office qui avait pour marque l'onction d'huile, l'office du roi ou celui du prêtre.[40]

While this seems appropriate in principle, one must also note that few scholars restrict the concept of 'messianism' in the Dead Sea Scrolls to only those figures explicitly called משיח in the Qumran texts or explicitly depicted as anointed. Rather, primary attention is placed by most scholars on the particular roles exercised by a figure, the

---

36 Craig A. Evans, "Messianic Hopes and Messianic Figures in Late Antiquity," *JGRChJ* 3 (2006): 9-40, esp. 18.

37 Evans, "Messianic Hopes," 18-19.

38 Evans, "Messianic Hopes," 18-22.

39 Examples are numerous, but see recently Joseph A. Fitzmyer, *The One Who is to Come* (Grand Rapids: Eerdmans, 2007), 1-2.

40 Andre Caquot, "Le messianisme Qumrànien," in *Qumrân: Sa piété, sa théologie et son milieu* (ed. M. Delcor.; BETL 46; Paris-Gembloux: Duculot/Leuven University Press, 1978), 231-47, esp. 231-32.

Scripture quotation on which the figure's significance is explained and established, and the name given the figure in comparison with names given to figures in other texts. As is discussed further in the following chapter, for example, Florentino García Martínez argues that Melchizedek should be understood as a messianic figure in 11QMelchizedek because his duties are those normally associated with a messiah.[41] Likewise, harmonization of texts that seem to describe equivalent figures is essential because of the nature of the textual evidence; it often is the only way to make sense of such references in manuscripts which often have not survived well enough to provide the context necessary for comprehensive internal study of these figures.[42]

Still, this approach has critics. Fitzmyer scolds scholars taking such a view as guilty of "rubber-band" messianism.[43] Géza Xeravits prefers to jettison the terminology of 'messiah' and 'messianism' altogether, arguing that both terms imply a standardization of roles or a "coherent system of 'expectations'" that belie the evidence at Qumran.[44] Instead, Xeravits proposes that the term 'positive eschatological protagonist' be used to describe various leaders who act on behalf of God's people in the eschatological age.[45] Certainly Xeravits is correct to note that use of the terms 'messiah' and 'messianism' for widely-varying figures is not ideal, and his assertion that their use may imply false impressions

---

[41] Florentino García Martínez, "Las tradiciones sobre Melquisedec en los manuscritos de Qumrán," *Bib* 81 (2000): 70-80. For a similar approach, see Zimmermann, *Messianische Texte*, 15-18.

[42] Shemaryahu Talmon and Lawrence H. Schiffman urge caution when seeking to equate messianic figures from various documents and argue that two different views of the eschaton are present in the Qumran documents. Some documents seem to teach a restorative vision for the eschaton in which the golden days of Israel's past are restored, often by a Davidic messiah, a concept similar to what Evans finds in the Hebrew prophets. Other documents have a utopian apocalyptic vision and expect a radical, cataclysmic arrival of the eschaton. Both Talmon and Schiffman caution that interpreters must take care not to conflate messianic descriptions from these two different frameworks. See Talmon, "Types of Messianic Expectation at the Turn of the Era," in *King, Cult and Calendar in Ancient Judaism* (Jerusalem: Magnes, 1986), 202-24; and Schiffman, "Messianic Figures and Ideas in the Qumran Scrolls," in *The Messiah: Developments in Earliest Judaism and Christianity* (ed. J. H. Charlesworth; Minneapolis: Fortress, 1992), 116-29.

[43] Fitzmyer, *The One Who is to Come*, 6. Fitzmyer specifically levels the charge against Johannes Zimmermann in Joseph A. Fitzmyer, review of Johannes Zimmermann, *Messianische Texte aus Qumran*, *TS* 60 (1999): 750-51.

[44] Géza G. Xeravits, *King, Priest, Prophet: Positive Eschatological Protagonists of the Qumran Library* (STDJ 67; Leiden: Brill, 2003), 2; cf. 8-9.

[45] Xeravits, *King, Priest, Prophet*, 2-3.

of consistency in the Qumran texts certainly is valid. What is not clear, though, is how his alternate terminology avoids the same pitfalls.

In summary, while one might argue that the term 'messiah' should be reserved for figures explicitly identified as such in the texts, other figures discussed in the Qumran texts certainly factor into the community's 'messianic' expectations, as evidenced by the roles assigned to them and the biblical interpretation that undergirds their identification. It is imperative, however, that the diversity of messianic expectations in the Qumran texts be recognized, a point that also is at stake in the second prefatory issue.

1.2. *Evolutionary Development of Messianic Conceptions at Qumran*

A second prefatory issue to consider is that of the chronology of messianic expectations at Qumran. In other words, did various members of the Qumran community hold a variety of messianic and eschatological views simultaneously (perhaps reflecting a variety of opinion wider than what any 'official' Qumran stance might embrace), or did these views fluctuate or even evolve in various periods of the community's history, with different ideas alternately embraced or dispatched based on a variety of factors?

Jean Starcky argued for the latter idea rather early in the history of Qumran scholarship. In 1963 he wrote a very influential—and subsequently controversial—article proposing a logical development of messianic beliefs of the sect.[46] Starcky sought to correlate the various messianic views expressed in the Qumran texts, his theories on the dating of various Dead Sea Scrolls manuscripts, and archaeologist Roland de Vaux's theories about the various stages of settlement of the Qumran community.[47] Starcky proposed the following schema, which is recounted here because of its influence on subsequent scholarship:

Stage 1: Maccabean era (de Vaux's phase Ia)—According to Starcky, the Qumran community had no messianic expectations in this

[46] Jean Starcky, "Les quatre étapes du messianisme à Qumrân," *RB* 70 (1963): 481-505.

[47] Though de Vaux never published final reports on his Qumran excavations, his theory of the phases of Qumran's occupation was presented in de Vaux, *Archaeology and the Dead Sea Scrolls: The Schweich Lectures of the British Academy, 1959* (rev. ed.; London: Oxford University Press, 1973).

era. The *Rule of the Community* was written during this time (as represented by the fragmentary 4QS^{e} [4Q259]) by the Teacher of Righteousness, who was more concerned with ethics than eschatology. This original version of the *Rule of the Community* lacked the reference to 'messiahs of Aaron and Israel' that subsequently was added by a redactor to 1QS IX in stage 2 (see further below). Also, 1QpHab, 4QpPs, and 1QH were written during this period.[48]

Stage 2: Hasmonean era (the first part of de Vaux's phase Ib)—Starcky proposed that numerous Pharisees, having fallen into poor relations with the Hasmoneans, fled to Qumran and swelled the ranks of the community. The Qumran community was opposed to the Hasmonean usurpation of the political and priestly offices, especially because the Hasmoneans lacked both Davidic and Zadokite pedigrees, and community members with Hasidic sentiments began expressing their hope for a Davidic messiah in contrast to the purely ethical interests previously espoused by the Teacher of Righteousness. As evidenced in 1QS IX, 11, the *Rule of the Community* was redacted to include a messianic expectation of an eschatological prophet and two other figures, משיחי אהרון וישראל ('the messiahs of Aaron and Israel'); this messianic outlook was formulated polemically against the impious combination of political and cultic power by the Hasmoneans in Jerusalem.[49]

Stage 3: Pompeian era (the second part of de Vaux's phase Ib)—Starcky proposed that the *Damascus Document*, extant in several Cave 4 copies, was written during this time of Roman hegemony sometime after Pompey's arrival in Jerusalem and between the death of the Teacher of Righteousness and the expected messianic age. Messianic expectations in this period were consolidated from the bifurcated royal and priestly expectations of stage 2 into the hope for one priestly messiah. According to Starcky, this is demonstrated by references in the *Damascus Document* to the singular משיח in the phrases 'the messiah of Aaron and Israel' (משיח אהרון וישראל) and 'the messiah from Aaron and from Israel' (משיח מאהרון ומישראל).[50] An eschatological prophet, now understood as the Teacher of Righteousness *redivivus*, was expected as a forerunner of the messianic priest.[51]

---

[48] Starcky, "Les quatre étapes," 482-87.
[49] Starcky, "Les quatre étapes," 487-92.
[50] See below for further discussion of these phrases.
[51] Starcky, "Les quatre étapes," 493-99.

Stage 4: Herodian era (de Vaux's phase II)—Starcky notes that Josephus reports positive relations between Herod the Great and the Essenes (*Ant.* 15:348) and surmises that this positive relationship contributed to the Essenes' lack of urgency about returning to Qumran to rebuild after the earthquake. Later (as proposed by Józef Milik) the Essenes resettled Qumran in the chaotic days after Herod's death until the Romans arrived at the site c. 68 C.E. Starcky attributes the more aggressive messianic views of this period, as evidenced in the *War Scroll* (1QM), to influences of newcomers "d'un spirit anti-romain et zélote." The messianic priest was accorded great significance in 1QM, but other texts of the era placed great emphasis again on the Davidic royal messiah. Likewise, the expectation of the Teacher of Righteousness *redivivus* as the eschatological prophet remained. Many of the Cave 4 *pesharim* (including 4QpIsa), 4QpGen (*Patriarchal Blessings*), and 4QFloriligium were written during this time. Some contemporary texts, including 4QMess ar and *Parables of Enoch* (the latter not found among the Dead Sea Scrolls), placed great emphasis on an otherworldly eschatological figure, perhaps one modeled on the 'son of man' in Dan 7.[52]

As noted above, this schema was very influential, and Starcky is to be credited with emphasizing the link between historical events and the ideas expressed in various documents, an approach that most scholars assume today.[53] Starcky should also be recognized for taking seriously the differences between the various messianic visions in the documents and for seeking to give them a cogent interpretation.

On the other hand, numerous scholars have disputed certain aspects of Starcky's dating of texts and his interpretations of significant words and phrases, especially pertaining to *Rule of the Community* and the *Damascus Document*. Few today would even accept the validity of Starcky's conclusions regarding the entire third stage. Starcky was prone to date and classify documents according to the date of the particular *manuscript*, seemingly failing to consider that certain

---

[52] Starcky, "Les quatre étapes," 499-504.

[53] While recognizing the strong likelihood that messianic ideas at Qumran did evolve, Florentino García Martínez notes that the nature of the textual evidence does not allow one to confidently reconstruct the nature of this development. See Florentino García Martínez, "Messianic Hopes in the Qumran Writings," in *The People of the Dead Sea Scrolls* (ed. F. García Martínez and J. Trebolle Barrera; Leiden: Brill, 1995), 159-89, esp. 189.

documents were composed much earlier than the extant copies were made. This is most glaring with his approach to one fragmentary copy of the *Damascus Document*, 4QD^b [4Q267], whose Pompeian era dating (second quarter of the first century B.C.E.) forms the cornerstone of his third period and is the sole evidence for his idea that the royal messiah faded for a time and was consumed by the priestly messiah.

His thesis also faced other severe challenges. Raymond Brown demonstrated that Starcky misread the *Damascus Document* when, for example, he equated the foreign invaders of *Yawan* (CD VIII, 11) with the Romans (thus allowing him to date the *Damascus Document* to the era of Pompey) rather than the Greeks. Brown noted instead that *Yawan* normally is the cipher for Greeks in the Qumran literature, whereas the Romans are the *Kittim*. As a result of such challenges, Starcky's entire third phase of messianism is to be discarded, leaving the new stress put on the Davidic nature of the royal messiah as the only significant distinction between the messianism of the Hasmonean and Herodian eras.[54] Also, Jodi Magness has recently called into question parts of de Vaux's historical framework on which Starcky based his four stages, including the existence of his phase Ia (Starcky's Maccabean era).[55]

Despite these problems and criticisms, the aforementioned admirable qualities of Starcky's theory continue to find wide acceptance and influence discussions of messianism at Qumran and even for the entire Second Temple period. Though arriving at different conclusions, Hartmut Stegemann used similar means as Starcky to propose his theory of the three-stage development of Qumran messianism, though his preference is to speak of sequential 'stages' of development of messianic tied to more loosely-demarcated historical periods.[56] Stegemann finds in the first stage, up to c. 150 B.C.E.,

---

[54] Raymond E. Brown, "J. Starcky's Theory of Qumran Messianic Development," *CBQ* 28 (1966): 51-57.

[55] Jodi Magness, *Archaeology of Qumran and the Dead Sea Scrolls* (Grand Rapids: Eerdmans, 2003), 63-66.

[56] Hartmut Stegemann, "Some Remarks to 1QSa, to 1QSb, and to Qumran Messianism," *RevQ* 17 (1996): 479-505. For criticism of this proposal, see Michael A. Knibb, "Eschatology and Messianism in the Dead Sea Scrolls," in *The Dead Sea Scrolls after Fifty Years: A Comprehensive Assessment* (vol. 2; eds. P. W. Flint and J. C. VanderKam; Leiden: Brill, 1999), 379-402. See also Gerbern S. Oegema, *The Anointed and his People: Messianic Expectations from the Maccabees to Bar Kochba* (JSPSup 27; Sheffield: Sheffield Academic Press, 1998), an even more ambitious effort to trace the development of messianism more generally in Second Temple

messianic thought centered on a figure representing the collective people of Israel. Evidence is found in collective images such as the 'one like a son of man' in Dan 7:13, and observes that the quotation of Num 24:1 in 1QM XI, 6f is interpreted to point to the collective people, not distinct figures indicated by the 'star' and 'scepter' (or 'staff') as found later in CD VII, 19f. Indeed, Stegemann asserts that in this period the Qumran community saw Hasmonean political rule as legitimate so long as it conformed to the models of David and Solomon. He finds this implicit in 4QMMT and proposes that the Teacher of Righteousness could not have expected a royal messiah because he acquiesced to Jonathan's political (but not priestly) authority.[57]

Stegemann's second stage emphasizes the royal messiah, as evidenced in 1QSa and 1QSb, and he proposes the possibility that the Teacher of Righteousness was responsible for the creation of this concept in response to his hostilities with Jonathan c. 150 B.C.E., subsequent to 4QMMT.[58] Finally, three figures—royal messiah, priestly messiah, and prophet—appear in Stegemann's third stage by about 100 B.C.E., evidenced by 4QTestimonia (4Q171); an addition to 1QS (VIII, 15b-IX, 11); and the *Damascus Document*. Of these, only the expectation of the prophet—evidenced elsewhere in 1 Macc 4:46—was introduced into the thought of the Qumran community from outside sources.[59]

Judaism, not just in the Qumran texts and community. He addresses the Qumran texts on pp. 86-97, 108-27. This volume is a translation and expansion of his monograph titled *Der Gesalbte und sein Volk: Untersuchungen zum Konzeptualisierungsprozeß der messianischen Erwartungen von den Makkabäern bis Bar Koziba* (Göttingen: Vanderhoeck & Ruprecht, 1994). Oegema offered a revised version of his discussion of messianic expectations at Qumran in Gerbern S. Oegema, "Messianic Expectations in the Qumran Writings: Theses on the Development," in *Qumran-Messianism: Studies on the Messianic Expectations in the Dead Sea Scrolls* (ed. J. H. Charlesworth, H. Lichtenberger, and G. S. Oegema; Tübingen: Mohr Siebeck, 1998), 53-82.

[57] Stegemann, "Some Remarks," 501-03.

[58] Stegemann, "Some Remarks," 503-04. Stegemann notes that the royal messiah is also present in *Pss. Sol.* 17, but he dates that text a century later than 1QSa and 1QSb. Also, he proposes that no priestly messiah is proposed at this point because the priestly Teacher expected to see the arrival of the royal messiah in his lifetime.

[59] Stegemann, "Some Remarks," 504-05.

Rather similar—but more complex—is the recent proposal of Heinz-Josef Fabry.[60] Fabry finds six stages of development, again understanding them primarily as reactions to external factors. The first stage is the pre-Essene era of opposition to Hellenization; a priestly messiah is expected as indicated by 4Q375 and 4Q376, both of which concern Moses, and 4Q541, an apocryphal text concerning Levi.[61] Next, in the pre-Qumran Essene period, opposition to Antiochus IV is expressed with the expectation of a messianic figure representing the collective people of God, a development similar to (but dated differently than) Stegemann's first stage. Like Stegemann, Fabry finds the roots of this imagery in Dan 7 and evidence of its acceptance among the Essenes in 1QM.[62] The third stage, in the era of the Maccabean revolt and the early years of the Qumran settlement, saw the rise of a dual royal and priestly expectation (1QS V, 1-IX, 26; 1QSa II, 11-22), though subsequently the two roles were fused into one figure in CD (perhaps in response to the combination of powers under Jonathan, Simon, or John Hyrcanus I).[63] This expectation also corre-sponds with a stage proposed by Stegemann, but Fabry dates it several decades later. Next (as for Stegemann), in the Qumran era three figures—the aforementioned royal and priestly figures, now joined by a prophet; i.e., the '*munus triplex*' of 1QS IX, 11—appear in response to John Hyrcanus' appropriation of all three offices.[64] Also, the portrait of Melchizedek as a messianic figure in 11QMelchizedek may be a response to perceived Hasmonean misuse of Melchizedek imagery beginning with Simon.[65] Fabry finds three more stages: an expansion in the early first century B.C.E. of the royal messianic expectation to incorporate the biblical imagery of a Davidic royal figure, countering the cruel reigns of Alexander Janneus and Aristobulus but also useful in subsequent historical situations; development later in the century for an apocalyptic expectation of an eschatological prophet to be accompanied by a teacher of the Law; and

---

[60] Heinz-Jozef Fabry, "Die Messiaserwartung in den Handschriften von Qumran," in *Wisdom and Apocalypticism in the Dead Sea Scrolls and in the Biblical Tradition* (ed. F. García Martínez; BETL 168; Leuven: Peeters, 2003), 357-84.

[61] Fabry, "Die Messiaserwartung," 368-69.

[62] Fabry, "Die Messiaserwartung," 369-71. Fabry also finds this understanding in 4Q491, 4Q471b, and 4Q427.

[63] Fabry, "Die Messiaserwartung," 371-72.

[64] Fabry, "Die Messiaserwartung," 372-75.

[65] Fabry, "Die Messiaserwartung," 375-77.

expectation of David *redivivus* in the first century C.E. as seen in 11QPs[a].[66]

In addition to Stegemann and Fabry, numerous other scholars similarly have analyzed the development of messianic thought at Qumran.[67] It is sufficient to note at this point, however, that Starcky's examination established the precedent for subsequent Qumran scholars to address the messianic expectations in the Dead Sea Scrolls as developing and morphing over the years, especially as the community adapted its expectations in light of changing historical circumstances. Though no one scholarly reconstruction of the details of development presently has emerged as the scholarly consensus, nevertheless the varying proposals serve as a reminder that messianic expectations were fluid and far from standardized in Second Temple Judaism—both at Qumran and more broadly.

Likewise, one cannot dismiss the possibility that differing messianic expectations existed simultaneously in the community, as John Collins notes:

> This is not to suggest that there was a requirement of orthodoxy in the matter of messianism at Qumran. Individual authors or members of the community may have focused their attention on one messiah, or on none at all. The authoritative rule books, however, which are surely our best guide to the general beliefs of the sect, reflect the expectation of both a royal messiah of Israel and a priestly messiah of Aaron.[68]

Similarly, Xeravits notes the diversity of 'positive eschatological protagonists' present in the Qumran literature, whether in sectarian texts or those from wider Judaism, and concludes that even in the sectarian texts one finds "no indication that they considered any aspects as an 'authoritative doctrine.'"[69]

With the recognition that much still remains to be understood about messianic thought at Qumran, attention now turns to discussion of those passages noted above as evidence for the expectation at Qumran of a messianic priest.

---

[66] The respective developments are addressed in Fabry, "Die Messiaserwartung," 377-79; 379-81; and 381-82.

[67] See the survey of previous proposals in Fabry, "Die Messiaserwartung," 360-65; Collins, *Scepter*, 77-83.

[68] Collins, *Scepter*, 83.

[69] Xeravits, *King, Priest, Prophet*, 224.

2. THE MESSIANIC PRIEST IN THE QUMRAN TEXTS

2.1. *Rule of the Community* and *Damascus Document*

As implied above in the survey of Starcky's theory, the *Rule of the Community* and *Damascus Document* are the twin epicenters of interpretation of Qumran messianism.[70] Much of the discussion has focused on a few short phrases with ambiguous grammar that are alternately present or missing from extant manuscripts of these two texts. Interpretations of these phrases lie at the heart of scholarly arguments concerning both the number of messiahs expected by the Qumran community and the evolution of their messianic thought. Because the consequences of the interpretation of certain passages from these two rule books are so intertwined, it seems appropriate to address them together.

The histories and contents of these two texts are very well known among scholars of Second Temple Judaism, so brief introductory comments will suffice. The former, found in a substantially-complete manuscript among the original Cave 1 scrolls (1QS, on a scroll also

[70] Discussions of both of these texts are complicated by the presence of conflicting editions of each among the Qumran manuscripts and, in the case of the *Damascus Document*, from other earlier manuscript discoveries. For overviews of the critical issues, see Michael A. Knibb, "Rule of the Community," *EDSS* 2:793-97, and Joseph M. Baumgarten, "Damascus Document," *EDSS* 1:166-70. The major manuscripts of these two texts were published in their *editio princeps* outside the DJD series. For 1QS, see Millar Burrows, ed., *The Dead Sea Scrolls of St. Mark's Monastery, Volume II, Fascicle 2: Plates and Transcription of the Manual of Discipline* (New Haven: American Schools of Oriental Research, 1951) [plates and transcription only]; Jacob Licht, *The Rule Scroll: A Scroll from the Wilderness of Judaea—1QS, 1QSa, 1QSb: Text, Introduction and Commentary* (Jerusalem: Bialik Institute, 1957) [Hebrew]; and more recently Elisha Qimron and James H. Charlesworth, PTSDSSP 1, 1-51. The latter includes the copies from Caves 4 and 5. For the DJD editions of these texts, see the Cave 4 fragments in Philip S. Alexander and Geza Vermes, *Qumran Cave 4, XIX, Serekh ha-Yaḥad and Two Related Texts* (DJD XXVI; Oxford: Clarendon, 1998); and 5Q11 in Maurice Baillet, Józef T. Milik, and Roland de Vaux, *Les 'petites grottes' de Qumrân* (DJDJ III; 2 vols.; Oxford: Clarendon, 1962). For CD, see Solomon Schechter, *Documents of Jewish Sectaries, Vol. 1: Fragments of a Zadokite Work* (Cambridge: Cambridge University Press, 1910); more recently Magen Broshi, *The Damascus Document Reconsidered* (Jerusalem: Israel Exploration Society, 1992); and Joseph M. Baumgarten and Daniel R. Schwartz, PTSDSSP 2, 17-57. The DJD editions of the Cave 4 texts are found in Joseph M. Baumgarten, *Qumran Cave 4, XII, The Damascus Document (4Q266-273)* (DJD XVIII; Oxford: Clarendon, 1996), an edition based on the transcriptions of Milik. Milik earlier had published 5Q12 in DJDJ III, and 6Q15 was published by Baillet in the same volume.

containing 1QSa and 1QSb; see further on these texts below), is popularly called the *Manual of Discipline* but is more accurately titled the *Rule of the Community* (סרכ היחד). This manuscript normally is dated to 100-75 B.C.E. Portions of this text were also preserved in ten fragmentary Cave 4 manuscripts (4Q255-264, ranging in date from the second half of the second century B.C.E. to the first half of the first century C.E.) and 5Q11. The language of composition was Hebrew, and variations from the text of 1QS among the Cave 4 witnesses indicate that the text has a history of redactions. It also is a composite text, as its eleven columns include sections on admission into the community, the community's dualistic beliefs, rules for community life, and a hymn of praise.[71]

The latter, the *Damascus Document*, was known for several decades prior to the discovery of the Dead Sea Scrolls. Two medieval manuscripts of this text were discovered among the Cairo geniza scrolls, one (mss. A) a tenth-century copy with sixteen columns and the other (mss. B) a twelfth-century manuscript with only two extant columns. These were published in 1910 by Solomon Schechter as *Fragments of a Zadokite Work*. Eight Qumran manuscripts of the work have been recovered from Cave 4—4Q266-273, variously dated between the first century B.C.E. and the first century C.E.—and other caves yielded the very fragmentary 5Q12 and 6Q15. This text too includes community rules, but it also addresses briefly the history of the community and includes numerous regulations that do not seem to address the all-male communal life typically proposed for the inhabitants of the Qumran site.[72] The most common explanation for the existence of these two similar sectarian rules is that they addressed two different types of Essene commitments—the *Damascus Document* was intended to guide Essenes living conventional family lives in various villages of Israel, whereas the *Rule of the Community* was specifically for those undertaking the rigorous demands of life at Qumran.[73]

---

[71] Knibb, "Rule of the Community," 2:793-94. On the redactional history of the text, see especially Sarianna Metso, *The Textual Development of the Qumran Community Rule* (STDJ 21; Leiden: Brill, 1997); and Philip S. Alexander, "The Redaction-History of Serekh ha-Yaḥad: A Proposal," *RevQ* 17 (1996): 437-57.

[72] Baumgarten, "Damascus Document," 1:166-67.

[73] See, for example, James VanderKam and Peter Flint, *The Meaning of the Dead Sea Scrolls: Their Significance for Understanding the Bible, Judaism, Jesus, and Christianity* (New York: Harper San Francisco, 2002), 215-18.

2.1.1. *Rule of the Community*

In 1QS IX, 11, three figures seem evident when the author mentions נביא ומשיחי אהרון וישראל, 'the prophet and the messiahs of Aaron and Israel.' Nothing is said here about what these figures will do, but the context clearly seems eschatological; the community members are said to be obligated to the law and community rule until the arrival of these figures. However, this key phrase is omitted—along with several lines of its context—in 4Q259 (4QS^{e}), a copy of this document dated on paleographical grounds to 50-25 B.C.E.[74] The 19 lines of 4Q259 col. III contain the equivalent of 1QS VIII, 10-15 and IX, 12-20 but clearly lack the intervening materials of 1QS.[75] (On the other hand, 4Q258 VII much more closely parallels this section in 1QS.)

As mentioned above, Starcky in large part based his theory that the Teacher of Righteousness lacked eschatological (and messianic) interests on the absence of this key phrase in 4Q259, which he deemed an older manuscript than 1QS. He surmised that a later scribe responsible for 1QS incorporated mention of the prophet and messiahs in response to the rise of the Hasmoneans to political and priestly power.[76] Scholars today tend to reject Starcky's assertion that 4Q259 is an older copy than 1QS, but naturally the more important issue is which manuscript preserves the older version of the work. While rejecting Starcky's relative dating of the manuscripts, Sarianna Metso nevertheless mounts a complimentary challenge to the priority of 1QS. She argues that the original version of *Rule of the Community* is not preserved in any extant manuscript, but that 4Q259 and 4Q256, 258 represent two different revisions of the original edition. Though a

[74] On the dating, see Frank Moore Cross, "Appendix: Paleographical Dates of the Manuscripts," PTSDSSP 1, 57; accepted with nuance by Alexander and Vermes, DJD XXVI, 133-34.

[75] This was not due, as earlier suggested by some, to an incorrect join of two fragments. Instead, the part of the manuscript in question is preserved in toto. James H. Charlesworth attributes the suggestion of an incorrect join to Lawrence Schiffman in James H. Charlesworth, "From Messianology to Christology: Problems and Prospects," in *The Messiah: Developments in Earliest Judaism and Christianity* (ed. J. H. Charlesworth; Minneapolis: Fortress, 1992), 3-35, esp. 26-27, but he repudiates the suggestion in James H. Charlesworth, "Challenging the *Consensus Communis* Regarding Qumran Messianism (1QS, 4QS MSS)," in *Qumran-Messianism: Studies on the Messianic Expectations in the Dead Sea Scrolls* (ed. J. H. Charlesworth, H. Lichtenberger, and G. S. Oegema; Tübingen: Mohr Siebeck, 1998), 120-34, esp. 123.

[76] Starcky, "Les quartre étapes," 482-92.

significantly older manuscript than 4Q256 or 4Q258 (and perhaps older than 4Q259), 1QS represents a conflation of the divergent trajectories of those two revisions, both when it was composed and later again when corrections were added to 1QS VII-VIII.[77]

Metso mounts a significant argument that offers much to explain the redactional history of the text. Prior to the publication of her thesis, most rejected Starcky's position and remained convinced of the priority of 1QS. Several scholars, including VanderKam, Schiffman, and Collins, argued that the reading of 1QS is to be preferred and attributed the omission of this key passage in 4Q259 to scribal error.[78] Though Philip Alexander remains unconvinced, arguing that 4Q259 just as likely was a contracted version of 1QS, James Charlesworth earlier pointed to a similar conclusion as Metso that 1QS stood at the latter end of the developmental history of this text, as has more recently Xeravits.[79]

What can be stated with certainty in light of the final form of 1QS IX, 11 is that at some (perhaps relatively late) point in the community's history, its constitutional document expressed an expectation for three figures—an eschatological prophet, a priestly 'messiah of Aaron,' and a royal (presumably Davidic) 'messiah of Israel'—without defining their tasks.

---

[77] For a convenient summary of this proposal in diagram form, see Metso, *Textual Development*, 147.

[78] VanderKam, "Messianism," 213; Schiffman, "Messianic Figures," 120; and Collins, *Scepter*, 82-83.

[79] Alexander, "Redaction-History"; Charlesworth, "Challenging the *Consensus Communis*"; Xeravits, *King, Priest, Messiah*, 20-21. Charlesworth developed his thesis independently of Metso; this chapter was derived from an earlier conference presentation and does not reference Metso's work. As noted by Charlesworth elsewhere, however, Milik also had proposed that 4Q259 was the earliest copy of the work and lacked the messianic material of 1QS IX, 11. Milik's comments were sparse, however, and appeared in a book review rather than an edition of 4Q259. See Józef T. Milik, review of P. Wernberg-Møller, *The Manual of Discipline Translated and Annotated, with an Introduction*, *RB* 67 (1960): 411. Charlesworth discusses this comment in James H. Charlesworth, "From Jewish Messianology to Christian Christology: Some Caveats and Perspectives," in *Judaisms and Their Messiahs at the Turn of the Christian Era* (ed. J. Neusner, W. S. Green, and E. Frerichs; Cambridge: Cambridge University Press, 1987), 225-64, esp. 232; and in his similarly-titled article from *The Messiah*, James H. Charlesworth, "From Messianology to Christology," 26, n. 79.

2.1.2. *Damascus Document*

A phrase quite similar to 'the messiahs of Aaron and Israel' also appears in the text of the *Damascus Document*, and once it appears in the context of a discussion of atonement.[80] The phrase is preserved four times in CD (slight variations in the phrase are underscored):

CD A XII, 23-XIII, 1 — משוח אהרון וישראל
CD A XIV, 19 — משי]ח אהרון וישראל
CD B XIX, 10-11 — משיח אהרון וישראל
CD B XX, 1 — משיח מאהרון ומישראל

Internal variations aside (with משוח presumably a scribal error for משיח), these phrases from *Damascus Document* chiefly differ from that of 1QS IX, 11 in their use of the singular משיח. In contrast, the plural משיחי appears in 1QS. This has led to much discussion about whether the phrase in CD should be read as denoting one messiah, as the grammar would seem to indicate, or two messiahs as demanded by the plural משיחי in 1QS.[81] To complicate the issue further, proponents of both views can cite passages in CD—albeit from different manuscripts from the geniza—that lend support to their differing interpretations.[82]

(It should be reiterated here that the textual evidence for this discussion of the *Damascus Document* is that chiefly of the medieval Cairo geniza scrolls, not the Qumran manuscripts. Of the four examples of the phrase משיח אהרון וישראל cited above, only that of CD XIV, 19 is also extant—albeit in reconstructed forms—in the Qumran fragments, at 4Q266 10 i 12 and 4Q269 11 i 2.[83])

Those who argue that the term refers to two messiahs usually cite the correspondence with the similar phrase in 1QS. VanderKam argues

[80] The word משיח appears twice in CD outside of this phrase—II, 12 and V, 21-VI, 1—but clearly in reference to figures of the past. See Xeravits, *King, Priest, Prophet*, 36.

[81] Such discussion, of course, presumes that messianic figure(s) are in view in these passages and their contexts. Xeravits demurs: "Their only role is to mark the temporal delimitation of certain ages. However, none is a 'messianic passage' in the strict sense. Their aim is not to speak of positive eschatological protagonists; rather, they serve as an auxiliary topic for the better understanding of another, more fundamental message of the author." See Xeravits, *King, Priest, Prophet*, 37.

[82] VanderKam, "Messianism," 228-31; compare Abegg, "Messiah at Qumran," 125-44.

[83] Baumgarten, DJD XVIII, 72, 134. See DJD XVIII, 3-5, for charts comparing the contents of the Qumran Cave 4 fragments with the contents of the Cairo geniza texts.

that even though משיח in משיח אהרון וישראל is in a singular construct form, the phrase clearly refers to two different individuals. Otherwise 'Aaron' and 'Israel' are redundant, because the former is certainly part of the latter. Also, analogous expressions that clearly refer to multiple figures—despite having singular nouns in construct—can be cited elsewhere (Gen 14:10; Judg 7:25; 1QM III, 13; V, 1).[84]

Those who hold to the view that only one figure is intended propose significant counterarguments. The fact that the term משיח is singular each time the phrase משיח אהרון וישראל appears in Damascus Document would seem on the surface to be a strong point in their favor, and admittedly יכפר in CD A XIV, 19 (see further below) is also singular.[85] (Alternately, יכפר could be pual, rendering this passage useless for proponents of both interpretations.[86] This would require the verb to be in a separate phrase from משיח אהרון וישראל and that the subject be עונם, 'their iniquity,' as read by Baumgarten and Schwartz.[87]) Likewise, Abegg argues that phrases with a singular noun in construct followed by multiple absolutes take a plural meaning only when the word in construct refers to body parts. As for Gen 14:8-9, both internal evidence (plural verbs elsewhere in the context) and external evidence (the MT appears defective because the Samaritan Pentateuch and ancient translations support the reading 'king of Sodom and king of Gomorrah') negate that possible parallel.[88]

Certainly one might question the appropriateness of appealing to 1QS—itself a manuscript that may reflect expansions of an earlier version of *Rule of the Community*—in order to settle disputes over a reading in the *Damascus Document*. It ultimately is more significant, therefore, that proponents of the bifurcated interpretation can cite CD A VII, 9-VIII, 1 as further—and internal—evidence for the expectation

---

[84] VanderKam, "Messianism," 230.

[85] See, for example, Abegg, "Messiah at Qumran," 130. Unfortunately this word is not extant in the Qumran fragments of the *Damascus Document*.

[86] L. Ginzberg, *An Unknown Jewish Sect* (Moreshet Series 1; New York: Jewish Theological Seminary of American, 1976), 252-53. According to VanderKam ("Messianism," 230, n.33), Ginzberg earlier published this idea in 1914 and 1922.

[87] Baumgarten and Schwartz, PTSDSSP 2, 57.

[88] Abegg, "Messiah at Qumran," 129-30. Zimmermann attempts to span the contrasting positions, concluding that two messiahs are intended in the phrase but that the singular משיח may point to the combination of both roles in one figure. See Zimmermann, *Messianische Texte*, 45.

of two messiahs elsewhere in the *Damascus Document* itself.[89] The passage, a complex midrashic discussion of God's eschatological judgment on the wicked, mentions both royal and priestly figures:[90]

VII, 9 וכל המואסים בפקד אל את הארץ להשיב גמול רשעים
10 עליהם בבוא הדבר אשר כתוב בדברי ישעיה בן אמוץ הנביא
11 אשר אמר יבוא עליך ועל עמך ועל בית אביך ימים אשר <לא>
12 באו מיום סור אפרים מעל יהודה בהפרד שני בתי ישראל
13 שר אפרים מעל יהודה וכל הנסוגים ה'סגרו לחרב והמחזיקים
14 נמלטו לארץ צפון *vacat* כאשר אמר והגליתי את סכות מלככם
15 ואת כיון צלמיכם מאהלי דמשק *vacat* ספרי התורה הם סוכת
16 המלך כאשר אמר והקימותי את סוכת דוד הנופלת *vacat* המלך
17 הוא <נשיא> הקהל <וכיניי הצלמים> וכיון הצלמים הם ספרי הנביאים
18 אשר בזה ישראל את דבריהם *vacat* והכוכב הוא דורש התורה
19 הבא דמשק כאשר כתוב דרך כוכב מיעקב וקם שבט
20 מישראל השבט הוא נשיא כל העדה ובעמדו וקרקר
21 את כל בני שת אלה מלטו בקץ הפקודה הראשון
VIII, 1 והנסוגים הסגירו לחרב

VII, 9. But those who reject the commandments and the rules (shall perish). When God judged the land bringing the just deserts of the wicked

10. to them that is when the oracle of the prophet Isaiah son of Amoz came true,

11. which says, '*Days are coming upon you and upon your people and upon your father's house that*

12. *have never come before, since the departure of Ephraim from Judah*' (Isa 7:17), that is, when the two houses of Israel separated,

---

[89] Portions of this passage are preserved in 4Q266 3 iii 18-22 and 4Q269 5 1-4. See Baumgarten, DJD XVIII, 44, 128. Unlike the משיח passages in CD noted above, Xeravits does consider this passage to be 'messianic.' See Xeravits, *King, Priest, Prophet*, 37.

[90] The CD manuscripts (rightly) have not been published in a DJD edition. The transcription (by Martin Abegg, Jr.) and translation (by Edward Cook) cited here are those from Emanuel Tov, ed., *The Dead Sea Scrolls Electronic Library, Revised Edition 2006* [CD-ROM] (Dead Sea Scrolls Electronic Reference Library; Leiden: Brill, 2006).

13. Ephraim departing from Judah. All who backslid were handed over to the sword, but all who held fast

14. escaped to the land of the north, *vac* as it says, '*I will exile the tents of your king*

15. *and the foundation of your images beyond the tents of Damascus*' (cf. Amos 5:26-27). *vac* The books of Law are the '*tents of*

16. *the king*' (cf. Amos 5:26), as it says, '*I will re-erect the fallen tent of David*' (cf. Amos 9:11). *vac* '*The king*' (cf. Amos 5:26) is

17. <Leader of> the nation and the <? of your images> '*foundation of your images*' (cf. Amos 5:26) is the books of the prophets

18. whose words Israel despised. *vac* '*The star*' (Amos 5:26) is the interpreter of the Law

19. who comes to Damascus, as it is written, '*A star has left Jacob, a staff has risen*

20. *from Israel*' (Num 24:17). The latter is the leader of the whole nation; when he appears, he will shatter

21. all the sons of Sheth (Num 24:17). They escaped in the first period of God's judgement,

VIII, 1. but those who held back were handed over to the sword.

In the immediate context the author of CD has been discussing the commitment to the Torah required of those (presumably Essenes) who live in the land of Israel among others not so committed. To distinguish the fates of these parties, he cites Isa 7:17 (CD A VII, 11-12), which recalls the hardships of the period in which Israel and Judah divided. Those devoted to the Torah are said to have escaped לארץ צפון, 'to the land of the north,' presumably to Syria. Perhaps the author introduces this element under the influence of Jer 31:8, which prophesies a future act of gathering God's remnant מארץ צפון, 'from the land of the north.' This possibility is especially appealing because of the 'new covenant' overtones in both Jer 31 and CD. Thus, for example, CD A VIII, 20-21: 'This is the word that Jeremiah spoke to Baruch son of Neriah, and Elisha to Gehazi his servant. So it is with all the men who entered the new covenant in the land of Damascus.'

The author then draws on the reference to Syria and adapts a citation from Amos 5:26-27 (in lines 14-15) that differs significantly from the MT.[91] In Amos this too (like the earlier citation from Isaiah)

---

[91] Unfortunately this passage is not otherwise extant among the Qumran Scrolls (MT וּנְשָׂאתֶם אֵת סִכּוּת מַלְכְּכֶם וְאֵת כִּיּוּן צַלְמֵיכֶם כּוֹכַב וְהִגְלֵיתִי אֶתְכֶם מֵהָלְאָה לְדַמָּשֶׂק).

is a passage about hardships in a time of political upheaval, explicitly linked here to idolatry. As noted by Baumgarten and Schwartz, however, the author of this section of CD has recast the passage to speak of an exile to, not beyond, 'Damascus.'[92] As such, it is transformed into a positive reference from the perspective of the community. The סכות and כיון originally were references to the Mesopotamian deities Sakkuth and Kaiwan; Jörg Jeremias notes that in a later era "the Masoretes distorted the Assyrian-Babylonian divine names with the vowels of *šiqqûṣ*, 'abomination.'"[93] In CD, however, both סכות and כיון are positive images. The reference to סכות is read in light of God's promise to restore 'the fallen tent [סוכת] of David' (Amos 9:11). This points to the reestablishment of the 'books of the Law.' The 'king' appears to be identified with the 'assembly' (קהל) in lines 16-17, though the Davidic parallel instituted by the סוכת/סכות correlation and the later identification in lines 19-20 of the 'staff' (of Num 24:17) with 'the leader [or prince, נשיא] of the whole nation [כל העדה]' tempts one to seek a more messianic interpretation in lines 16-17 beyond its *prima facie* reading.[94]

This introduction of Num 24:17 into the midrash is facilitated by appeal to כוכב in Amos 5:26, despite the fact that this part of the verse had not earlier been included in the quotation of lines 14-15.[95] Before this, however, כיון is recast as a reference to 'the books of the prophets' (line 17). This further appeal to Amos 5:26 then allows for an explication of two figures from Num 24:17. The aforementioned 'staff' will emerge from and lead the nation. This leader explicitly comes 'from' or 'out of' Israel (מישראל) and so arises is a royal figure, perhaps even Davidic.[96] As such, perhaps one need not then be so concerned about finding a leader—as opposed to the people themselves—already in line 17.

More important for this investigation, however, is the 'star,' who is identified as is the interpreter of the Law—reflecting a traditional priestly function—relocated from 'Jacob' to Damascus (lines 18-20).

---

[92] Baumgarten and Schwartz, PTSDSSP 2, 27.

[93] Jörg Jeremias, *The Book of Amos* (trans. D. W. Stott; OTL; Louisville: Westminster John Knox, 1998), 98.

[94] Cook, for example, inserts 'leader of' into his translation in line 17.

[95] Xeravits assumes the phrase including כוכב did appear in the original version of this midrash. See Xeravits, *King, Priest, Prophet*, 45.

[96] Cf. VanderKam, "Messianism," 229.

Though grammatically it is possible to interpret the Hebrew participle הבא in line 19 to mean this figure had come in the past, a future interpretation is equally possible.[97] (The latter certainly accords well with expectations of an eschatological interpreter in other Qumran literature.) If a priest is expected in CD, this would seem to explain CD A XIV, 19, where one reads of atonement perhaps made by the messiah(s): [עד עמוד משי]ח אהרן וישראל ויכפר עונם מ[נחה וחטאת].[98]

Thus on the basis of internal argumentation, one may conclude that CD A VII, 9-VIII, 1 presents two messianic figures, one royal and one priestly. The presence of a priestly messianic figure may also be supported by the discussion of atonement in CD XIV, 19.[99]

Additionally, this *may* lend credence to the bifurcated interpretation of משיח אהרון וישראל. Admittedly one must be cautious here. The foregoing midrash appears only in manuscript A from the Cairo geniza. Manuscript B has instead a very different midrash in CD B XIX, 5-14 that need not be addressed in detail here beyond the following observations. The argument there uses entirely different verses than those utilized in CD A VII, 9-VIII, 1, instead discussing Zech 13:7 and Ezek 9:4. The midrash is significantly shorter than that in CD A, and the point is that the משיח אהרון וישראל will save the righteous but bring judgment on the wicked. Here a martial task for the figure(s) is implied, something that has minimal relationship to a priestly role; yet, even if only one figure is anticipated, as 'messiah *of Aaron* and Israel' the terminology requires that he be a priest. As would be expected, scholarly debate about how to understand the origins of these alternate midrashic sections has been vigorous; proposals include redactions due to changing messianic views in the community and various sorts of haplography.[100]

Regardless of whether the midrash of CD A was an original element of the *Damascus Document*, it is documented in the Cave 4 fragments

---

[97] Xeravits, *King, Priest, Prophet*, 45-46.

[98] The reconstruction is that of Abegg and is very similar to those offered by Broshi, *Damascus Document*, 37; and García Martínez and Tigchelaar, *DSSSE* 1:574. Baumgarten and Schwartz (PTSDSSP 2, 57) do not seek to reconstruct the missing words in this line.

[99] Cf. VanderKam, "Messianism," 229. The verb יכפר is singular, presumably in grammatical conformity to the singular משיח.

[100] See discussion in Collins, *Scepter*, 80-82; and Xeravits, *King, Priest, Prophet*, 38-41.

(unlike the alternative midrash of CD B).[101] But because one may not know at what point the midrash of CD A appeared in the redactional history of the *Damascus Document*, one cannot state with complete confidence that its expectation of two messianic figures was also reflected in the phrase משיח אהרון וישראל when it appears in other sections of the text. On the other hand, if the CD A midrash was a later addition to the text, it may be significant that its redactor felt no compulsion to modify the phrase משיח אהרון וישראל to bring the rest of the document into harmony with its bifurcated messianism. Furthermore, VanderKam noted the redundancy of the disputed phrase if only one figure is expected, and one should yet again be reminded that a solitary messiah in CD would by necessity be a priest since he would be 'of Aaron.' Since also the contexts in which the phrase appears normally concern teaching or keeping the law, this further implies at a minimum the expectation of a messiah priest.

2.2. *Rule of the Congregation*

This text is preserved in only the two lacunae-filled columns of 1QSa (1Q28), in the same scribal hand as 1QS and following that important text on the same scroll.[102] As such, the copy is dated on paleographical grounds, like 1QS, to 100-75 B.C.E. Also, Stephen Pfann has identified several fragments from Cave 4 (4Q249[a-i]) as 4Qpap cryptA Serekh ha-ᶜEdah[a-i]. As indicated by the sigla, these are papyrus manuscripts written in a cryptic alphabet. They are very poorly preserved, but Pfann has identified all but two of the 23 fragments with a parallel in the two columns of 1QSa and dates them to the second century B.C.E.[103] Others are less convinced of these identifycations.[104] Dating the composition of *Rule of the Congregation* is

[101] Xeravits, *King, Priest, Prophet*, 41.

[102] Major editions of 1QSa include D. Barthélemy, DJD I, 107-18 and pls. XXIII-XXIV; Licht, *Rule Scroll*; and James H. Charlesworth and Loren T. Stuckenbruck, PTSDSSP 1, 108-17. See also the short monograph on the book, Lawrence H. Schiffman, *The Eschatological Community of the Dead Sea Scrolls: A Study of the Rule of the Congregation* (SBLMS 38; Atlanta: Scholars Press, 1989).

[103] Stephen J. Pfann, DJD XXXVI, 515-72.

[104] So Xeravits, who states that the poor state of preservation requires demands that Pfann's identifications "must remain hypothetical." See Xeravits, *King, Priest, Prophet*, 22-23.

difficult; it clearly is sectarian, and the text appears to be a composite work. Xeravits asserts a date in the second century B.C.E., while Charlesworth and Stuckenbruck more cautiously state "sometime before 75 B.C.E."[105]

Despite the fact that the major extant witness to the text was appended by the scribe to 1QS, *Rule of the Congregation* is a text distinct from *Rule of the Community*. Nevertheless, *Rule of the Congregation* does have conceptual affinities both with it and the *War Scroll*. The latter, as will be discussed more fully below, describes the great eschatological battle expected by the Qumran community, and presumably the *Rule of the Congregation* describes community life thereafter. Lawrence Schiffman sees such a connection and writes further on the relationship between the rules of 1QSa and 1QS:

> When read in comparison with the Rule of the Community (1QS), it becomes clear that the Rule of the Congregation presents a messianic mirror image of the life of the sectarians in the present, premessianic age. Once can conclude that life in the present sectarian community is seen as an enactment of what will be the order of the day at the End of Days. At the same time, the life of the eschatological community reflects a transformation of the present order into the life of the End of Days.[106]

Others find even closer connections in some passages with the *Damascus Document*, which includes directives for Essenes engaged in normal family relations outside of Qumran, because *Rule of the Congregation* assumes women and children will be included in the eschatological assembly.[107]

The text opens with notice of an assembly 'in the end of days' at which numerous regulations are enumerated, classified by Charlesworth and Stuckenbruck as "stages of life" (1QSa I, 6-18) and "disqualifications" (1QSa I, 19-22). Comments on duties of the Levites (1QSa I, 22-25), consecration for the assembly (1QSa I, 25-27), and who may (1QSa I, 27-II, 3) or may not participate (1QSa II, 3-10) then follow. Most significant for the present study, however, is 1QSa II, 11-22, which concludes the text. The scene is of a banquet at the time when God has provided the משיח ישראל ('messiah of Israel'), clearly

---

[105] Xeravits, *King, Priest, Prophet*, 23; Charlesworth and Stuckenbruck, PTSDSSP 1, 108.

[106] Lawrence Schiffman, "Rule of the Congregation," *EDSS* 2:797-99, esp. 797.

[107] Charlesworth and Stuckenbruck, PTSDSSP 1, 109, particularly in light of 1QSa I, 4.

a lay figure and presumably militaristic.[108] The 'chief priest of the congregation' is never called a 'messiah,' but he takes precedence over the 'messiah of Israel' in two ways.[109] The high priest, other priests, and finally the 'men of renown' all take their places in the banquet hall before the messiah of Israel and other military chiefs enter. After pronouncing the blessing on the bread and wine, the priest is the first to take the bread, followed by the messiah; both then bless the members of the congregation. The eschatological setting and the priest's preferential status over the messiah of Israel have prompted many interpreters to infer that this priest is also a 'messianic' figure. Admittedly the text suffers from unfortunate lacunae in places that *might* have included more information about this priest, but as the text stands he is never explicitly identified as a messianic figure, nor does anything in the context indisputably point to this.[110] The priest's activities in the text are limited to preeminent standing and leadership in the messianic banquet.

2.3. *Rule of the Blessings*

The nomenclature for this text, 1QSb (1Q28b), indicates that it too is preserved on the same scroll as 1QS and 1QSa.[111] The extant text includes much of five columns of 28 lines each, though much of the middle portion of each column has not survived. While 1QS is preserved almost completely, it was on the interior of the scroll; 1QSb was on the outside and suffered much more deterioration.[112]

---

[108] Much debate concerns the verb denoting God's action vis-à-vis this 'messiah' at the end of 1QSa II, 11. Barthélemy read יוליד in the transcription of the text (DJD I, 110), a reading supported by Xeravits because of the biblical precedent of God 'begetting' the king of Israel in Ps 2:2 (*King, Priest, Prophet*, 26-27). In his notes on the line, however, Barthélemy accepted an emendation (which he credited to Józef Milik) to יוליך and thus the idea that God 'will bring' the messiah (DJD I, 117). This emendation was also accepted by Charlesworth and Stuckenbruck in their recent edition (PTSDSSP 1, 109, 116-17).

[109] Absence of the term 'messiah' for the priest is emphasized in Schiffman, "Messianic Figures and Ideas," 121.

[110] VanderKam, "Messianism," 223-24.

[111] Major editions of 1QSb include Milik, DJD I, 118-30 and pl. XXV-XXIX; Brooke, DJD XXVI, 227-33 and pl. XXIV; Licht, *Rule Scroll*, 273-89; and Charlesworth and Stuckenbruck, PTSDSSP 1, 119-131.

[112] Milik, DJD I, 119.

The text is marked by a series of blessings pronounced on various groups or figures, though multiple proposals for the identity of those addressed have been offered. While the text seems to discuss a messianic priest, its fragmentary condition allows for even less certainty than is possible for 1QSa. Infused with the language of the priestly blessing of Num 6:24-25, 1QSb contains sections that clearly can clearly be identified as prescribing blessings on the entire community, priests, and the 'Prince of the Congregation' (who clearly seems to be a Davidic messiah; cf. 'prince' in Ezek 34:24). Whether blessings for other figures or groups are also seem to be present, but identifications of those being blessed have not survived, and scholars lack a consensus about how to reconstruct the text.

Milik, the original editor of the text, proposed the following outline for the text, which still finds support from several scholars:[113]

I, 1-21	blessing on members of the Qumran community
I, 21-III, 21	blessing on the high priest
III, 22-V, 19	blessing on the Zadokite priesthood
V, 20-29	blessing on the Prince of the Congregation[114]

In spite of the absence of any surviving text for I, 11-25, Milik asserted that a blessing on the high priest began in I, 21 primarily because of a marginal notation that survived to the left of 1QSa II, the column that would have preceded 1QSb I on a scroll that began with 1QS. Milik interpreted this as a paragraph marker indicating the beginning of a new blessing.[115] Citing language in col. III which he felt could not describe mortal priests, he reasoned that this text was consistent with other texts (including 1QS, 1QSa, 1QM, 4Q175, and CD) in presenting an eschatological high priest who would function alongside a 'messiah of Israel' figure, here identified as the Prince.[116]

Licht proposed a different reading of the text, charging that Milik's reconstruction of the blessing on the eschatological high priest was too

---

[113] Martin G. Abegg, Jr., notes that Milik's outline has been followed by Jean Carmignac, Geza Vermes, and Michael Wise. See Abegg, "1QSb and the Elusive High Priest," in *Emanuel: Studies in Hebrew Bible, Septuagint, and Dead Sea Scrolls in Honor of Emanuel Tov* (eds. S. M. Paul, R. A. Kraft, L. H. Schiffman, and W. W. Fields; Leiden: Brill, 2003), 3-16, esp. 3.

[114] Milik DJD I, 120-29. Presumably the blessing on the Prince continued in col. VI. Several other small fragments of the document were recovered but were not incorporated into the extant columns by Milik.

[115] Milik, DJD I, 119, 122.

[116] Milik, DJD I, 121-22.

long and out of place. Licht proposed that the blessing on an eschatological high priest instead appeared at the beginning of col. IV, not in col. I, and he argued that this placement immediately before the blessing on the Prince was more consistent with other Qumran texts that present the two messianic figures as a pair:[117]

I, 1-9	blessing of the faithful
II, 22-28	blessing of an unidentified group
III, 1-6	blessing of an official or group of importance
III, 22-28	blessing of an unidentified group
IV, 22-28	blessing of the high priest
V, 18-19	unidentified
V, 20-29	blessing of the Prince of the Congregation[118]

Overall Licht's reconstructions were more cautious than those of Milik. Phrases in IV, 24-25, such as ואתה כמלאך הפנים במעון קודש ('but you are like the angel of the presence in an abode of holiness'), lend strong support to his proposal.[119]

Building on the work of Licht (and to an extent Milik), Abegg has proposed the following outline for 1QSb:

I, 1-20	blessing on the faithful
I, 21-II, 20?	blessing on an unidentified group or individual
II, 21?-III, 21	blessing on an unidentified group or individual
III, 22-IV, 19	blessing on the Zadokite priests
IV, 20-V, 19	blessing on the high priest
V, 20-VI, 20?	blessing on the Prince of the Congregation[120]

Abegg finds three major phrases in IV, 20-V, 19 that validate his theory that a blessing on the eschatological high priest stood here. The phrase from IV, 24-25 cited above is significant because the figure blessed here is described as an 'angel of the presence,' not simply as being with the angels as the community as a whole is described in 1QH[a] XIV, 13. Also, in 1QSb IV, 23, one finds the phrase ולשאת ברוש קדושים, which Abegg translates as 'to place [you] at the head of the Holy Ones.' The 'holy ones' are the angels; their leader

[117] Licht, *Rule Scroll*, 273-89.

[118] Licht, *Rule Scroll*, 277-89, following here the translation of Wayne Baxter, "*1QSB*: Old Divisions Made New," *RevQ* 21 (2004): 615-29, esp. 617. Note that Licht (unlike Milik) did not attempt to classify the missing lines of the text. Licht's outline generally is followed by Schiffman, *Eschatological Community*, 72-76; and Charlesworth and Stuckenbruck, PTSDSSP 1, 119.

[119] VanderKam, "Messianism," 225; cf. Abegg, "1QSb," 4-5.

[120] Abegg, "1QSb," 10-12.

here must be the high priest because earlier the Zadokite priests as a group are blessed by being בתוך קדושים ('in the midst of the holy ones'; III, 25). Finally, in IV, 25-26 the figure is said to serve in the היכל מלכות ('temple of the kingdom') with the angels.[121] Abegg, following Licht, concludes that these blessings would have been pronounced annually at Qumran's covenant renewal ceremony.[122] As for the identity of the messianic priest, Abegg surmises that he would be whichever human priest happened to be serving as high priest at the time of the Prince's appearance.[123]

All of these readings have been recently criticized by Wayne Baxter, who allows only for blessings of the three types listed above:

I, 1-III, 21	blessing on the faithful
III, 22-V, 19	blessing on the Zadokite priesthood
V, 20ff	blessing on the royal messiah[124]

Baxter takes his cues for the divisions chiefly from the introductory formula that appears at the beginning of each of his three sections (דברי ברכה למשכיל לברך את).[125] More importantly, however, he finds a particular form of blessing in each section, each derived from a particular biblical text: Num 6:24-26 in the first; Deut 33:8-11 in the second (with Num 25:7-13); and Isa 11:2-5 in the third.[126] This is key for Baxter; he is most concerned with the second section, and use there of biblical blessings for the priesthood indicates that the priesthood also is in view in this portion of 1QSb. This in turn is important because it disallows the idea that a messianic high priest is being blessed.[127] Whereas, for example, Abegg found a blessing on this figure in IV, 20-V, 19 (but considered him to be a mortal high priest of the community), Baxter considers separate blessings on the priests collectively and on the high priest individually to be redundant.[128] A greater concern, though, is his rejection of the idea that the two

[121] Abegg, "1QSb," 11.

[122] Abegg, "1QSb," 12-14. In contrast, Bilha Nitzan proposes an eschatological setting for the blessings because no corresponding curses are mentioned; the presence of the 'Prince of the Congregation' would also imply such a setting. See Nitzan, "Blessings and Curses," *EDSS* 1.95-100, esp. 99.

[123] Abegg, "1QSb," 15.

[124] Baxter, "*1QSB*: Old Divisions Made New," 618.

[125] The initial two words of the formula are omitted in V, 20.

[126] Baxter, "*1QSB*: Old Divisions Made New," 618-20.

[127] Baxter, "*1QSB*: Old Divisions Made New," 620, 625-28.

[128] Baxter, "*1QSB*: Old Divisions Made New," 625.

messiahs of 1QS and 1QSa must also be found in this text, especially since terminology for the supposed figures varies significantly among these three texts.[129]

In the end, though, Abegg's reading (following Licht) of 1QSb IV 20-V, 19 is persuasive, and Baxter's suffers due to his overconfidence in the idea that all of the division markers in the text have survived. The terms 'high priest' and 'messiah' are not extant and much of the context is missing, yet the language seems best directed to an individual figure, not the entire priesthood, and seems to indicate a high priest who leads the angelic temple worship. As such, it implies cultic worship in the very presence of God, i.e. in a heavenly context, at the time when God has sent the Prince and the distinction between earthly and heavenly worship has been obliterated. Certainly caution must be exercised, but the pairing of the priestly and royal messianic figures matches the diarchy evidenced in several other Qumran texts. Though such language is not extant, one might with only a little imagination propose (especially in light of CD A XIV, 19) that the author of 1QSb conceived of a high priest who would make an eschatological sacrifice of atonement in the heavenly temple. That, though, is only an assumption of what might have appeared in the lost lines, and ultimately little can be concluded for this study on the basis of 1QSb.

2.4. *War Scroll*

This text, published by the first editor of its major manuscript as *The War of the Sons of Light with the Sons of Darkness*, is represented in 1QM (=1Q33), 4Q491-96, and perhaps in 4Q285 and 11Q14.[130] Text

---

[129] Baxter, "*1QSB*: Old Divisions Made New," 625-26.

[130] The first publication of 1QM (brief introduction, transcription, and photographs) was the posthumous edition of E. L. Sukenik, ed., *The Dead Sea Scrolls of the Hebrew University* (Jerusalem: Magnes, 1955 [Hebrew 1954]), 35-36, pl. 16-34. Subsequent major editions of 1QM include Yigael Yadin, *The Scroll of the War of the Sons of Light against the Sons of Darkness* (Oxford: Oxford University Press, 1962); and J. Duhaime, PTSDSSP 2, 80-141. For 4Q491-96, see M. Baillet, DJD VII, 12-68 and pls. V-VII, X, XII, XIV, XVI, XVIII, and XXIV; and J. Duhaime, PTSDSSP 2, 142-97. In addition, see 4Q497, called a "War Scroll-Like Fragment," in J. Duhaime, PTSDSSP 2, 198-203. For 4Q285, see P. Alexander and G. Vermes, DJD XXXVI, 228-46 and pls. XII-XIV. For 11Q14, see F. García Martínez, E. Tigchelaar, and A. S. van der Woude, DJD XXIII, 243-51 and pl. XXVIII.

from 20 columns is relatively well preserved in 1QM, a manuscript dated to the latter decades of the first century B.C.E.[131] The Cave 4 materials are much more fragmentary and range in date from the first half of the first century B.C.E. (4Q493) to the early first century C.E. (4Q494). The fragments of 4Q496 are of papyrus rather than skin. Some divergences in the Cave 4 fragments from the extant text of 1QM imply a history of literary development for the work, and 4Q497 may include fragments of a related but different work from 1QM.[132] Scholars remain divided between proposals for dating the text to the second or first century B.C.E., but final redaction before 150-100 B.C.E. is unlikely because of the text's dependence on Daniel and *Jubilees*.[133]

As the title implies, the text concerns the eschatological war between the 'sons of light' and 'sons of darkness,' respectively led by the 'Prince of the Congregation' and Belial. The war spans a period of 35 years, interrupted every seven years for a sabbatical year of rest (1QM II). A high priest and other priests are mentioned frequently in the document; tasks of priests include blowing horns to signal various stages in the battle (1QM VII, 9-IX, 9; XVI, 3-XVIII, 4; cf. Num 10:9) and pronouncing numerous words with the high priest.

The most intriguing discussion of priests is found in 1QM II, 1-6, where the high priest and rotating groups of priests and Levites are said to take up their cultic duties:

> These shall take their station at the holocausts and at the sacrifices to prepare a soothing incense for the good pleasure of God, to atone [לכפר] on behalf of all his congregation and to grow fat before him steadily at the table of glory. They shall arrange all these during the appointed time of the year of remission [במועד שנת השמטה]. (1QM II, 5-6, PTSDSSP)

The high priest, then, appears to lead a temple service in an eschatological sabbatical year.[134] This is reminiscent of Melchizedek's role in 11QMelchizedek (a text discussed in much detail in the following chapter of this study), though there Melchizedek is a

---

[131] Duhaime, PTSDSSP 2, 80.

[132] These issues are surveyed in Duhaime, PTSDSSP 2, 80-83. See especially the chart of correspondences on 82-83. For a summary of discussion of recensions of the text, see Philip R. Davies, "War of the Sons of Light Against the Sons of Darkness," *EDSS* 2:965-968, esp. 2:965-66. Davies considers the redactions so significant that he restricts use of the term 'War Rule' to 1QM (2:966).

[133] Xeravits, *King, Priest, Prophet*, 75-77.

[134] The sabbatical year is a שנת השמטה in Deut 15:1; 31:10; etc.

heavenly figure combining the priestly and militaristic roles (which clearly are distinguished in 1QM) in an eschatological Jubilee year.

The high priest participates in the eschatological war in numerous other ways, sometimes in the company of other priests and Levites. As in Deut 20:2-5, the high priest (הכוהן) exhorts and encourages the warriors with promises of God's presence with them (1QM X, 2-5). Explicit mention of the high priest almost certainly has been lost in the lacunae at the end of 1QM XII, because one finds in 1QM XIII, 1-6 that 'his brothers . . . with him' (ואחיו . . . עמו), the priests, Levites, and elders, pronounce blessings on God and the righteous, and curses on Belial and his lot; this is followed by a prayer of thanksgiving and deliverance (XIII, 7-18 extant, perhaps through XIV, 1).[135] Included here is an explicit thanksgiving for God's provision of 'the commander of light' (שר מאור; XIII, 10), the leader of God's forces, i.e., the Prince.

In XV, 4-XVI, 1 the high priest again speaks, this time reading a prayer as he walks among the warriors and reiterating the themes of encouragement and the certainty of the destruction of the wicked. Even more striking is XVI, 13-XVII, 9; after the trumpeting priests have signaled a retreat, the high priest goes to the front of the line again to encourage the warriors, this time drawing heavily on biblical imagery of God's wrath on the wicked, his miraculous provisions for Israel in battle, and the reassurance of angelic help in the battle. Finally, in 1QM XVIII, 5-XIX, 8(?) the high priest, priests, and Levites bless God and utter a prayer of thanksgiving as the conclusion of the battle—and thus the realization of 'everlasting redemption' (פדות עולמים; XVIII, 11)—draws near.

This text is also striking for two things it does *not* say about the high priest in 1QM XI. Numbers 24:17-19, whose 'star' was understood in CD A VII as the messianic priest, is cited in 1QM XI, 6-7 but with no elaboration on the identity of any figures. Instead, the emphasis is on God's deliverance. This use of Num 24:17-19 is nevertheless significant; its use here, in CD VII, and 4Q175 all testify to its eschatological interpretation.[136] Similarly, in 1QM XI, 7 mention

[135] An almost-identical phrase is preserved in 1QM XV, 4; the leading figure is the כוהן הראש. Compare also 1QM XVIII, 5-8.

[136] Xeravits, *King, Priest, Prophet*, 78.

is made of משיחיכה, 'your anointed ones,' but this clearly refers to prophets in the Hebrew Bible.

Finally, another passage in the *War Scroll* may contain words of the high priest, but the poor state of preservation of the text makes confident identification of the speaker impossible. In 4Q491 11 I, 8-19, the speaker boastfully describes his exalted state; he declares, among other things, 'I reckon myself among the divine beings [אלים], and my place (is) in the holy congregation' (line 14; PTSDSSP) and that he alone has 'a powerful throne in the congregation of the divine beings' (line 12; PTSDSSP). Baillet, the DJD editor of the text, considered the speaker to be the archangel Michael, but Morton Smith argued that the speaker is a human who claims to have been exalted into heaven. Collins proposes that the speaker is the eschatological high priest but that this saying, paralleled in 4Q471b and 4Q427, was interpolated into the *War Scroll*.[137] Martin Abegg denies that this passage is even part of the *War Scroll* for paleographical, orthographical, and literary reasons, and he instead associates it with the *Hodayot*.[138] Finally, Israel Knohl proposed that the speaker is the failed messianic figure Menahem, an Essene acquaintance of Herod the Great according to Josephus (*Ant.* 15.372-79); he further proposes that this Menahem was the role model for Jesus' later messianic self-consciousness.[139] Needless to say, few have followed this interpretation.[140]

As noted above, evaluation of this passage is difficult because of the poor preservation of 4Q491. If one could confidently conclude that the declaration was a secondary insertion in the *War Scroll*, one would be inclined to follow Collins' suggestion that the redactor intended to present these as the words of the high priest because of the context into which the passage was inserted. The high priest certainly is presented

---

[137] See M. Baillet, DJD VII, 26-30; Morton Smith, "Ascent to the Heavens and Deification in 4QM[a]," in *Archaeology and History in the Dead Sea Scrolls* (ed. L. Schiffman; Sheffield: JSOT, 1990), 181-88; and Collins, *Scepter*, 136-53, esp. 138, 148-49.

[138] Previous scholars had noticed similarities between this saying and the hymns but nevertheless understood it as part of the *War Scroll*. See Martin G. Abegg, Jr., "Who Ascended to Heaven? 4Q491, 4Q427, and the Teacher of Righteousness," in *Eschatology, Messianism, and the Dead Sea Scrolls* (eds. C. A. Evans and P. W. Flint; SDSSRL 1; Grand Rapids: Eerdmans, 1997), 61-73.

[139] See Israel Knohl, *The Messiah Before Jesus: The Suffering Servant of the Dead Sea Scrolls* (Berkeley: University of California Press, 2000), esp. 51-71.

[140] For critiques of this and a similar attempt by Michael Wise to find a failed messianic figure in the Qumran texts, see VanderKam and Flint, *Meaning*, 268-72.

as speaking in the first person on several occasions in the *War Scroll*, though in such cases, as noted above, his purpose is exhorting the troops, not boasting of his own status. Indeed, the arrogant tone of the exaltation saying clashes with that of the high priest's words elsewhere in the text, and one wonders why a high priest would boast of receiving a throne. In the end, too little can be confidently asserted about this passage to allow one to draw on it for information about the eschatological priest.

In summary: though never called משיח in 1QM, the high priest has liturgical responsibilities, including making atonement, and plays a significant role in the Prince's eschatological war. His purity requirements prevent him from taking a combat role, yet the high priest nevertheless has the crucial responsibility of rallying the troops with prayers, blessings, and exhortations, often drawing on war materials from Scripture.[141] Even the courses of the battle are dictated by the trumpet blasts of the priests of whom he has oversight. Amazingly, more is said explicitly about the role of the high priest in this battle than is said about the role of the Prince. Since the outcome of this war has already been determined by God, one might perceive that the high priest is its real leader. The Prince has an important role to play because it cannot begin until he arrives, but it is the priest who has ultimate oversight of the troops.

2.5. *Florilegium* (4Q174) *and Catena*[a] (4Q177)

Most commonly called 4QFlorilegium, 4Q174 is sometimes also classified as an 'eschatological midrash,' an appellation introduced by its original editor, John Allegro.[142] The poorly-preserved text is a

---

[141] In 1QM IX, 7-9, priests blowing trumpets to signal various phases of the battle are said to avoid the corpses of the slain so as not to 'profane the oil of their priestly anointing [שמן משיחת כהונתם] through the blood of nations of vanity' (lines 8-9; PTSDSSP translation).

[142] The *editio princeps* is that of John M. Allegro in DJDJ V, 53-57 and pls. XIX-XX. He used the term 'eschatological midrash' in an earlier publication, John M. Allegro, "Fragments of a Qumran Scroll of Eschatological *Midrašim*," *JBL* 77 (1958): 350-54. Allegro's edition has been much criticized, especially in John Strugnell, "Notes en marge du volume V des 'Discoveries in the Judaean Desert of Jordan,'" *RevQ* 7 (1969-70): 163-276 and pls. I-VI, esp. 220-25. A new DJD edition of the text is in preparation. The text was edited in the Princeton edition by Jacob Milgrom, PTSDSSP 6b, 248-263. Major monographs on the text include George J. Brooke,

thematic midrash incorporating numerous passages of Scripture, including materials from Deut 33; 2 Sam 7; and Pss 1, 2, and 5. It is represented by 26 fragments dating to the second half of the first century B.C.E.[143] Because of the poor state of preservation, most editors have been content to transcribe and translate the materials on the several fragments; Steudel, however, has proposed the reconstruction of six columns, incorporating all but eight small fragments.[144]

Similarly, 4Q177 (4QCatena[a]) is preserved in 34 fragments dating from the second half of the first century B.C.E.[145] Of these, 20 were incorporated by Steudel into an arrangement of five columns.[146] The poor condition of the manuscript makes comprehension difficult, but numerous passages from Psalms and the Hebrew prophets are cited and interpreted; clearly the context is eschatological. As indicated by the traditional sigla, this text has long been associated with 4Q182 (4QCatena[b]).

More recently Annette Steudel has argued that 4Q174 and 4Q177 (4QCatena[a]) preserve different parts of the same text from two different manuscripts with differing physical qualities. As such, she proposes that these two texts should be reclassified as 4QMidrEschat[a,b], with 4Q178, 4Q182, and 4Q183 perhaps also being additional copies of the book, and that the text was composed between 72-63 B.C.E.[147] Steudel proposes that portions of the first six (of an unknown number of) columns of the work are preserved in 4Q174; she

---

Exegesis at Qumran: 4QFlorilegium in Its Jewish Context (JSOTSup 29; Sheffield: JSOT, 1985); and Annette Steudel, *Der Midrasch zur Eschatologie aus der Qumrangemeinde (4QMidrEschat[a,b]): Materielle Rekonstruktion, Textbestand, Gattung und traditionsgeschichtliche Einordnung des durch 4Q174 ('Florilegium') und 4Q175 ('Catena A') repräsentierten Werkes aus den Qumranfunden* (STDJ 13; Leiden: Brill, 1994). For a brief overview, see Brooke, "Florilegium," *EDSS* 1:297-98.

[143] Brooke, "Florilegium," 1:297.

[144] Steudel, *Der Midrasch*, 23-29.

[145] George J. Brooke, "Catena," *EDSS* 1:121-22, esp. 121.

[146] Steudel, *Der Midrasch*, 71-76.

[147] See Steudel, *Der Midrasch*; and Annette Steudel, "4QMidrEschat: «A Midrash on Eschatology» (4Q174+4Q177)," in *The Madrid Qumran Congress: Proceedings of the International Congress on the Dead Sea Scrolls, Madrid 18-21 March, 1991* (2 vols.; ed. J. Trebolle Barrera and L. Vegas Montaner; STDJ 11; Leiden: Brill, 1992), 2:531-41. Steudel argues that col. I-VI of the manuscript are preserved in 4Q174 and col. VIII-XII in 4Q177 ("4QMidrEschat," 2:532). For earlier considerations of this connection, see Strugnell, "Notes en marge," 237. See Steudel, *Der Midrasch,* 152-57; and Steudel, "4QMidrEschat," 2:536 on the possibility that the other three manuscripts preserve the same text, though admittedly there is no extant textual overlap among these manuscripts. On the date, see Steudel, "4QMidrEschat," 2:540.

further suggests that 4Q177 originally included 18 columns, of which remains of columns VII-XII are extant.[148] Reasons for assuming both manuscripts contained the same text include their sequential citations of texts from Psalms (with minor variations) and the consistency of their citation formulae and other terminology.[149] Reception to her proposal has been mixed, and it was not reflected in the most recent major edition of these manuscripts by Jacob Milgrom.[150]

'The interpreter of the law' (דורש התורה) is mentioned in 4Q177 11 5, but the context is so poorly preserved that one cannot determine his function. The same phrase appears in 4Q174 1-2 I, 11, where the author states that the 'shoot [צמח] of David' will arise with 'the interpreter of the law' in the last days. The only extant word on 4Q174 23 is דורש.

While much is said about a Davidic figure, no further description of the 'interpreter of the law' is given. Nevertheless, what has survived leads many scholars to propose that this text presents a messianic diarchy of priest and king. As such, VanderKam points to a fragmentary citation of Deut 33:8-11, the blessing on Levi that says he will teach the law, in 4Q174 6-7 and notes the potential messianic significance of such a passage in an eschatological context.[151] Unfortunately, however, little else can be said because of the poor condition of the manuscript.

2.6. *Testimonia* (4Q175)

This text is of a very different sort than anything addressed above.[152] Consisting almost entirely of four quotations—with marginal notations

---

[148] Steudel, "4QMidrEschat," 2:532-33.

[149] Steudel, "4QMidrEschat," 2:533-35.

[150] For example, Xeravits accepts Steudel's proposal, but Brooke, who accepts Steudel's arrangement of the 4Q174 fragments as superseding his own edition, nevertheless rejects her proposal involving 4Q177. As noted, 4Q177 was published separately from 4Q174 in thc PTSDSSP edition; see Jacob Milgrom and Lidija Novakovic, "Catena A (4Q177=4QCat[a])," PTSDSSP 6b, 286-303. The Milgrom editions of both 4Q174 and 4Q177 are those included in *The Dead Sea Scrolls Electronic Library, Revised Edition 2006*.

[151] VanderKam, "Messianism," 227-28.

[152] Again the *editio princeps* is that of Allegro, DJDJ V, 57-60 and pl. XXI. See also Strugnell, "Notes," 225-29; Brooke, *Exegesis*, 309-19; Steudel, *Der Midrasch*, 179-81; Fitzmyer, "4QTestimonia," 59-89; and Steudel, "Testimonia," *EDSS* 2:936-38. See also the recent edition of Frank Moore Cross, "Testimonia (4Q175=4QTestim)," PTSDSSP 6b, 308-28.

demarcating each of these—this short text is one column of 30 lines on a single sheet of leather. The scribe is the same person responsible for 1QS, but the handwriting here is far less careful. The manuscript is dated to about 100 B.C.E.; Strugnell surmises that it may be the autograph because of its distinctive format, slipshod handwriting, and numerous corrections.[153]

No eschatological figure is specifically named in the text, which also lacks a narrative context. Instead, 4Q175 normally has been approached as a list of proof texts, with its first three quotations evoking a future prophet (Exod 20:21 SamPent, = MT Deut 5:28-29 plus Deut 18:18-19); king (Num 24:15-17; cf. CD and 1QM above); and priest (Deut 33:8-11; cf. 4Q174 above).[154] The text concludes with a quotation (Josh 6:26) pronouncing a curse on anyone who rebuilds Jericho and a vague application of the curse, presumably directed at a Hasmonean figure. John Hyrcanus may have been the target; he was described (admittedly much later) by Josephus as having held a combination of the offices of prophet, king, and priest (*Ant.* 13.299-300).[155] This Joshua material is paralleled in 4Q379 22 II, 7-14 (*Apocryphon of Joshua*^{b}) and likely is cited from that text.[156]

Testimonia is distinguished by its lack of commentary and elaboration on the quotations of Scripture other than sparse introductory formulae. Because of this, one cannot be entirely sure that the text has messianic implications. While most scholars do understand it as a collection of messianic proof texts, admittedly interpretation of the concluding Joshua material is more problematic.[157] In light of the latter, John Lübbe argued that the text is not messianic at all but instead functioned as rebuke for apostates in the early years of the

---

[153] Strugnell, "Notes," 225; Steudel, "Testimonia," 936.

[154] Theoretically the two Deuteronomy citations could be independent rather than drawn from Exod 20:21 in the SamPent, but the lack of an introductory formula before Deut 18:18-19—as appears before the quotation of Deut 5:28-29 and before quotations concerning the king and priest—implies that the materials originally from Deuteronomy are being cited as a unit. See further below the significance of this for John Lübbe's argument.

[155] Virtually every Hasmonean leader has been suggested, as surveyed by Steudel. Collins, following Hanan Eshel, asserts that John Hyrcanus most likely is intended. See Collins, *Scepter*, 94-5; and Eshel, "The Historical Background of the Pesher Interpreting Joshua's Curse on the Rebuilder of Jericho," *RevQ* 15 (1992): 409-20.

[156] Steudel, "Testimonia," 2.936-37. Eshel argues for dependence in the opposite direction; see Eshel, "Historical Background," 412.

[157] See, for example, VanderKam, "Messianism," 226; Oegema, *Anointed*, 93-94.

community's existence.[158] Lübbe observes that the citations are all presented as statements in the past and that each concludes with a curse or other negative; as such, he proposes they were intended to offer warnings of judgment on those who would ignore God's commands. Whereas most scholars have found messianic figures in the first and third quotations, Lübbe understands the prophet as the Teacher of Righteousness and the priest as symbolic of "the sect itself in its contemporary priestly role."[159] As for the second quotation, he does admit that messianism may be present, but not in the way normally explained: "although something of the sect's messianic expectations underlie this text, neither the sect's messianism in general, nor particular details thereof are of primary concern here."[160] Instead, he wishes to stress the pattern he finds in each of the first three quotations—a figure, representing the sect, is evoked, then judgment is pronounced on the sect's opponents. The dualistic presentation of the faithful community over against those outside their covenant is reminiscent of the blessings and curses of the *Rule of the Community*.[161]

Ultimately, however, Lübbe's argument falters. He opens the article by challenging the scholarly assumption that *Testimonia* must point to a prophet and two messianic figures (presumably under the influence of 1QS IX, 11), and certainly that is a valid caution. Likewise, he criticizes the standard view that the quotation of Num 24:15-17 in 4Q175 9-13 points only to a royal figure, whereas in CD VII, 18-21 the 'scepter' (or 'staff') and 'star' clearly are two figures, a king and priest, the latter of whom is also 'the interpreter of the law." Lübbe demands that both a king and priest are intended by this quotation in *Testimonia*, but he explains away the priest: because the 'star' in CD VII is the 'interpreter of the law,' he assumes he must also be that in *Testimonia*, even though such is never stated.[162] Instead, the quotation cuts off in 4Q175 13 with talk of violence; no priestly tasks are demanded or even implied by this particular quotation of Num 24:15-17 unless one has an *a priori* expectation that the 'scepter' and 'star'

---

[158] John Lübbe, "A Reinterpretation of 4Q Testimonia," *RevQ* 12 (1986): 187-97. This argument is cited with approval in Abegg, "Messiah at Qumran," 133.
[159] Lübbe, "A Reinterpretation," 190-91.
[160] Lübbe, "A Reinterpretation," 189.
[161] Lübbe, "A Reinterpretation," 191.
[162] Lübbe, "A Reinterpretation," 188-89.

must be distinct figures here. Having found a priest in the quotation, Lübbe then effectively eliminates him by assimilating this 'interpreter of the law' with the prophet of the first quotation, i.e., the Teacher of Righteousness, because of the priest's presumed function borrowed from the interpretation of the 'star' in the *Damascus Document*.[163] His argument is further weakened by his assertion that the compiler of the *Testimonia* intentionally joined Deut 5:28-29 and Deut 18:18-19 to create the image of the prophet (on behalf of the community) who indirectly—through the rejection of his message—brings God's judgment on those outside the community.[164] The intentionality of this arrangement is crucial for Lübbe's argument, especially since he finds in this composite quotation features that solidify the comparison to the blessings and curses of 1QS I, 1-10.[165] As noted above, however, this same combination of elements from Deuteronomy appears in the SamPent of Exod 20:31, and manuscripts exhibiting features of that textual tradition are present among the scrolls. Though this particular verse is not extant, 4QpaleoExod^{m} (4Q22) preserves a version of the text otherwise consistent with the SamPent in this particular context.[166]

Lübbe correctly emphasizes the element of judgment in each of the first three citations; he also was correct to seek ties with 1QS, but not for the proper reasons. His rejection of the idea that the first three citations evoke three eschatological figures seems contrived. Instead, the observation that the same scribe is responsible for the references to the prophet and the messiahs of Aaron and Israel in 1QS IX, 11 and this collection of quotations that seem clearly to evoke a prophet, king, and priest strongly implies that *Testimonia* is a messianic proof-text. As Xeravits notes, "This fact hypothetically allows us to suppose that the *Testimonia* could even have been compiled by this scribe, seeking to collect biblical passages supporting this theological concept."[167]

As noted above, the polemical nature of the text seems clear, and hostilities between the Hasmonean house and Qumran leadership certainly are evident in other Dead Sea Scroll texts. Likewise, the

---

[163] Lübbe, "A Reinterpretation," 189, 191.

[164] Lübbe, "A Reinterpretation," 191, following John M. Allegro, "Further Messianic References in Qumran Literature," *JBL* 75 (1956): 174-87, esp. 186.

[165] Lübbe, "A Reinterpretation,"191.

[166] The DJD edition is that of Patrick W. Skehan, Eugene Ulrich, and Judith E. Sanderson, DJD IX, 53-130 and pls. VII-XXXII. Exodus 20:18-19 is extant in col. XXI, and col. XXII resumes with Exod 21:5-6.

[167] Xeravits, *King, Priest, Prophet*, 58.

correspondences of these particular offices and citations of Scripture with other Qumran texts that clearly are messianic appears decisive—even if in *Testimonia* the actions of Yahweh, not the prophet or priest themselves, are described. Perhaps a *via media* may be proposed—*Testimonia* is a polemical text against an arrogant Hasmonean facing divine wrath and whose legitimacy pales in comparison to that of the eschatological figures whose combined offices he currently claims. Collins comes to a similar conclusion: "The plurality of the messianic figures in question, however, was in itself a political statement, since it implicitly rejected the combination of royal and priestly offices by the Hasmoneans."[168]

Thus the text seems to indicate the expectation of a messianic priest (along with a political figure and a prophet) without clearly addressing the figure's own future activities. Admittedly, though, no commentary is present to indicate exactly what the compiler wishes to emphasize.

2.7. *Other Possible References to a 'Messianic' Priest*

A few other very fragmentary texts *may* be relevant for discussion of a priestly messiah, but their poor states of preservation make interpretation impossible.[169] Also, some texts discuss a priest but not a figure relevant for this survey. The latter category includes 4Q375 and 4Q376, both of which mention an 'anointed priest' but do not appear to be eschatological, and the similar 4Q374 and 4Q377, reflections on the exodus and conquest events.[170]

Two other texts, though, can be addressed briefly. In 4Q161 (4QpIsa[a]; *Pesher Isaiah*), a Davidic messiah is clearly discussed, and he is described in 4Q161 8-10 11-24 with a quotation from Isa 11:1-5.[171] In line 24 this royal figure said to be accompanied by

[168] Collins, *Scepter*, 95.

[169] VanderKam lists 4Q167, 4Q173, 1Q30, 4Q252, 4Q375-6, and 4Q521. Another candidate is 4Q285. See VanderKam, "Messianism," 232-33.

[170] The DJD editions of 4Q374-4Q376 were published by Carol Newsom (4Q374) and John Strugnell (4Q375-4Q376) in DJD XIX; and 4Q377 was published by James VanderKam and Monica Brady in DJD XXVIII. For further discussion of 4Q375-4Q376, see Zimmermann, *Messianische Texte*, 233-46. On 4Q374 and 4Q377, see Xeravits, *King, Priest, Prophet*, 121-27.

[171] The *editio princeps* is that of Allegro, DJDJ V, 11-15, pls. IV-V. See also Strugnell, "Notes," 183-86 and pl. I; Maura P. Horgan, *Pesharim: Qumran Interpretations of Biblical Books* (CBQMS 8; Washington, D.C.: Catholic Biblical

אחד מכוהני השם ('one of the priests of repute') carrying some sort of garments, but the manuscript breaks off just after that point. Similarly, in the preceding lines 21-23 the interpreter apparently reveals the identity of those who would teach the royal figure how to judge properly: 'and according to what they teach him [וכאשר יורוהו] so shall he judge, and according to their command' (line 23). Priests likely are described, but the lacunae prevent certainty. Regardless, clearly the reference is to multiple persons who teach, not a single priest.

Potentially more significant is 4Q541 (4QapocrLevi-b? ar), though again the poor state of preservation does not allow any firm conclusions.[172] The manuscript dates to the late second or early first century B.C.E., but because it is an Aramaic text and does not reflect sectarian distinctives, it likely was not composed at the Qumran community.[173] Also, though it normally is assumed to be an apocryphal Levi text, it does not appear to be directly related to the *Aramaic Levi Document*, a text discussed in detail below.[174] Much attention has been given to latter portions of the text, which discuss hostility toward the central figure, but what is of interest for this examination is the language of 4Q541 9 i 2. Here the figure is presented as a teacher but also as having another priestly function: ויכפר על כול בני דרה ('he will atone for all the sons of his generation').[175] The figure's significance certainly is exalted in the text, but he also faces much opposition in his era, a time in which many will go astray (4Q541 9 i 7). Presumably the text is eschatological, but one gets the impression that the priestly figure described in 4Q541 fills a different role than the messianic priestly figures discussed in the texts surveyed above. In the other texts the priestly figure is active in the era during or after the

Association, 1979), 70-89; and more recently Horgan, "Isaiah Pesher 4 (4Q161=4QpIsa[a])," PTSDSSP 6b, 83-98. Citations above are to the DJD edition; the passage cited corresponds to III, 15-29 in Horgan's reconstruction.

[172] The DJD edition was published (with that of 4Q540) by Émile Puech in DJD XXXI.

[173] Xeravits, *King, Priest, Prophet*, 111.

[174] Jonas C. Greenfield, Michael E. Stone, and Esther Eshel, eds., *The Aramaic Levi Document: Edition, Translation, Commentary* (SVTP 19; Leiden: Brill, 2004), 31-32.

[175] The translation is adapted from that of García Martínez and Tigchelaar, *DSSSE* 2:1081.

triumph over Belial and his lot, whereas here the priest himself faces active opposition.[176]

3. Antecedents to the Qumran Expectations of a Messianic Priest

The texts surveyed above clearly demonstrate an expectation of a priestly, eschatological messianic figure who would appear alongside a lay figure, often explicitly identified as Davidic. An eschatological prophet also appears occasionally, but more typical is the pairing of king and priest. When one looks at these several texts and the quotations from Scripture from which they are drawn, one is struck by how little exegetical support can be found for the priestly messiah. Indeed, the only passages of Scripture invoked in this manner are Deut 33:8-11; Num 24:17-19; and Amos 5:26-27. Those not sharing the exegetical methods and eschatological doctrines of the Qumran community might be hard-pressed to decipher a priestly messiah figure from these texts.

It is perhaps surprising that no passages about Zadok or even Phinehas are cited in these texts to support the expectation for a priestly messiah.[177] Perhaps even more glaring is the absence of references to the several passages of Scripture which seem to stress a bifurcated or even priestly leadership. Passages in Zechariah immediately come to mind, especially Zech 4:14, where Zerubbabel and the high priest Joshua are called the 'two sons of oil,' and Zech 6:9-14, where according to most scholars Joshua's name has been inserted as the messiah in the place of Zerubbabel's.[178] Similarly in Haggai, Zerubbabel and Joshua are repeatedly mentioned in tandem, though at the end of the book Zerubbabel alone is told that he will be God's signet ring. Attention should also be given to Jer 33:14-26, where the eternal nature of both the Davidic throne and Levitical priesthood are

[176] Possible allusions in this text to the 'suffering servant' of Isa 52:13-53:12 are beyond the scope of this study but are discussed by Zimmermann, *Messianische Texte*, 247-77.

[177] Among texts not unique to the Qumran community but nevertheless found among the Dead Sea Scrolls, Num 25:11-13 is significant for the portrayal of Levi in *Jubilees* and *Aramaic Levi* (see below).

[178] For a dissenting view of Zech 6:9-14, see Stephen L. Cook, *Prophecy & Apocalypticism: The Post-Exilic Social Setting* (Minneapolis: Fortress, 1995), 123-34.

discussed. One could also point to the dual leadership of Moses (as political leader) and the priest Aaron, the strong connection between the Davidic and Zadokite houses, and the long Persian-era theocracy headed by the high priests.[179]

It seems especially telling that the Qumran discussions do not build on the models of Zerubbabel and Joshua.[180] If the manifold theories about the Persian removal of Zerubbabel to nip messianic pretensions are correct, perhaps disappointment led to the de-emphasis of this paradigm in subsequent generations. One might also approach the issue by noticing that in some ways the Qumran community seems to ignore the Restoration community. The oft-cited CD I, 3-11 dates the community in relationship to the destruction of Jerusalem in 587/86 B.C.E.: a 'root' sprang up 390 years after this event, and the members 'groped' until God sent the Teacher of Righteousness 20 years later. While there is much debate about the historicity and/or potential symbolism of these numbers, one is struck by their point of reference. The Restoration community, with its strong priestly influence and rebuilt temple, is ignored in this chronology. Certainly it is clear in several of the Qumran writings that the Qumran community saw itself as the 'true' Israel; perhaps it also saw itself as the 'true' restoration community as well.

One must consider whether this messianic bifurcation at Qumran was a conceptual 'leap' or whether it was simply a step in a series of progressions—whether under literary or historical influences—toward the expectation of a priestly messianic figure. Certainly one should consider that their avoidance of especially the Zerubbabel and Joshua model may have been a subtle form of protest, perhaps against compliance with Persian hegemony. However, clearly books other than 'Scripture'—as such later would be defined by the rabbis and the early church—were considered as authoritative at Qumran. Some of these books present an exalted view of Levi and demand attention.

[179] For more comprehensive surveys, see José R. Villalón, "Sources vétéro-testamentaires de la doctrine qumrânienne des deux Messies," *RevQ* 8 (1972): 53-63; and Joachim Becker, *Messianic Expectation in the Old Testament* (Philadelphia: Fortress, 1980).

[180] Admittedly the phrase 'two sons of oil' appears in 4Q254 4 1, but the context is too fragmentary to draw conclusions about its significance there. See Collins, *Scepter*, 98-99, n. 55.

Scholars have long noticed the esteem with which Levi is presented in *Jubilees*, the *Aramaic Levi Document*, and *Testament of Levi* (from the larger work *Testaments of the Twelve Patriarchs*). As discussed further below, however, study of this common theme is complicated by numerous perplexing issues. Chief among these issues are questions concerning the textual reconstruction of the *Aramaic Levi Document* and the nature of the relationships between these three texts. Critical opinion on these issues is surveyed as relevant below, though for the examination at hand discussion of the themes of the texts, not their textual histories, takes precedence.

Details of the presentations of Levi vary in these three texts, and these discrepancies are very important data for discussions of literary relationships between the three. Yet, more importantly for the study at hand, all three explain the divine establishment of the Levitical priesthood as the fulfillment of a bequest to the tribal ancestor. One encounters the phenomenon of rewritten Scripture in these accounts, as the central narrative setting for these stories clearly is derived from Gen 34 and its context.[181] Jacob and his family have migrated to the city of Shechem among the Canaanites, and the patriarch has purchased property (Gen 33:18-20). At some point Dinah, Jacob's daughter by Leah, goes out to visit the women of the area and is raped by Shechem, son of Hamor the Hivite. Smitten with Dinah, Shechem desires her as his wife, so he solicits his father to make this request of Jacob (Gen 34:1-4).[182] Jacob, aware of the violence against his daughter, nevertheless receives Hamor and Shechem to consider their request. This occurs to the chagrin of Jacob's sons, who are outraged that their sister has been treated in such a way by an outsider. Hamor and Shechem plead with Jacob and his sons, pledging peaceful relations between the peoples and a bountiful marriage price for Dinah (Gen 34:5-12). The sons of Jacob respond that their daughter could only be given to one who was circumcised, and they propose that Shechem and his people be circumcised in order to foster the

[181] The passage and its context have attracted much scholarly discussion. As Robert Kugler notes about Gen 34, "The account is set within the cycle of narratives about Jacob, and appears intrusive since it shifts the focus from Jacob's generation to that of his sons." For further discussion, see Robert A. Kugler, *From Patriarch to Priest: The Levi-Priestly Tradition from* Aramaic Levi *to* Testament of Levi (SBLEJL 9; Atlanta: Scholars Press, 1996), 9-12, esp. 9.

[182] As noted by Kugler, this suggestion is in harmony with the prescription of Deut 22:28-29. See Kugler, *From Patriarch to Priest*, 12.

intermarriage they desire (Gen 34:13-17). In the biblical account, this clearly is proposed as a ruse, so Gen 34:13—'The sons of Jacob answered Shechem and his father Hamor deceitfully [MT בְּמִרְמָה]' (NRSV). Nevertheless, Hamor and Shechem prevail on all the men of the city to submit to circumcision, citing the necessity of this action for future social integration with Jacob's clan (Gen 34:18-24). Simeon and Levi, full brothers of Dinah by Jacob and Leah, attack the city on the third day, while those recently circumcised are still recovering. They kill all of the males, including Hamor and Shechem, and retrieve their sister. Jacob's other sons then take spoils of the women, children, livestock, and wealth in the city (Gen 34:25-29). Jacob is enraged by these actions, fearing retribution from the inhabitants of the region, but the sons are indignant that their sister's honor must be defended (Gen 34:30-31).[183]

Clearly nothing in this passage—as it stands in Genesis—points to an eternal priesthood for Levi, and even here he shares the spotlight of vengeance for his sister's shame with his brother Simeon. This passage is transformed into the setting for a priestly endowment, however, through midrashic interpretations that incorporate several other passages from the Hebrew Scriptures. Robert Kugler notes other texts from the Hebrew Bible that seem to have been read with Gen 34 to produce this explanation for Levi's reception of the priesthood:

a. Exod 32:25-29—in the wake of the golden calf episode at Mount Sinai and the resulting frenzy, Moses calls for those who will stand for the LORD to rally to him; the Levites respond and are given a divine command through Moses to slaughter their fellow Hebrews. Thus they are granted an ordination for the LORD's service and a divine blessing. For Kugler, this passage, read in conjunction with Gen 34, begins to justify a Levitical priesthood based on the tribe's zeal for purity.[184]

b. Num 25:6-15—as in the previous passage, again Israel struggles with idolatry. In Num 25:1-5, the specific enticement is the Baal of Peor at Shittim; this draws the wrath of the Lord, who commands that all participating in such relationships be killed. Another account about idolatry follows in 25:6-15; here the punishment is a plague. While the masses gathered in the assembly were weeping near the tent of

---

[183] This action is condemned both here and in Gen 49:5-7, as noted by Kugler, *From Patriarch to Priest*, 13.

[184] Kugler, *From Patriarch to Priest*, 12-14.

meeting, an Israelite man (interestingly, of the tribe of Simeon) openly brought a Midianite woman into his tent. Phinehas, son of Eleazar, son of Aaron, sees this and springs to action, spearing the couple in one strike and thus halting a plague that had claimed 24,000 Israelites. Because of his zeal, Phinehas and his descendants are promised 'a covenant of perpetual priesthood' (NRSV; MT בְּרִית כְּהֻנַּת עוֹלָם), and Phinehas is credited as having 'made atonement [וַיְכַפֵּר] for the Israelites.' Kugler finds here the important theme that God has specifically chosen the Levites to hold the priesthood in light of the actions of Phinehas, the descendant of Aaron.[185]

c. Deut 33:8-11—this passage, of a very different nature than those surveyed above, is Moses' blessing on the tribe of Levi, though as Kugler notes, it opens as if addressed only to Levi himself.[186] Moses calls on God to grant the priesthood to members of this tribe because their ancestors' faithfulness even to the detriment of their kin. Presumably the example cited evokes the Sinai incident of Exod 25 surveyed above, where Levites slaughtered their kin out of zeal, yet here the grammar implies a singular actor, not a group. (While it is common in the entire list of blessings for tribes to be referenced by their eponymous ancestor in the singular, such an observation need not impede the creative approaches of ancient interpreters.) Kugler finds in this passage the final building blocks needed to establish the divine origins of Levi's priesthood:

> With these verses the connection is finally made among the Levi/Levite texts of the Hebrew Bible between Levi's violent past and his appointment to the priesthood. The references to Levi alone in Deut 33:8-9a, 11 are sufficient evidence for his own divine election to the priesthood. The bonus is that Deut 33:8, 10a also link Levi with the priestly roles of making judgment and teaching the law; thus the passage

[185] Kugler, *From Patriarch to Priest*, 14-16.

[186] Kugler, *From Patriarch to Priest*, 16. Kugler also notes that Qumran versions of this text tend to have singular verbs, not the plurals of the MT, which further complicates interpretation of the passage, but concludes that it is not possible to determine which is the more primitive reading. See Kugler, *From Patriarch to Priest*, 17. Henryk Drawnel agrees that Gen 34(-37), along with Deut 33:8-11 and Mal 2:4-7 (see further below) provide the materials from which "the beginning of the Levitical tradition according to which Levi as an individual has a priestly status may be deduced." He denies, however, that the latter two texts directly influence the *Aramaic Levi Document*, and he asserts that "the image of Levi as a priest and scribe is never attested in the biblical texts, and is unique to the presentation contained in this Aramaic work." See Henryk Drawnel, *An Aramaic Wisdom Text from Qumran: A New Interpretation of the Levi Document* (JSJSup 86; Leiden: Brill, 2004), 3.

> contributes a new element to the biblical materials available for a portrait of Levi, the priest.[187]

For Kugler, the first extant example of such creative interpretation at work is found in Mal 2:4-7. This late passage signals a new phase in perception of Levi, one in which all four of the passages previously survey have been utilized to present the idea that Levi himself personally was chosen by God as priest. So Kugler:

> Declaring that God had a priestly covenant with Levi, the passage depicts Levi as an ideal priest. In 2:4bα and 5aα we encounter the phrases, בריתי את לוי, "My covenant with Levi," and בריתי היתה אתו, "My covenant was with him" . . . it is only by admitting the influence on Mal 2:4-7 of all four Pentateuchal passages addressed above that we can comprehend the origin of such a covenant.[188]

As such, Kugler rejects proposals that the passage is to be understood only in light of other texts that discuss covenants with Levites, not the eponymous ancestor himself.[189]

In summary, subsequent discussions of Levi's elevation to the priesthood are indebted to a midrashic interpretative tradition concerning Gen 34. The Shechem incident of this chapter provides the narrative framework for these accounts, read through the lens of Deut 33 and its motifs of blessing and an eternal priestly covenant. God's granting of these honors is justified by retroverting statements of praise for the zeal of Levi's descendents in Exod 32 and Num 25 to reinterpret Levi's own act in Gen 34 as zeal for righteousness. Such an interpretation of Levi is first found in Mal 2 but subsequently undergirds the presentations of Levi in three texts— *Aramaic Levi Document*, *Jubilees*, and *Testament of Levi* from *Testaments of the Twelve Patriarchs*—texts to which closer attention now turns.

3.1. *Aramaic Levi Document*

It is unfortunate that this document (hereafter *ALD*) must be treated first, because it exists only in fragmentary form reconstructed from

[187] Kugler, *From Patriarch to Priest*, 16-18, esp. 18.
[188] Kugler, *From Patriarch to Priest*, 18-21, esp. 18-19.
[189] Kugler, *From Patriarch to Priest*, 18-19. He articulates what each passage contributes to the portrait of Levi in Mal 2:4-7 in pp. 19-21.

disparate textual sources. Nothing approximating a complete copy has survived. Instead, the document is preserved in two fragments of a Cairo Geniza manuscript (discovered and published in the early 1900s); fragments found at Qumran cave 1 (1Q21) and cave 4 (4Q213; 4Q213a; 4Q213b; 4Q214; 4Q214a; and 4Q214b); passages incorporated into *Testament of Levi* in a Greek manuscript of *Testaments of the Twelve Patriarchs* from the Koutloumous monastery at Mount Athos, Greece; and a small Syriac fragment housed in the British Museum.[190] Several scholars have sought to reconstruct the entire *ALD* on the basis of these disparate manuscripts; recent major editions include those of Kugler, Henryk Drawnel, and the team of Jonas Greenfield and Michael Stone (editors of the Cave 4 Levi texts for DJD) in conjunction with Esther Eshel.[191] Such attempts have been complicated by the nature of the textual evidence and the need for

[190] The geniza fragments, unfortunately separated and further identified as Cambridge Geniza and Bodleian Geniza, were first published respectively by H. L. Pass and J. Arendzen, "Fragment of an Aramaic Text of the Testament of Levi," *JQR* 12 (1900): 651-61; and R. H. Charles and A. Cowley, "An Early Source of the Testaments of the Patriarchs," *JQR* 19 (1907): 566-83. Additions to the Mt. Athos manuscript of *Testaments of the Twelve Patriarchs* that Charles identified as having originated with *Aramaic Levi* were also discussed in the latter article. Fragments from Qumran cave 4 were first published by Józef T. Milik, "Le testament de Lévi in araméen: Fragment de la grotte 4 de Qumrân," *RB* 62 (1955): 398-406, and continued to appear in various publications, culminating with the DJD edition of Michael E. Stone and Jonas C. Greenfield in DJD XXII, 1-72 and plates I-V. Only a few words remain of 1Q21, published in 1955 by Milik, DJD I, 87-91 and plate XII. Émile Puech has argued that 4Q540-41 should also be identified with Aramaic Levi, but he has found few followers. See Puech, "Fragments d'un apocryphe de Lévi et le personnage eschatologique, 4QTestLévi^{c-d} (?) et 4QAJa," in *The Madrid Qumran Congress: Proceedings of the International Congress on the Dead Sea Scrolls, Madrid, 18-21 March 1991* (eds. J. Trebolle Barrera and L. Vegas Montaner; 2 vols.; STDJ 11; Leiden: Brill, 1992), 449-501. The Syriac fragment, B Add. 17, 193, was first identified in W. Wright, *Catalogue of Syriac Manuscripts in the British Museum Acquired Since the Year 1838: Part II* (London: Gilbert and Rivington, 1871), 997; subsequently it was published with the Cambridge geniza fragments in the aforementioned article by Pass and Arendzen. Editions of all of these manuscripts are included in the reconstructions of *ALD* in Drawnel, *Aramaic Wisdom Text*; and Greenfield, Stone, and Eshel, *Aramaic Levi Document*. For overviews of scholarly publication and discussion of *Aramaic Levi*, see Drawnel, *Aramaic Wisdom Text*, 14-21; Greenfield, Stone, and Eshel, *Aramaic Levi Document*, 1-6; Michael E. Stone, "Levi, Aramaic," *EDSS* 1:486-88; and Kugler, *From Patriarch to Priest*, 227-29.

[191] See Kugler, *From Patriarch to Priest*; Drawnel, *Aramaic Wisdom Text*; and Greenfield, Stone, and Eshel, *Aramaic Levi Document*. Greenfield was deceased before work specifically began on the latter volume, but his credit here represents his work on the texts for DJD publication. Note also that this and the Drawnel volume both appeared in 2004, in different series but from the same publisher (Brill).

scholars to impose artificial sigla on the source texts in order to reflect their distinctive reconstructions of *ALD*.[192] Likewise, confusion arises from the differing decisions made as to how to correlate the fragmentary evidence (especially the Qumran manuscripts) within the relatively more contiguous evidence from the medieval geniza texts.

Very detailed discussions of the physical characteristics of the several manuscripts relevant for this examination are available elsewhere, so only the most important issues will be addressed here.[193] The Cairo Geniza manuscripts are the starting point for any reconstruction of *ALD*. Though accidentally separated into holdings at Cambridge and Oxford when the manuscripts were removed to Britain, they are parchment, double-leaf *folia* from the same medieval manuscript. They are in the same scribal hand, present a semi-cursive style from the eastern Mediterranean, and are dated to the late ninth or early tenth century C.E. Each page originally had two columns on both the *recto* and *verso*. Of the two extant Cambridge folia, the first is very poorly preserved, with only about a third of one column (nine lines) from each side remaining; thus a full column and about 14 lines from a second are missing from each side. In contrast, the four columns of the attached second page are missing only a total of four lines. The Oxford manuscript has only one double-sided page, but the columns are intact.

Supplementing—and in several cases, overlapping—the textual contents of the geniza manuscripts are several sources from the Dead Sea Scrolls. All of these manuscripts are in poor states of preservation. Drawnel counts 88 individual fragments among 1Q21 (itself with 60 fragments); 4Q213; 4Q213a; 4Q213b; 4Q214; 4Q214a; and 4Q214b. The largest of these fragments easily is 4Q213 frag. 1, at 10 x 13 cm.[194] Editors of the respective DJD editions have dated most of these manuscripts to the first century B.C.E. in late Hasmonean or early

[192] This difficulty is recognized by the scholars themselves. Note, for example, the comments of Greenfield, Stone, and Eshel: "We are conscious of the problems that renumbering ancient texts creates, but this action was forced upon us by the multiple and conflicting numbering systems that had become customary" (*Aramaic Levi Document*, 10).

[193] Most of what follows on the physical characteristics of the various manuscripts is summarized from Drawnel, *Aramaic Wisdom Text*, 21-32. See also discussions in the critical editions of each text cited above.

[194] See his careful descriptions of the fragments in Drawnel, *Aramaic Wisdom Text*, 21-29.

Herodian hands. The chief exception is 4Q214b, dated perhaps as early as 150 B.C.E.[195]

The three Mount Athos insertions, found in MSS Koutloumousiou 39, are present in a well-preserved eleventh-century C.E. minuscule Greek manuscript of *Testaments of the Twelve Patriarchs*. They are included in the main body of the manuscript, not as scribal additions. The aforementioned Syriac source for *ALD* consists of only a few lines included in an anthology of brief passages from biblical and patristic texts. This manuscript is dated to 874 C.E.[196]

Like the extant sources themselves, the reconstructed composite text of *ALD* derived from these various manuscripts is riddled with lacunae. Enough remains, however, to reveal a retelling of the Shechem incident and its aftermath in which Levi receives a priesthood with heavenly commission. Though the earliest manuscript evidence for *ALD* is found in the various Qumran texts, most interpreters date the composition of *ALD* to about a century earlier in the third century or early second century B.C.E.[197] Several early scholars argued that *ALD* was originally written in Hebrew and later translated into Aramaic, but the modern consensus is that language of composition was Aramaic.[198] Also, the dialect is largely consistent in the Qumran and geniza witnesses, though, as noted by Greenfield, Stone, and Eshel, "the Geniza manuscript exhibits features which are to be expected in a medieval 'modernization' of a text from antiquity."[199]

Naturally any reconstruction of *ALD* is fraught with speculation because of the fragmentary nature of the textual evidence. Kugler's work is particularly ambitious because it was undertaken by necessity before the appearance of the DJD editions of the Cave 4 Qumran manuscripts. He argues for the existence of a Levi apocryphon predating *ALD* and utilized by the author of *ALD*. His assertion that *ALD* contains one lengthy vision of Levi, rather than two shorter ones, is a significant point of his work but one that has not generally been

---

[195] This data is conveniently gathered in table form from the various DJD sources in Greenfield, Stone, and Eshel, *Aramaic Levi Document*, 4.

[196] Drawnel, *Aramaic Wisdom Text*, 31-32.

[197] See, for example, Kugler, *Patriarch*, 23; and Stone, "Levi, Aramaic," 2:486. Drawnel opts for an earlier date in the late fourth century/early third century; see his extensive discussion in Drawnel, *Aramaic Wisdom Text*, 63-75.

[198] For a survey, see Drawnel, *Aramaic Wisdom Text*, 55-63.

[199] Greenfield, Stone, and Eshel, *Aramaic Levi Document*, 22-25, esp. 25.

followed in subsequent scholarship.[200] Kugler understands the text as emphasizing Levi as the model priest, one with a "passion for purity and attachment to the roles of scribe and sage"; the text's provenance is understood as intra-priestly polemics.[201]

Drawnel also discerns a priestly polemic, but one of a different sort, and he emphasizes the influences of Mesopotamian wisdom traditions on *ALD*. The proposed historical context is the early Hellenistic period, when Shechem was rebuilt and the rival temple at Mount Gerizim proved tempting for certain Jewish Levites. Thus reflection on Levi's exploits at Shechem would serve as a fitting call to Jewish zeal and endogamy. In his view, the text is "didactic in nature and intends to transmit an idealized image of a wise priest."[202]

Both Kugler and Drawnel are relatively bold in their reconstructions of *ALD*, whereas Greenfield, Stone, and Eshel decline to speculate on the placement of several fragments with significant extant text.[203] Likewise, they cautiously approach the issue of provenance, preferring instead to list "a number of characteristics of the document that may hint at the character of the group that produced it." These include use of a solar calendar (but non-polemically; here and elsewhere the sectarianism of the Qumran community is not evident); great stress on the centrality of the priesthood, the purity of the Levitical line, and transmission of teachings to subsequent generations; and distinctive positions on dualism, exorcism, and demonology.[204]

Because of the incomplete nature of the manuscript evidence, it is not possible to speak definitively about the flow of the text. A comparison of the reconstructions of Drawnel and Greenfield, Stone, and Eshel—both undertaken with full access to the DJD editions of the Levi texts—is instructive. The former reconstructs eleven sections of

---

200 So states Drawnel, who offers an extensive critique of Kugler's position in *Aramaic Wisdom Text*, 45-49. He notes in a review of Greenfield, Stone, and Eshel's edition, however, that their treatment of the vision materials is a "tacit acknowledgment of Kugler's one-vision theory." See Henryk Drawnel, review of J. Greenfield, M. Stone, and E. Eshel, *The Aramaic Levi Document: Edition, Translation, Commentary*, *RB* 113 (2006): 127-31, esp. 129.

201 Kugler, *From Patriarch to Priest*, 136.

202 Drawnel, *Aramaic Wisdom Text*, 74.

203 See their treatment of 'unplaced fragments' at *Aramaic Levi Document*, 216-34. The major of the fragments treated here, especially small remains with only a few extant letters or words from 1Q21, also do not figure prominently into Drawnel's reconstruction.

204 Greenfield, Stone, and Eshel, *Aramaic Levi Document*, 19-22, esp. 20.

material, whereas the latter find thirteen.[205] The materials present in Drawnel's §§6-11 do accord quite well with those of Greenfield, Stone, and Eshel's §§5-13—testifying in large part to the value of the geniza evidence for this continuity—but this high level of agreement is not the norm in the remaining columns.

In both reconstructions (§3 for Drawnel, but §1 for Greenfield, Stone, and Eshel), an early section of *ALD* narrates the Dinah episode of Gen 34. The text is extremely fragmentary here, and only a reflection on defilement and the proposal that the Shechemites be circumcised remain. Blame for the defilement of the sons of Jacob is shifted in *ALD* from Shechem to Dinah.[206]

Whether placed before or after the Dinah passage, both reconstructions also find among the early sections materials concerning a report to Jacob about actions of Simeon and Levi. Greenfield, Stone, and Eshel place this text subsequent to the Dinah passage above, assuming the flow of the Gen 34 account. Drawnel, however, positions this passage at the very beginning of his reconstruction. In both alignments, however, this passage is following by an account of Levi washing his clothes and self so that he could proclaim that 'I made all my paths upright' (GSE 2:5; cf. D 1:2; the phrase in full is preserved only in Greek). Next one encounters in both reconstructions an extended prayer of Levi (replete with biblical allusions) for holiness, direction, protection, and purity, concluding with a petition to remain in God's presence eternally.

This is followed in both reconstructions with a very fragmentary account of Levi's heavenly vision. Greenfield, Stone, and Eshel diverge from Drawnel and also place here materials concerning the priority of 'the kingdom of the priesthood' (GSE 4:7, utilizing text from 1Q21 1) over another sort of kingdom. This is followed (immediately in GSE; after other materials in D) by further visionary

---

[205] Note that the sigla created for both reconstructions refers to topical sections, not columns.

[206] Due to the complexity of the differing sigla and reconstructions, references will be made to the section and paragraph numbers assigned in the relevant reconstructions, which will allow access to further examination of the source materials. Drawnel will be referenced as D; Greenfield, Stone, and Eshel as GSE. Note that Drawnel uses his section numbers only in his translation of the entire reconstructed text (*Aramaic Wisdom Text*, 353-73), not in his commentary on the text; his paragraph numbers are in a running system (i.e., not restarting with each section), and these are used in both the commentary and full translation sections.

materials concerning conflicts of 'the kingdom of the sword,' but Levi's special status is affirmed, as is his reception of רבות שלם עלמא ('anointing [GSE 4:12]/greatness [D 5:6] of eternal peace'; 4Q213b).

The reconstructions largely converge for the remaining materials due to the more sustained nature of textual evidence from the geniza text. Levi travels to visit Isaac and receives a blessing. Presumably there is a shift of scene (to Bethel), then Levi is recognized as priest by his father and brothers when Jacob pays him a tithe, invests him in priestly attire, and consecrates him. Levi responds by offering sacrifices for his father and by blessing him and his brothers; then the blessings are reciprocated. Subsequently the scene shifts yet again, as Jacob and his sons are back in the company of Isaac at the residence of Abraham. When Isaac learns of Levi's experience, he instructs him in the 'law of the priesthood.' Such instruction includes the following: warnings about purity and sin; exhortation to practice endogamy; procedures for ritual purity in preparation for offering sacrifices; information on proper woods for use in burnt offerings; logistical procedures for burnt offerings; proper measures of wood, salt, flour, oil, wine, and frankincense to use with sacrifices; and concluding miscellaneous exhortations and reminders concerning his sacrificial office and dynasty.[207]

The remaining materials in both reconstructions are devoted to discussions of Levi's children and subsequent progeny and a wisdom poem, delivered in his old age to his descendents, in which Joseph is extolled as an example. The text concludes with what appear to be instructions on significance of wisdom and learning for Levi's descendants.

Two issues in the genealogical discussion deserve further attention. A list of ages at which Levi experienced particular things is preserved (in whole or in part) in the Cambridge geniza, Greek, and Syriac sources (GSE 12:6-9/D 9:78-81). Of particular interest are the following: Levi was 18 during the Shechem incident, when he 'destroyed the workers of violence'; he received the priesthood at 19.

Even more significant are Levi's comments about the birth of his son Kohath, preserved in both the Cambridge geniza and Greek texts (GSE 11:5-6/D 9:66-67). The text is presented by Greenfield, Stone, and Eshel as follows:

---

[207] These materials constitute GSE 5-10, D 6-8.

> And she conceived again and she bore by me according to the proper time of women [Greek]/another son [geniza] and I saw that to him would be an assembly of all the people and that he would have the high-priesthood; he and his seed will be the beginning of kings, a priesthood for all Israel.[208]

This passage is important because it underscores the dynastic nature of Levi's priestly office. Furthermore, Greenfield, Stone, and Eshel find special significance in the appropriation here of royal dynastic language from Abraham's blessing for Judah in Gen 49:10 through the use of etymology. The son 'Kohath' (קהת) receives 'an assembly of all the people' (Aramaic כנשת כל עמא), whereas in Gen 49:10 MT one reads of Judah that לו יקהת עמים. Though traditionally translated as 'the obedience of the peoples is his,' Greenfield, Stone and Eshel mount an impressive argument (citing evidence in targumim and Aquila's Greek translation) that many ancient Jewish interpreters instead read in Gen 49:10 something more akin to 'the assembly of the peoples is his.'[209] Because the overwhelming emphasis in the text is on Levi's reception of the priesthood, this argument that his priesthood may be described using dynastic language drawn from royal contexts is preferable to that espoused by Drawnel, who demands that the author introduces here a combination of royal and priestly roles.[210]

One finds then a major move beyond the *prima facie* information about Levi in the HB. Little text remains concerning his role in the Dinah affair, but shortly thereafter he is divinely invested with a dynastic priesthood. If Greenfield, Stone, and Eshel's reconstruction is deemed appropriate, the presence of Levi's prayer immediately after the Shechem account is significant. The prayer does not have the tone of confession, nor would such be expected in light of the commentary on his action ('destroyed the workers of violence') later in the text when his age at this episode is given. Instead, it appears to be a prayer of commitment and resolve, something fitting for a figure of righteous zeal, and is sets the stage for his investiture with a heavenly-ordained (something implied at a minimum by his visionary reception of 'anointing/greatness of eternal peace'), dynastic priesthood.

---

[208] This quotation has been adapted to represent the alternate versions presented by the editors, and brackets indicating partial words have been omitted. See Greenfield, Stone, and Eshel, *Aramaic Levi Document*, 95.

[209] Greenfield, Stone, and Eshel, *Aramaic Levi Document*, 184-88, esp. 184-85.

[210] Compare the discussion in Drawnel, *Aramaic Wisdom Text*, 307-09.

3.2. *Jubilees*

More familiar to most interpreters of Second Temple Judaism is the book of *Jubilees*, and as such fewer introductory comments will suffice. *Jubilees* purports to record Moses' reception of much of the narrative of Gen 1-Exod 12—now recast with a chronology based on 49-year Jubilee units—chiefly from 'the angel of the presence.'[211] As such it is a major example of the 'rewritten Scripture' genre in Second Temple Jewish literature. The text, which espouses a priestly perspective, most likely was written c. 170-150 B.C.E.[212] Fragments of 14 (or perhaps 15) manuscripts of *Jubilees* were found among the Qumran scrolls (1Q17-18; 2Q19-20; 3Q5 frgs. 3, 1; 4Q176a frgs. 19-21; 4Q216; 4Q218-24; 11Q12; perhaps also 4Q217); their orthographies are Hasmonean or Herodian, and they provide verification for earlier speculation that the text originally was written in Hebrew. The text was translated into Greek, which served as the basis for Latin and Ethiopic versions, and perhaps also into Syriac. The complete text is extant only in Ethiopic (in 27 manuscripts), no doubt preserved because of its canonical status in the Abyssinian Church.[213]

Jubilees 30-32 has much to say about Levi and the institution of the Levitical priesthood. As expected in *Jubilees*, the angelic narrator reports that the deeds and destiny of Levi and his descendents are recorded on heavenly tablets. In *Jub.* 30:1-20, the vengeance of Jacob's sons on the Shechemites for the rape of Dinah (Gen 33-34) is recounted. As in Genesis, the sons attack and kill all the males of the city, but discussion of the circumcision scheme is suppressed in *Jubilees*; in the latter only Simeon and Levi (rather than *all* the sons of Jacob) are explicitly said to execute the slaughter and plundering (*Jub.*

---

211 The standard critical text is that of VanderKam, *Book of Jubilees*, a two-volume edition which also includes an introduction and translation. All quotations of *Jubilees* are from VanderKam's translation. This edition supplanted the venerable work of R. H. Charles, published as *The Book of Jubilees or the Little Genesis* (London: A&C Black, 1902) and in a slightly revised form as "The Book of Jubilees," *Apocrypha and Pseudepigrapha of the Old Testament* (ed. R. H. Charles; 2 vols.; Oxford: Clarendon, 1913), 2:1-82. Recent introductions and translations include those by O. S. Wintermute, *OTP* 2:35-142; and R. H. Charles and C. Rabin, *AOT* 1-139 (the latter a revised version of Charles' *APOT* translation).

212 VanderKam, *Book of Jubilees*, 2:V-VI.

213 James C. VanderKam, "Book of Jubilees," *EDSS* 1:434-38. esp. 435, 437. See also VanderKam, "Jubilees, Book of," *ABD* 3.1030-32, and VanderKam, *The Book of Jubilees* (Guides to Apocrypha and Pseudepigrapha; Sheffield: Sheffield, 2001).

30:1-6). *Jubilees* then departs from the biblical narrative, as two theological points are derived from this story of vengeance. In *Jub.* 30:7-17, the rape of Dinah is presented as an illustration of the dire necessity of preventing sexual intermingling of Israelites and Gentiles. Execution of the guilty persons is the only means to restore purity to Israel, because no cultic sacrifice is sufficient for such an offense. In *Jub.* 30:18-20, Levi's zeal on behalf of Israel is then praised; rewards include a hereditary priesthood and a righteous accounting. Most striking is the angelic narrator's statement about the reward for Levi's zeal:

> Levi's descendants were chosen for the priesthood and as levites to serve before the Lord as we (do) for all time. Levi and his sons will be blessed forever because he was eager to carry out justice, punishment, and revenge on all who rise against Israel. (30:18)

Since the angel revealing this information to Moses uses the first-person plural in reference to the eternal priestly service, this clearly connects Levi's priesthood with the heavenly angelic cult.

An exhortation for subsequent generations of Israelites to imitate the righteousness of Levi follows in *Jub.* 30:21-23.[214] In 30:24-25 the discussion returns to the Genesis narrative, recounting the restoration of Dinah to the house of Jacob and the patriarch's concern about future relations with their Gentile neighbors. Jacob's protest of Gen 34:30 is much tamed in *Jub.* 30:25, and there the author of *Jubilees* adds (or displaces from Gen 35:5) notice that God prevented any possible retribution against the Israelites.

The Gen 35 account of Jacob's call to travel to Bethel is retold in *Jub.* 31 but with numerous details added. As in Genesis, Jacob calls for any idols in his household to be left at Shechem before the journey begins; this is intensified in *Jubilees*, as Rachel turns over those she had stolen from her father Laban (*Jub.* 31:2; cf. Gen 31:19, 33-35) and Jacob utterly destroys any such items before hiding them under the oak. Genesis 35:6-8 records Jacob's arrival at Bethel and construction of an altar, then it abruptly reports the death and burial at Bethel of

---

[214] Reflecting more broadly, John Endres notes: "The second-century struggle for an uncontaminated priesthood bore powerful resemblance to the stories from earlier days of Israel's history. Thus, although the historical circumstances had certainly shifted, the indispensable ingredient (zeal for Israel's God) remained the same." See John C. Endres, *Biblical Interpretation in the Book of Jubilees* (CBQMS 18; Washington, D. C.: Catholic Biblical Association, 1987), 149-50.

Deborah, the nurse of Jacob's mother Rebekah. Missing in the biblical text, however, is an explanation of why this Deborah was now in the household of Jacob, and the author of *Jubilees* seizes this opportunity to postulate an explanation in *Jub*. 31:5-32—after arriving at Bethel, Jacob visits his parents Isaac and Rebekah.[215]

Rebekah greets Jacob and two of his sons who accompany him, Levi and Judah, but clearly the emphasis is on their encounter with Isaac. What follows is a thinly-veiled adaptation of Joseph's visit with the elderly Jacob in Gen 48 and the deathbed blessings on Joseph's two sons. In *Jubilees*, Isaac places a hand on each of his grandsons and first blesses the one at his right, Levi. Isaac's comments include another statement connecting Levi's office to the angelic priesthood:

> May the Lord give you and your descendents extremely great honor;
> may he make you and your descendants (alone) out of all humanity approach him
> to serve in his temple like the angels of the presence and like the holy ones.
> The descendants of your sons will be like them in honor, greatness, and holiness,
> May he make them great throughout all ages. (31:15)

Isaac then echoes Moses' blessing on the tribe of Levi from Deut 33:9-11 with an exhortation for Levi to provide instruction for 'Jacob' and 'Israel,' a blessing, and a call for God's vengeance on any who might oppose Levi (*Jub*. 31:15-17).[216]

In the subsequent blessing on Judah, Isaac strikes a Davidic note: 'Be a prince—you and one of your sons—for Jacob's sons . . . Then the nations will be frightened before you; all the nations will be disturbed; all peoples will be disturbed' (*Jub*. 31:18). Jacob and Isaac converse that night and the following morning, when Isaac sends Jacob on his way along with Rebekah and Deborah. Then Jacob reflects on the significance of his meeting with his father:

---

[215] See James Kugel, "Levi's Elevation to the Priesthood in Second Temple Writings," *HTR* 86 (1993): 1-64. Modern commentators attribute this mention of Deborah to traditions that connect a person of that name with the area around Bethel and/or trees, as the judge Deborah in Judg 4 is also associated with a tree. See, for example, Gerhard von Rad, *Genesis* (rev. ed.; OTL; Philadelphia: Westminster, 1972), 337-38; and Robert G. Boling, "Deborah," *ABD* 2:113-14.

[216] James C. VanderKam, "Jubilees and the Priestly Messiah of Qumran," *RevQ* 13 (1988): 353-65, esp. 363-64.

> He said, 'Now I know that I and my sons, too, have an eternal hope before the God of all'. This is the way it is ordained regarding the two of them, and it is entered for them as an eternal testimony on the heavenly tablets just as Isaac blessed them. (*Jub.* 31:32)

Clearly two eternal lines are intended: one priestly and one political.

Further elaboration follows on the honors granted to Levi. After the party returns to Bethel, Levi dreams that he receives a priesthood of the Most High God for himself and his descendents. Without further explanation, on the fourteenth day of the month he receives a tithe from his father Jacob (*Jub.* 32:1-2). Then, after the birth of Benjamin, Jacob counts his sons in reverse order so that Levi is reckoned his tenth, invests him with priestly robes, and provides a bounty of animals for sacrifice on the fifteenth day at Bethel (*Jub.* 32:3-9). An elaboration on the tithe follows (*Jub.* 32:10-15) before the narrative again intersects with the Genesis account at the death of Deborah (*Jub.* 32:30; cf. Gen 35:8) and the focus on Levi ceases.

With *Jubilees*, several significant themes present in *ALD* are made more explicit. As in *ALD*, Levi's reception of the priesthood seems in some way a product of his zeal against the Shechemites. The theme recurs in *Jubilees*, but with the additional theological justification for the appropriateness of such slaughter. The heavenly bestowal of Levi's priesthood is yet more explicit as well. The dynastic nature of Levi's office receives major stress, but whereas in *ALD* royal dynastic imagery was transferred to Levi's priestly status, in *Jubilees* more stress is placed on the *dual* dynastic lines of Levi and Judah.

3.3. *Testament of Levi*

Analysis of themes in the *Testament of Levi* is difficult because of the nagging questions about the extent of Christian redactions to this and the *Testaments of the Twelve Patriarchs* as a whole, but most scholars assume that the testaments have Jewish origins at some level.[217] Because their compositional history is so debated, proposals

[217] See the survey of proposals in Robert A. Kugler, *The Testaments of the Twelve Patriarchs* (Guides to Apocrypha and Pseudepigrapha; Sheffield: Sheffield, 2001); 31-38. For a broader (but considerably older) survey of scholarship, see H. Dixon Slingerland, *The Testaments of the Twelve Patriarchs: A Critical History of Research* (SBLMS 21; Missoula, Mont: Scholars Press, 1977). Kugler notes three major clusters

for dates of various supposed editions of the text vary widely. The oldest manuscript, in Greek, dates from the 10th century C.E., and the text survives in later Slavonic, Serbian, New Greek, and Latin translations. At best one can say with de Jonge that the extant version dates to c. 200 C.E. and likely was composed in Greek.[218]

Nine of the 12 testaments within *Testaments of the Twelve Patriarchs* (all but those attributed to Zebulun, Asher, and Benjamin) pair Levi and Judah as preeminent among their brothers.[219] Exaltation of Levi most certainly is an important Jewish motif in the work rather than a Christian creation. Scholars have proposed numerous explanations for the apparent relationship between *Testament of Levi* and *Aramaic Levi*; these are discussed briefly below.

As expected in the testament genre, *Testament of Levi* opens with an explanation that what follows are the words the patriarch delivered to his family members in anticipation of his death (*T. Levi* 1:1-2).[220] Judgment is introduced in this opening note as a major theme for the text. In *T. Levi* 2:1-4:1, the patriarch narrates an apocalyptic vision of heaven he received after praying for deliverance from sinful humanity in the context of the Dinah episode of Gen 34.[221] The angelic guide

---

of theories: since 1698 most scholars have assumed that the text has Jewish origins but was redacted at some point by Christians, but A. Dupont-Sommer and M. Philoneno argued in the mid-20th century that the supposed Christian redactions actually are Essene references to the Teacher of Righteousness. More recently Marinus de Jonge has argued that the *Testaments* are a Christian composition based on Jewish sources. Though these Jewish sources may have coagulated for a time in Jewish circles before being shaped into the extant version of the *Testaments*, it now is impossible to distinguish an original Jewish version from the final Christian form, nor is the attempt to do so worthwhile. Kugler notes that de Jonge's approach is gaining adherents (slowly). Though de Jonge certainly is correct that the *Testaments* are imbued with a Christian perspective, statements in the survey below that clearly present Christian views in contexts that otherwise are compatible with a Jewish perspective nevertheless are identified with the admittedly-problematic term 'interpolation.'

[218] Marinus de Jonge, "Patriarchs, Testaments of the Twelve," *ABD* 5:181-86, esp. 182.

[219] Hollander and de Jonge, *Commentary*, 56.

[220] The standard edition of the critical text of *Testaments of the Twelve Patriarchs* is Marinus de Jonge, in cooperation with H. W. Hollander, J. J. de Jonge, and Th. Korteweg, eds., *The Testaments of the Twelve Patriarchs: A Critical Edition of the Greek Text* (PVTG 1/2; Leiden: Brill, 1978). The translation used here is that of Hollander and de Jonge, *Commentary*. Other translations and introductions include those by Howard Clark Kee (*OTP* 1:775-828) and de Jonge (*AOT* 505-600).

[221] The number of levels of heaven is confused in the manuscript tradition. Kee asserts that an original schema of three levels was later edited to reflect a seven-level conception. See Kee, *OTP*, 788, n. d. Seven levels of heaven are mentioned in *T. Levi* 3:1 in the Cambridge manuscript. See Marinus de Jonge, *Testamenta XII*

announces that when Levi has reached the level of God's abode, he will enter God's priestly service and take up a significant role alongside Judah:

> For you will stand near the Lord and will be his minister and will declare his mysteries to men and will proclaim concerning him who will redeem Israel. And by you and Judah the Lord will appear among men, saving through them the whole race of men. And from the Lord's portion will be your life, and he will be your field, vineyard, fruits, gold, silver. (*T. Levi* 2:10-12)

This section exhibits obvious Christian interpolation with its discussion of 'him who will redeem Israel.'[222] Its description of Levi, however, including his selection as priest before God and his two-fold responsibilities to conduct liturgies ('stand near the Lord') and provide instruction to humanity, is consistent with other presentations in the Levi priestly tradition. (Though the details differ significantly, one might compare this vision with the narrating angel's statement in *Jub.* 30 that Levi has been granted a priesthood like the angelic priesthood.) The priestly language also is evident in the discussion of Levi's provisions.

The angelic guide proceeds to lead Levi through various levels of heaven, culminating in a description of God's dwelling in the celestial Temple:

> For in the highest of all dwells the Great Glory in the holy of holies far beyond all holiness. In the (heaven) next to it there are the angels of the presence of the Lord, those who minister and make propitiation to the Lord for all the sins of ignorance of the righteous, and they offer to the Lord a pleasant odour, a reasonable and bloodless offering. (*T. Levi* 3:4-6)

The angelic guide then announces that God has heard Levi's prayer and will appoint him 'son and a servant and a minister of his presence' (*T. Levi* 4:2), presumably meaning Levi will have a ministry in heaven itself. The angel elaborates on this appointment through line 6, though again Christian interpolations are evident as Levi's descendents are said to impale the son of the Lord (line 4). Then Levi is taken to the presence of the Lord, where he indeed receives his priestly

---

Patriarcharum: Edited According to Cambridge University Library MS Ff I.24 fol. 203a-262b with Short Notes (PVTG 1; Leiden: Brill, 1964), 11.

[222] See Hollander and de Jonge, *Commentary*, 135.

commission: 'Levi, I have given to you the blessings of the priesthood, until I come and sojourn in the midst of Israel' (5:2; the latter phrase may reflect Christian redaction). After this the tour of heaven immediately comes to an end; Levi is returned to the earth, given a shield and sword by the angel, and instructed to take vengeance on the Shechemites with angelic help (5:3-6). The implication is that because he is priest, he is to undertake this action. Levi then awakes from the vision, finds a brass shield, and travels to visit Jacob. He urges unsuccessfully that the Shechemites not be asked to be circumcised, then he slaughters the inhabitants of that city while Reuben attacks those of Hamor. This action raises the ire of Jacob, and Levi admits he sinned against his father. Levi nevertheless justifies his actions as the will of God and the just recompense for those who had oppressed nomadic Hebrews since the time of Abraham. Levi defends his actions to Jacob and prophesies the future conquest of Canaanite lands, then they travel to Bethel (5:7-7:4).

At Bethel, Levi receives another vision, this time of his investiture as high priest (*T. Levi* 8:1-19). Seven men, presumably angels, anoint and attire Levi with priestly garments, a crown, and a staff, and they proclaim him 'a priest of the Lord, you and your seed, for ever' (8:3). Prophecies are then spoken about the destiny of his descendants; three groups (likely corresponding to his three sons mentioned elsewhere) will have different offices. The second group inherits the priesthood; roles of the first and third are less clear. The first group is vaguely described (yet praised) as 'believing,' while the third will receive a new name because a king from Judah will establish a new priesthood for the Gentiles (8:11-17). Again Christian interpolations complicate the interpretation of the passage. Clearly, though, a dynastic priesthood is proclaimed: 'your seed will divide among themselves the table of the Lord. And from them there will be highpriests and judges and scribes, because the holy place will be guarded on their command' (8:16-17). Levi awakes but, as with his earlier vision, keeps secret the contents of his revelation.

Jacob, Levi, and Judah then visit Isaac, and the latter blesses Levi (*T. Levi* 9:1-2); this scene parallels accounts in *Jubilees* and *Aramaic Levi*, but here no further details are given. Jacob and his sons then return to Bethel, where Jacob has a vision revealing Levi's priesthood and offers his tithes, afterwards the family returns to Hebron and Isaac. Isaac then instructs Levi on purity, sexual mores and marriage, and proper woods and gifts for sacrifices (9:3-14). This discourse bears strong similarities to that in *Aramaic Levi*.

Levi pauses temporarily from narrating his past in *T. Levi* 10:1-5 to warn his offspring of their future apostasy and consequences, citing the book of Enoch as a source for his prophecy that the temple would be in Jerusalem.[223] The extant prophecy displays extensive Christian editing. Levi then recounts his personal and family chronology in *T. Levi* 11:1-12:7 before exhorting his offspring on the Law, righteousness, and wisdom in *T. Levi* 13:1-9. The salient points here are consistent with those in the parallel passages in *Aramaic Levi*—Levi received the priesthood at age 19, and the priesthood is passed through the line of his second son Kohath (Kaath).

In *T. Levi* 14:1-18:14, Levi prophesies (again claiming reliance on Enoch) about the future sinfulness of his descendants, the ensuing judgment, and their opposition to the figure sent by the Most High (clearly a Christian addition about Jesus). These prophecies climax in *T. Levi* 18 with an apocalyptic oracle—also clearly Christian—describing the supersession of the Levitical priesthood by the one sent by God (who will also execute the ultimate defeat of Beliar). The text concludes in *T. Levi* 19 with Levi's call for his offspring to choose to live either for the Lord or Beliar; Levi's death at age 137 is reported.

Themes that have been observed in *ALD* and *Jubilees*' discussion of Levi, such as the heavenly nature of his priesthood and the dual appointments of Levi and Judah, appear again in *Testament of Levi*. Perhaps most striking, however, are the discussion of Levi's service in heaven itself and the way this visionary experience fits with the Shechem incident. His selection as priest now seems to be the *reason* he acts against Shechem (with angelic aid at that), whereas in other traditions his priesthood *results from* this action against Shechem.

3.4. *Significance of the Levi Priestly Tradition*

The similarities of these accounts are evident in this survey, and scholars have made numerous proposals about the literary relationships among these texts, especially *ALD* and *Testament of Levi*.

[223] Kee, *OTP*, 792, n. d, comments that no such passage is extant in literature attributed to Enoch.

Despite the widely varying views on the origins of *Testaments of the Twelve Patriarchs*, most scholars agree that *ALD* very likely was *a* source for the later Greek testament, but *Testament of Levi* is not merely a translation and expansion of this earlier Semitic text. As for *Jubilees*, Stone asserts that *ALD* was a source for *Jubilees*, while James Kugel takes the unusual position that *Jubilees* was a source for *ALD*.[224] More convincing that either of these, however, is Kugler's argument that the authors of *Jubilees* and *ALD* independently drew upon a common Levi tradition, thus explaining the similarities (and differences) between these two texts and *Testament of Levi* (derived from *ALD*).[225] Regardless, it is clear that the presentations of Levi in these three texts are intertwined at some level.

Much more significant for our purposes is whether this elevation of Levi has any relation to the priestly messianism of Qumran or Hebrews' presentation of Jesus as priestly messiah. VanderKam has argued for the former, claiming that the Levi priestly tradition of *Jubilees*, clearly a highly esteemed book in the Qumran community, provided a significant intermediary step toward this expectation.[226] VanderKam is characteristically prudent not to overplay his hand: admittedly *Jubilees* never proclaims Levi or a descendent to be a messianic figure as several Qumran texts do for the 'messiah of Aaron,' but Levi nevertheless enjoys a divine appointment to the priestly office and is promised an eternal line. As demonstrated above, support from Scripture for the priestly messiah is meager at Qumran, and it seems quite unlikely that the Qumran community—so grounded in Scripture and exegesis—would unilaterally create such a figure without exegetical moorings. It seems feasible then to regard the understanding of Levi in *Jubilees*, itself derived from midrashic readings of several passages of Scripture as noted earlier, as a conceptual undergirding for Qumran's priestly messianism, all the more since *ALD* was also being read in the community.

Unfortunately, however, it is difficult to estimate how widely *Jubilees* was read in Second Temple Judaism outside of Essene circles. VanderKam notes, for example, that its literary influences on Jewish texts primarily are found in the Qumran corpus, where it has great

[224] Stone, "Levi, Aramaic," 1:486; James Kugel, "Levi's Elevation," 1-64.
[225] Kugler, *From Patriarch to Priest*, 222.
[226] VanderKam, "Jubilees and the Priestly Messiah," 353-65.

importance. Elements of *Jubilees*—such as the presence of an alternate liturgical calendar that may explain the discrepancies between the dating of events during the Passion week in the Synoptics and John, or agreements between *Jubilees* and NT books on minor details against the MT or LXX readings—*may* be reflected in the New Testament, but one cannot positively assert whether literary dependence or the presence of mere parallel themes provides the best explanations for the similarities. Influence on rabbinic Jewish texts is very late.[227] Similarly, the numerous questions surrounding the origins of the *Testaments of the Twelve Patriarchs* make it impossible to speculate on its influence on pre-Christian Judaism.

What can be asserted confidently, however, is that traditions of Levi's divine appointment to an eternal priesthood definitely predate Christianity and almost certainly influenced Qumran's priestly messianism. Likewise, early Christians found texts asserting this Levi tradition attractive for conveying Christian messages. More will be said in this regard in the final chapter, but at this point one other stream of thought, angelomorphic Christology, demands notice.

4. Angelomorphic Christology

A transition in focus from Levi priestly traditions to consideration of texts which describe heavenly angelic figures is only natural since Levi is told he will join such company during his tour of heaven in *Jubilees*. Furthermore, several Qumran texts describe angelic priestly activities, and even the heavenly Melchizedek of 11QMelchizedek (discussed in the next chapter) makes atonement and seems to be correlated with the archangel Michael.

Scholars occasionally have suggested that the understanding of Jesus in early Christianity was influenced by post-biblical Jewish angel speculation. This idea found its most prominent early spokesman in Wilhelm Bousset in the late 19th-early 20th centuries, was rejuvenated later in the 20th century, and has been espoused by a significant number of recent scholars.[228]

---

[227] VanderKam, *Book of Jubilees* (2001), 143-48.

[228] To borrow the terminology of Darrell Hannah, the "Pre-History" of such research is represented by Wilhelm Bousset, *Die Religion des Judentums im Späthellenistischen Zeitalter* (4th ed.; Tübingen: Mohr Siebeck, 1966), the first edition

Recent proponents of angelomorphic Christology who discuss Hebrews tend to focus on Heb 1-2 and whether either the author or the recipients can be understood as espousing the view that the Son was an angel, not whether the motif of Jesus as priest is dependant on texts with angelic liturgical themes. For example, Darrell Hannah and Loren Stuckenbruck argue that neither the author nor recipients of Hebrews

---

of which appeared in 1903; Bousset, *Kyrios Christos: A History of the Belief in Christ from the Beginnings of Christianity to Irenaeus* (trans. J. E. Steely; Nashville: Abingdon, 1970), which first appeared in German in 1913; and the work of his student Wilhelm Lueken, *Michael: Eine Darstellung und Vergleichung der jüdischen und der morgenländisch-christlichen Tradition vom Erzengel Michael* (Göttingen: Vandenhoeck & Ruprecht, 1898). Hannah dubs the next stage "The First Period: Angel Christology," characterized by adoptionistic Christology and best represented by Martin Werner, *Die Entstehung des christlichen Dogmas* (Bern/Leipzig: Haupt, 1941). An examination of patristic use of the term ἄγγελος also appeared in 1941, later revised as Joseph Barbel, *Christos Angelos* (2nd ed; Theophaneia 3; Bonn: Peter Hanstein, 1964). After several years the approach revived in what Hannah calls "The Second Period: Angelomorphic Christology," with the shift in titles reflecting the general (but not unanimous) trend away from adoptionism toward the idea that early Christians appropriated the framework of various Second Temple Jewish mediator figures for understanding Jesus. Major voices include Richard Longenecker, *The Christology of Early Jewish Christianity* (London: SCM, 1970); Hengel, *Cross*, 1-90; Alan F. Segal, *Two Powers in Heaven: Early Rabbinic Reports About Christianity and Gnosticism* (SJLA 25; Leiden: Brill, 1977); J.A. Bühner, *Der Gesandte und sein Weg im 4.Evangelium: Die kultur- und religionsgeschichtlichen Grundlagen der johanneischen Sendungs-christologie sowie ihre traditionsgeschichtliche Entwicklung* (WUNT 2/2; Tübingen: Mohr Siebeck, 1977); multiple articles by Christopher Rowland, including "A Man Clothed in Linen: Daniel 10.6ff and Jewish Angelology," *JSNT* 24 (1985): 99-110; Jarl Fossum, *The Name of God and the Angel of the Lord: Samaritan and Jewish Conceptions of Intermediation and the Origin of Gnosticism* (WUNT 2/36; Tübingen: Mohr Siebeck, 1985); and Larry W. Hurtado, *One God, One Lord: Early Christian Devotion and Ancient Jewish Monotheism* (London: SCM, 1988). (Now see also Hurtado, *Lord Jesus Christ: Devotion to Jesus in Earliest Christianity* [Grand Rapids: Eerdmans, 2003].) Recent works include Loren T. Stuckenbruck, *Angel Veneration and Christology: A Study in Early Judaism and in the Christology of the Apocalypse of John* (WUNT 2/70; Tübingen: Mohr Siebeck, 1995); Charles A. Gieschen, "The Different Functions of a Similar Melchizedek Tradition in *2 Enoch* and the Epistle to the Hebrews," in *Early Christian Interpretation of the Scriptures of Israel* (ed. C. A. Evans and J. A. Sanders; JSNTSup 148; Studies in Scripture in Early Judaism and Christianity 5; Sheffield: Sheffield, 1997), 364-79; Charles A. Gieschen, *Angelomorphic Christology: Antecedents and Early Evidence* (AGJU 42; Leiden: Brill, 1998); Darrell D. Hannah, *Michael and Christ: Michael Traditions and Angel Christology in Early Christianity* (WUNT 2/109; Tübingen: Mohr Siebeck, 1999); and Timo Eskola, *Messiah and Throne: Jewish Merkabah Mysticism and Early Christian Exaltation Discourse* (WUNT 2/142; Tübingen: Mohr Siebeck, 2001). See also Carey C. Newman, James R. Davila, and Gladys S. Lewis, eds., *The Jewish Roots of Christological Monotheism: Papers from the St. Andrews Conference on the Historical Origins of the Worship of Jesus* (JSJSup 63; Leiden: Brill, 1999). This survey is dependant on Hannah, *Michael*, 2-11.

understood Jesus as an angel, though they contend that the stress on Jesus' superiority to angels in those chapters implies that some contemporaries did.[229] Similarly, Timo Eskola assumes that opponents of the author of Hebrews—but not the author himself or the recipients—held to an angelomorphic Christology.[230]

A very different position is espoused by Charles Gieschen, who finds strong evidence of this motif in Hebrews, especially with the figure of Melchizedek. Gieschen's thesis is that early Christians understood Jesus through the lens of a composite group of divine hypostases and named angels familiar from Second Temple Jewish texts. He assumes authors of NT books understood Jesus in this light because patristic and Gnostic authors could list numerous titles of Jesus that he thinks reflect pre-Christian Jewish thought.[231] For Hebrews in particular, he proposes (among other things) that the author was strongly influenced by assertions about Moses in Samaritan religious texts (following the thesis of his dissertation director Jarl Fossum) and that Hebrews' discussion of Melchizedek parallels that of the same figure in *2 Enoch*.[232]

Gieschen's approach, however, is problematic. An initial impression when reading his discussion of Hebrews is that he is drawing on an almost limitless mélange of sources and motifs—whether from Qumran, Samaria, Philo, or beyond, and whether discussing personified Wisdom, angelic liturgical service, or the Logos, all roads lead to angelomorphic Christology. While it is unwise to assume the author of Hebrews was influenced by only one or two streams of thought, Gieschen implies that these numerous traditions express some semblance of unified thought under his preferred category. Also, rarely is distinctive language in Hebrews to be explained in conventional ways. Gieschen, for example, downplays the influence of Jewish discussions of Wisdom on the presentation of the Son in Heb 1:1-4, asserting instead that the antecedents for the Divine Name lie in the *Apocalypse of Abraham* and *3 Enoch*; designation of the Son as 'firstborn' is most closely paralleled by the appellation of the Angel Israel in the *Prayer of Joseph*.[233]

---

[229] Hannah, *Michael*, 138-39; Stuckenbruck, *Angel Veneration*, 139.
[230] Eskola, *Messiah and the Throne*, 210.
[231] Gieschen, *Angelomorphic Christology*, 122-23.
[232] Gieschen, *Angelomorphic Christology*, 294-314. For Fossum, see above.
[233] Gieschen, *Angelomorphic Christology*, 295-98.

Later Gieschen asserts, as noted above, that language used in Heb 3:1-6 in the comparison of Jesus and Moses must be seen as drawn from Samaritan praise of the latter. Left unexplained, however, is why one should assume that the author of Hebrews—presumably a Jewish Christian or at least a Christian highly trained in Jewish exegesis, writing to a Roman Christian readership with its traditional Jewish flavor—would need here to draw on Samaritan motifs.[234] This seems all the more unlikely since an explanation for this language can be found in the targumim.[235] Finally, Gieschen's frequent use of *2 Enoch* as a comparative source is questionable because of the numerous unanswered questions about the origins and dating of this text, problems to which he is not oblivious.[236] Note, for example, Francis I. Anderson's summary of scholarly appraisals of *2 Enoch*:

> The origins of 2 Enoch are unknown. Research has not reached any consensus about the time, place, or contents of its first published form. The options range from [R. H.] Charles' theory that the longer recension was written by an Alexandria [*sic*] Jew in the 1st century B.C. through belief that it was a Christian rewrite of 1 Enoch, probably in Gk, made anywhere from the 2d century A.D. (in Syria?) to the 10th (in Byzantium), up to the denial that it is anything more than a home-grown product of Slavic religious culture.[237]

While Anderson certainly cites some extremes of scholarly opinion on *2 Enoch*, still his point stands that great caution is necessary when

[234] On the Jewish nature of Roman Christianity, see Joseph A. Fitzmyer, *Romans: A New Translation with Introduction and Commentary* (AB; New York: Doubleday, 1993), 33-34; and Raymond E. Brown and John P. Meier, *Antioch and Rome: New Testament Cradles of Catholic Christianity* (New York: Paulist, 1983), 110.

[235] See Sverre Aalen, "'Reign' and 'House' in the Kingdom of God in the Gospels," *NTS* 8 (1962): 215-40, esp. 233-37; and Mary Rose D'Angelo, *Moses in the Letter to the Hebrews* (SBLDS 42; Missoula, Mont.: Scholars Press, 1979), 71-75.

[236] Gieschen briefly surveys important studies that have omitted consideration of *2 Enoch* because of its uncertain provenance yet insists on its value. See Gieschen, "Different Functions," 365, n. 6. In his book *The Melchizedek Tradition*, Fred Horton (whom Gieschen criticizes frequently) correctly excludes *2 Enoch* 69-73 from the examination of Melchizedek in the Second Temple Period because of these numerous questions. Such an approach is further criticized by Christfried Böttrich, "The Melchizedek Story of *2 (Slavonic) Enoch*: A Reaction to A. Orlov," *JSJ* 32 (2001): 445-70, esp. 445. Nevertheless *2 Enoch* also is excluded from the present study because of significant questions concerning its date and origins. Gieschen, however, cites *2 Enoch* even when its presentation of Melchizedek contradicts that of Hebrews. See, for example, discussion of Melchizedek's genealogy in the two texts in Gieschen, *Angelomorphic Christology*, 310.

[237] Francis I. Anderson, "Enoch, Second Book of," *ABD* 2:516-22, esp. 521.

arguing on the basis of such a text. Admittedly Anderson's position reflects scholarship of the 1980s, yet little has changed in the last two decades; Grant Macaskill could be no more definitive about the provenance of the book in a very recent survey of the scholarly landscape.[238] Perhaps the most fruitful approach to *2 Enoch* is that of Andrei Orlov. While he dates the book to the late first century C.E., Orlov does not attempt to position *2 Enoch* as a source for Hebrews. Instead, he approaches the Melchizedek materials there and in Hebrews as parallel appropriations of traditions about the figure.[239]

The significance of these priestly discussions relative to Hebrews will be considered more fully in the final chapter. Before reaching that point, however, there remains an examination of discussions of Melchizedek in Second Temple Judaism.

---

[238] Grant Macaskill, "Enoch, Second Book of," *NIDB* 2:265.

[239] His publications on *2 Enoch* are numerous, but see especially Andrei Orlov, "The Heir of Righteousness and the King of Righteousness: The Priestly Noachic Polemics in 2 Enoch and the Epistle to the Hebrews," *JTS* 58 (2007): 45-65, esp. 57; and his earlier article "Melchizedek Legend of 2 (Slavonic) Enoch," *JSJ* 31 (2000): 23-38.

CHAPTER FOUR

MELCHIZEDEK TRADITIONS IN SECOND TEMPLE JUDAISM

As discussed in the exegetical survey in chapter one, the figure of Melchizedek plays a very important role in Hebrews' discussion of Jesus as priest. Jesus' status as priest is legitimated by his relationship to the mysterious figure. Jesus is said to be 'in the order of Melchizedek,' and on several occasions Jesus is said to be *like* Melchizedek. Conversely, once the opposite is asserted, as Melchizedek is compared to the 'Son of God.' Melchizedek's reception of tithes from and pronouncement of blessing on Abraham are key parts of Hebrews' argument that Jesus holds a priestly status greater than that of the Levitical priests.

As noted above, scholars continue to investigate the possibility that further understanding of Melchizedek in biblical and subsequent traditions might shed light on understanding the motif of Jesus as priest in Hebrews. Some attention has already been given in chapter 1 to Hebrews' interpretation of Gen 14:18-20 and Ps 110:4, with brief comments also made there about Melchizedek traditions in other literature from the Second Temple period. Much more can be said in this chapter about these challenging biblical passages, their use in Second Temple Jewish literature, and potential connections between these Jewish portraits of Melchizedek and Hebrews' discussion of Jesus as priest.

1. Melchizedek in the Hebrew Scriptures and the Septuagint

Melchizedek is discussed in only two passages in the Hebrew Bible, Gen 14:18-20 and Ps 110:4. These passages are of very different natures. The former claims to recount a historical encounter between Melchizedek, a local priest-king, and Abram after the patriarch's military victory over Chedorlaomer and his allies.[1] The latter appears to be part of a divine oath to a Davidic king in a royal psalm. The precise relationship between the Melchizedek traditions in these two passages is difficult to evaluate.

1.1. *Genesis 14:18-20*

In order to understand the critical problems surrounding this passage, it is important first to examine it in its context of Gen 14:17-24, with vv. 18-20 in italics. The following translation (NJPS) reflects the MT; differences present in the LXX are discussed below:

> 17 When he returned from defeating Chedorlaomer and the kings with him, the king of Sodom came out to meet him in the Valley of Shaveh, which is the Valley of the King. *18 And King Melchizedek of Salem brought out bread and wine; he was a priest of God Most High. 19 He blessed him, saying,*
> *"Blessed be Abram of God Most High,*
> *Creator of heaven and earth.*
> *20 And blessed be God Most High,*
> *Who has delivered your foes into your hand!"*
> *And [Abram] gave him a tenth of everything.*
> 21 Then the king of Sodom said to Abram, "Give me the persons, and take the possessions for yourself." 22 But Abram said to the king of Sodom, "I swear to the LORD, God Most High, Creator of heaven and earth: 23 I will not take so much as a thread or a sandal strap of what is yours; you shall not say, 'It is I who made Abram rich.' 24 For me, nothing but what my servants have used up; as for the share of the men who went with me—Aner, Eshkol, and Mamre—let them take their share." (Gen 14:17-24 NJPS)

As noted above, several aspects of the passage differ in the MT and LXX. Joseph Fitzmyer notes five such differences:[2]

a. Whereas the MT of Gen 14:18 mentions Melchizedek's offering of 'bread and wine' (לֶחֶם וָיָיִן) in the singular, in the LXX the 'bread' is plural (ἄρτους καὶ οἶνον). This may have given rise to inter-

[1] Though the patriarch is still named Abram in Gen 14 and does not become Abraham until Gen 17:5, the author of Hebrews always refers to him as Abraham, as do most Second Temple Jewish writers who retell this encounter.

[2] Joseph A. Fitzmyer, "Melchizedek in the MT, LXX, and the NT," *Bib* 81 (2000): 63-69, esp. 67. I have rearranged Fitzmyer's points and added additional comments.

pretations in some Second Temple Jewish texts that Melchizedek fed all of Abram's party (see further below).

b. Whereas the king of Sodom tells Abram to keep 'the possession' (הָרְכֻשׁ; singular, *contra* NJPS translation) as spoils in the Gen 14:21 MT, in LXX he tells him to keep 'the horse' (τήν ἵππον).

c. In the same verse, MT refers to captives with the collective singular noun הַנֶּפֶשׁ, but LXX transforms it into the plural ἄνδρας.

d. The LXX does not translate the Tetragrammaton in Gen 14:22 (יְהוָה אֵל עֶלְיוֹן). Instead, it renders only the second of the two designations, 'God Most High' (τὸν θεὸν τὸν ὕψιστον).

e. The Hebrew יִקְחוּ in Gen 14:24, usually translated as a jussive, becomes the future λήμψονται in the LXX.

These variations aside, several issues pertaining to both versions deserve attention. First, Melchizedek is introduced only as the king of Salem and priest of God Most High. Salem (שָׁלֵם; Σαλημ) has typically been understood as Jerusalem, as evidenced in Ps 76:3 (EV 2), most Second Temple Jewish recountings of Gen 14 (see below), and all the extant targums on Gen 14.[3] Occasionally, however, Salem has been identified with Shechem.[4] This leads to the next point of attention.

---

[3] See Robert Hayward, "Shem, Melchizedek, and Concern with Christianity in the Pentateuchal Targumim," in *Targumic and Cognate Studies: Essays in Honour of Martin McNamara* (ed. K. J. Cathcart and M. Maher; JSOTSup 230; Sheffield: Sheffield Academic Press, 1996), 67-80, esp. 72.

[4] See, for example, John Gammie, "Loci of the Melchizedek Tradition of Genesis 14:18-20," *JBL* 90 (1971): 385-96, esp. 390-93, for an argument in favor of identifying Salem with Shechem. Gammie bases his argument largely on Samaritan sources and biblical texts that may associate Shechem with wine rites and El 'Elyon. Perhaps his strongest point concerns Gen 33:18 (MT וַיָּבֹא יַעֲקֹב שָׁלֵם עִיר שְׁכֶם אֲשֶׁר בְּאֶרֶץ כְּנַעַן). Whereas most translators understand שָׁלֵם here as an adjective or adverb ('safety,' 'safely,' etc.; the Samaritan Pentateuch—not mentioned by Gammie—similarly reads שלום), Gammie prefers to translate the relevant part of the phrase as "And Jacob came to Salem, a city of Shechem" ("Loci," 390). Surprisingly, Gammie fails to mention that the LXX supports his reading with the rendering καὶ ἦλθεν Ιακωβ εἰς Σαλημ πόλιν Σικιμων, ἥ ἐστιν ἐν γῇ Χανααν. Unfortunately this phrase is not extant in the Qumran texts according to Martin Abegg, Jr., Peter Flint, and Eugene Ulrich, *The Dead Sea Scrolls Bible* (New York: Harper San Francisco, 1999), 506, n. d. James Kugel notes that some ancient writers also associated Salem with the Samaritans and identified it as Shechem, a city near Shechem, or Mt. Gerizim. See Kugel, *Traditions of the Bible*, 283-84, 291-93. See also Martin McNamara, "Melchizedek: Gen 14,17-20 in the Targums, in Rabbinic and Early Christian Literature," *Bib* 81 (2000): 1-31, esp. 9-10; and the discussion below of Pseudo-Eupolomus.

Second, Melchizedek appears without introduction and just as quickly disappears again, playing no further role in the Pentateuch. This has fostered much discussion about the literary integrity of this passage, as it appears that the Melchizedek pericope interrupts a description of Abram's encounter with the king of Sodom. Indeed, the historical-critical problems in Gen 14 are manifold. The contents of the entire chapter do not correspond to any of the four major documentary sources.[5] Though some scholars argue that Gen 14 is a literary unit, most think that Gen 14:18-20 has been inserted into the chapter's preexisting narrative about Abram's military exploits, which may itself be a composite unit incorporating texts which originally had no reference to the patriarch.[6] Many scholars have understood this passage as dating from the period of the united monarchy and inserted into Gen 14 in order to legitimate the Jerusalem priesthood and/or Davidic dominion over the city.[7] Other scholars, however, argue that Gen 14:18-20 predates the Davidic era and note two features, a possible theophoric element in the name מַלְכִּי־צֶדֶק and the designation of his deity as אֵל עֶלְיוֹן. These scholars understand Melchizedek as priest of a Canaanite deity, either Sedeq or El 'Elyon, rather than a priest of Israel's deity, as most certainly is implied in the final edition of Genesis.[8] Still others date the passage to the divided monarchy or after the exile.[9]

---

[5] See S. R. Driver, *An Introduction to the Literature of the Old Testament* (New York: Scribner's, 1913; repr., Cleveland: Meridian, 1956), 15, and Martin Noth, *A History of the Pentateuchal Traditions* (Englewood Cliffs, N.J.: Prentice-Hall, 1972; repr., Atlanta: Scholars Press, 1981), 28 n. 84. See also von Rad, *Genesis*, 175, for a concise summary of the passage's difficulties.

[6] For thorough surveys of various historical-critical issues concerning Gen 14, see J. A. Emerton, "The Riddle of Genesis XIV," *VT* 21 (1971): 403-39; and Westermann, *Genesis 12-36*, 187-90. Also useful, but more selective, is Horton, *Melchizedek Tradition*, 13-23. Scholars who argue for the literary integrity of Gen 14 include Nahum Sarna, *Genesis* (JPS Torah Commentary; Philadelphia: Jewish Publication Society, 1989), 109; and Gordon J. Wenham, *Genesis 1-15* (WBC; Dallas: Word, 1987), 303-07. Fitzmyer allows that the Melchizedek pericope may derive from "an independent ancient poetic saga, as old as the rest of Gen 14" which nevertheless was inserted and interrupts the account of Abram's meeting with the king of Sodom ("Melchizedek," 64).

[7] See the discussion of Ps 110:4 below for similar theories.

[8] Martin Bodinger also identifies Melchizedek with a Canaanite god, proposing that Melchizedek was himself a solar deity. See his "L'Énigme de Melkisédeq," *RHR* 211 (1994): 297-333.

[9] See the aforementioned surveys by Emerton and Westermann for discussions of these various positions.

Beyond the disjunctive nature of the passage, one other issue should be noted. In the final phrase of v. 20, both the Hebrew וַיִּתֶּן־לוֹ מַעֲשֵׂר מִכֹּל and Greek καὶ ἔδωκεν αὐτῷ δεκάτην ἀπὸ πάντων are ambiguous about both who pays and who receives the tithe. This typically is obscured in English translations, as most (including the NRSV, NJPS, NAB, and NIV) name Abram as the one who pays the tithe in Gen 14:20.[10] One can only wonder how much translators have been influenced by Heb 7 and/or the dominant Second Temple Jewish interpretative tradition. For ancient authors, experience testified that priests receive rather than pay tithes. In fact, some Second Temple Jewish authors use this passage as an opportunity to discuss this practice.[11]

Though certainly important, these issues which are so prominent in historical-critical discussions of Gen 14 were not troubling in Second Temple discussions of the passage. As will be evident below, ancient interpreters sense problems with the passage, but these simply are rough spots to rectify in their retellings, not matters that raise concern about the historicity or legitimacy of Melchizedek and his encounter with the patriarch. Issues such as Melchizedek's abrupt arrival and departure in Gen 14 can be glossed over or else read as theologically significant.[12] Interpreters do differ on the identification of the city Salem, but they reflect one location or another and do not enter into a debate between various sites. Even the Canaanite origins of Melchizedek are acknowledged but are not seen as problematic—all Second Temple interpreters assume Melchizedek's 'God Most High' is synonymous with the God of Abram, and Melchizedek can even be credited as builder of Israel's temple.[13]

---

[10] To their credit, the NJPS translators do indicate the ambiguity of the Hebrew by placing 'Abram' in brackets in Gen 14:20. Fitzmyer thinks that in the original version of the story, Melchizedek was an allied king and thus paid the tithe to Abram ("Melchizedek," 67). Robert Houston Smith also argues that Melchizedek paid the tithe in the original form of the story, but he considers it a ransom paid to avert a siege by Abram's army. See Smith, "Abram and Melchizedek (Gen 14 18-20)," *ZAW* 77 (1965): 129-53, esp. 131-39.

[11] See Kugel, *Traditions*, 276, and the discussion of relevant texts below.

[12] Kugel relates the latter practice to "the doctrine of 'omnisignificance,'" or seeking meaning in every detail of Scripture because of a belief that nothing there is superfluous. See Kugel, *Traditions*, 17.

[13] While Jewish sources that clearly can be dated to the Second Temple period exhibit no impulse to avoid identifying Melchizedek as a Canaanite, a different understanding of the figure is dominant in the targumim and rabbinic traditions (and is occasionally reflected in patristic literature). Here Melchizedek normally is identified

1.2. *Psalm 110:4*

Melchizedek is evoked in this royal psalm addressed to a ruler of the Davidic dynasty, perhaps as part of an enthronement or other similar ritual. The relevant verse, Ps 110:4 (Ps 109:4 LXX), reads:

MT: נִשְׁבַּע יְהוָה וְלֹא יִנָּחֵם
אַתָּה־כֹהֵן לְעוֹלָם
עַל־דִּבְרָתִי מַלְכִּי־צֶדֶק

LXX: ὤμοσεν κύριος καὶ οὐ μεταμεληθήσεται
Σὺ εἶ ἱερεὺς εἰς τὸν αἰῶνα
κατὰ τὴν τάξιν Μελχισεδεκ

NRSV: The LORD has sworn and will not change his mind,
"You are a priest forever
according to the order of Melchizedek."

An eternal priesthood somehow related to that of Melchizedek is bestowed on the king. The exact nature of this relationship, stated in the final phrase of Ps 110:4 (Hebrew עַל־דִּבְרָתִי מַלְכִּי־צֶדֶק; LXX κατὰ τὴν τάξιν Μελχισεδεκ) is somewhat ambiguous. It has been understood by interpreters in several ways.[14]

---

as Seth, the firstborn son of Noah (who, by virtue of birth order, held a priesthood). Though all the extant sources for such traditions postdate the Second Temple period, Martin McNamara proposes that the traditions date as early as the second century B.C.E. A talmudic tradition attributed to Rabbi Ishmael (early second century C.E.) in *b. Nedarim* 32b presents Melchizedek/Seth as surrendering his priesthood to Abram because he blessed the patriarch before blessing God. Psalm 110:4 is then quoted in the tradition as addressed to Abram and accomplishing the transferal. McNamara, following J. J. Petuchowski, argues that such a position is polemical, but not a response to early Christian use of Melchizedek as in Hebrews. Rather, the tradition is understood as arising in response to Hasmonean appropriation of Melchizedek imagery to legitimate their combination of priestly and political power, as with Simon (1 Macc 14:35-41). On this, see especially McNamara, "Melchizedek," 10-13, 16-17; and J. J. Petuchowski, "The Controversial Figure of Melchizedek," *HUCA* 28 (1957), 127-36, esp. 130-36. For further discussion of Melchizedek in the targumim and rabbinic sources, see Horton, *Melchizedek Tradition*, 114-30; and Claudio Gianotto, *Melchisedek e la sua tipologia: Tradizioni giudaiche, cristiane e gnostiche (sec. II a.C.-sec. III d.C.)* (SRivBib 12; Brescia: Paideia Editrice, 1984), 171-85.

[14] For a recent survey of the manifold problems concerning the setting, dating, and interpretation of Ps 110, see Leslie C. Allen, *Psalms 101-50, Revised* (WBC 21; Nashville: Nelson, 2002), 108-20. (Unfortunately Allen's commentary is plagued by printing errors with its Hebrew font.) See also Horton, *Melchizedek Tradition*, 23-34, and Hay, *Glory*, 19-22. See Hans-Joachim Kraus, *Theology of the Psalms* (Minneapolis: Fortress, 1992), 107-23, for a discussion of the genre of royal psalms.

One interpretation of the MT's reading is that the passage (and hence the entire psalm) was addressed *to* Melchizedek. Thus the end of Ps 110:4 would be translated, 'You are a priest forever by my order [or 'on my account'], O Melchizedek.'[15] A second option understands מַלְכִּי־צֶדֶק as a comment on the nature of the addressee's position rather than a proper name. The latter half of Ps 110:4 then could be rendered as presented in the NJPS (and essentially suggested as early as 1937 by T. H. Gaster), 'You are a priest forever, a rightful king by My decree.' Similarly, some have rendered the phrase as 'may justice reign' or the imperative 'reign in justice.'[16] Such translations are problematic because clearly most ancient interpreters understood מַלְכִּי־צֶדֶק as a personal name.[17] Several interpreters in the Second Temple period—who initially read the personal name Melchizedek here—do then proceed to interpret the meaning of his name as an indicator of something about his character or status.[18] In such cases, though, the interpreter always first presumes that Melchizedek is a personal name before elaborating in an etymological manner.

The dominant interpretation of Ps 110:4 is that reflected in the LXX—an eternal priestly office in some manner related to that of Melchizedek is bestowed on the king addressed in the royal psalm. Typically it has been asserted that the king is granted a priesthood like, or 'in the order of,' that of Melchizedek, often with the implication that association of the Davidic ruler with the ancient Canaanite

---

The following survey includes only interpretations which see some application of the psalm in ancient Israel and not those which see its original context as messianic or prophetic. For an example of the latter, see M. J. Paul, "The Order of Melchizedek (Ps 110:4 and Heb 7:3)," *WTJ* 49 (1987): 195-211.

[15] See David Flusser, "Melchizedek and the Son of Man (A preliminary note on a new fragment from Qumran)," *Christian News from Israel* (April 1966): 23-29, esp. 26-27; and Kugel, *Traditions*, 279. Kugel cites several Second Temple Jewish texts that he thinks reflect such a reading of Ps 110:4. See further discussion of this approach below.

[16] A third possibility is to understand Melchizedek as the speaker. See Józef T. Milik, "*Milkî-sedek* et *Milkî-reša'* dans les anciens écrits juifs et chrétiens." *JJS* 23 (1972): 95-144, esp. 125. See Allen, *Psalms 101-50*, 116, for a survey of interpretations that omit a personal reference to Melchizedek, which he deems "unconvincing attempts to evade this reference."

[17] Actually, no extant Second Temple period translations or interpretations of Ps 110:4 that do not find a reference to the *person* Melchizedek have been encountered in the course of preparing this study.

[18] Philo, Josephus, and the author of Hebrews all do this, as discussed briefly in chapter 1 above and in more detail below.

monarchy was politically expedient.[19] Formal ties between Gen 14:18-20 and Ps 110:4 are limited to the name Melchizedek and the assertion that he is a priest; also, Melchizedek clearly is a king in Genesis, and most understand Ps 110 as a royal psalm. In the words of Theo de Kruijf, "An attempt to establish a link between the Psalm and Gen 14 whereby one text is seen as dependent upon the other can at best be only conjectural."[20] Nevertheless, most—but admittedly not all—scholars agree that the same king-priest is being evoked in both passages.[21]

Much historical-critical scholarship has been devoted to Ps 110. Form critics have long debated the *Sitz im Leben* of the psalm, with most seeing it as either a liturgy from or reflection of a ceremony (especially of installation) for a Davidic king. This naturally has led to queries about the sacerdotal prerogatives held by monarchs in ancient Israel. A few scattered passages in the Hebrew Bible portray Israelite and Judean kings performing priestly functions like their royal peers in other ancient Near Eastern societies.[22] These passages, however, appear almost as anomalies in the biblical tradition, as most texts emphasize—or at least assume—a division of political and religious leadership between the Hebrew kingship and priesthood during the monarchial period. Similarly, the date of composition for the psalm is much disputed, though the majority of scholars propose preexilic rather than postexilic origins.[23] The difficulties of this issue have been minimized by those interpreters who date the original context of Ps

---

[19] A variation of this view is presented by Th. Booij, "Psalm CX: 'Rule in the Midst of Your Foes!'" *VT* 41 (1991): 396-407, esp. 402. Booij agrees that the psalm functioned to legitimate Israelite rule in Jerusalem, but the appeal is to Gen 14's presentation of Melchizedek as a priest of Yahweh who was already resident in the city, not Canaanite traditions. Though this view is fraught with historical-critical problems (especially concerning the identity of Melchizedek's deity, which in turn assumes that Gen 14 preserves actual history), it finds affirmation in Second Temple Jewish texts in which Melchizedek is recognized as the first priest of Israel's God.

[20] Theo de Kruijf, "The Priest-King Melchizedek: The Reception of Gen 14,18-20 in Hebrews Mediated by Psalm 110," *Bijdr* 54 (1993): 393-406, esp. 396.

[21] Fitzmyer, "Melchizedek," 64, says there is "little doubt" about this and cites numerous scholars holding this view. As noted above, however, some scholars deny a personal reference to Melchizedek in Ps 110:4.

[22] For a convenient list and brief discussion of such cases, see Roland de Vaux, *Ancient Israel: Its Life and Institutions* (London: Darton, Longman & Todd, 1961; repr. Grand Rapids: Eerdmans, 1997), 113-14. A particularly interesting example is 2 Sam 8:18, where David's sons are said to be כֹּהֲנִים; they instead are הָרִאשֹׁנִים לְיַד הַמֶּלֶךְ in 1 Chron 18:17.

[23] Hay, *Glory*, 19.

110 as early as David's conquest of Jebusite Jerusalem and see the psalm as providing legitimation for David's reign in the tradition of ancient Canaanite king-priests. Others have considered Ps 110 as addressed to a historic Israelite king who is a 'priest' in the sense of overseer of the state religion, not as a cultic figure.[24] At the other end of the spectrum, some scholars have proposed a postexilic setting for Ps 110, finding its combination of political and priestly authority most feasible in the period when high priests were recognized by Israel's imperial rulers as political representatives for the Jewish people. In the 20th century several scholars were inclined to date the psalm as late as the Hasmonean period, but such a proposal is fraught with problems.[25]

Again, as important as such investigations are for historical reconstructions of ancient Israel, they are less than crucial for understanding Second Temple interpretations and adaptations of Ps 110:4 because ancient interpreters did not read Scripture like modern historical critics. Clearly those responsible for the LXX translation of Ps 110:4 read here a reference to Melchizedek. The author of Hebrews noted that his priesthood was eternal and that in Ps 110 kingship and priesthood were united. As will be evident, few other Second Temple writers on Melchizedek seem to have been influenced by Ps 110, though the authors of 11QMelchizedek and Hebrews seem to share an interest in this psalm.

2. Melchizedek in Nonbiblical Second Temple Jewish Literature

Melchizedek is mentioned in numerous Jewish texts of the Second Temple period. Usually he is mentioned in texts that rewrite his encounter with Abraham from Gen 14 with relative exegetical restraint, and occasionally elements of these rewritings are comparable to statements about Melchizedek in Hebrews. As will be evident, however, Melchizedek is never presented as a heavenly figure in Jewish texts outside of the Dead Sea Scrolls. That stands in contrast

---

[24] De Vaux, *Ancient Israel*, 114.

[25] As noted above, Allen provides a useful survey of these positions. For further critique of the idea that Ps 110 has Hasmonean origins, see Petuchowski, "Controversial Figure," 135-36.

with his treatment in the Qumran texts, which are discussed in the latter part of this chapter.

2.1. *Genesis Apocryphon*

The *Genesis Apocryphon* was discovered in cave 1 near Qumran and as such was among the earliest Dead Sea Scrolls to come to light. The text was written in Aramaic, and it is extant in only one very fragmentary manuscript. Portions of 23 columns have survived; only three columns (1QapGen XX-XXII) are essentially intact, and 13 others contain varying numbers of lines or words.[26] Like several other texts from that cave, it has not been published in the official Discoveries in the Judean Desert series and instead has appeared in other venues.[27]

The text consists chiefly of expansions of accounts from Genesis concerning two characters, Noah and Abram. As Fitzmyer notes, "The conventional title, Genesis Apocryphon . . . is a misnomer."[28] Instead, the book is more accurately appraised as 'parabiblical literature,' incorporating paraphrase and the sorts of expansions common in later rabbinic *midrashim* (so Fitzmyer), or as 'rewritten Scripture.'[29] The manuscript is dated to roughly 25 B.C.E-50 C.E. on paleographical grounds, but its composition could be dated as early as the mid-second century B.C.E.[30] Though preserved only at Qumran, the text does not

---

[26] Joseph A. Fitzmyer, "Genesis Apocryphon," *EDSS* 1:302-04, esp. 1:302.

[27] The exception to this statement concerns portions of two columns published in DJD I as 1Q20, 'Apocalypse of Lamech.' See D. Barthélemy and J. T. Milik, eds., DJD I, 86-87, Pl. XVII. Major publications of other sections of the work include Nahman Avigad and Yigael Yadin, *A Genesis Apocryphon: A Scroll from the Wilderness of Judaea: Description and Contents of the Scroll, Facsimiles, Transcription and Translation of Columns II, XIX-XXII* (Jerusalem: Magnes, 1956); Joseph A. Fitzmyer, *The Genesis Apocryphon of Qumran Cave I: A Commentary* (3d ed.; Biblica et Orientalia 18B; Rome: Pontifical Biblical Institute, 2004 [1966; 1971]; Jonas C. Greenfield and Elisha Qimron, "The Genesis Apocryphon Col. xii," in *Studies in Qumran Aramaic* (ed. T. Muraoka; AbrNSup 3; Leuven: Peeters, 1992), 70-77; and M. Morgenstern, E. Qimron, and D. Sivan, "The Hitherto Unpublished Columns of the Genesis Apocryphon," *AbrN* 33 (1995): 30-54.

[28] Fitzmyer, "Genesis Apocryphon," 1:302.

[29] Fitzmyer, "Genesis Apocryphon," 1:302.

[30] Fitzmyer, *Genesis Apocryphon*, 23, following James C. VanderKam, *Textual and Historical Studies in the Book of Jubilees* (HSM 14; Missoula, Mont.: Scholars Press, 1977), 287. Earlier Fitzmyer proposed the date of 100 B.C.E. in "Genesis Apocryphon," 1:303. Ultimately this determination hinges largely on whether the

hint of community distinctives like its characteristic sectarianism. This factor and the text's composition in Aramaic likely serve as evidence that it originated outside Qumran.[31]

At first glance it appears that 1QapGen ar XXII, 12-17 narrates the encounter from Gen 14 quite faithfully. Subtle interpretative comments are introduced, however, that transform the tenor of the account. One might say *Genesis Apocryphon* 'demythologizes' it.

> [12] The king of Sodom heard that Abram had brought back all the captives [13] and all the booty, and he went up to meet him. He came to Salem, that is Jerusalem, while Abram was camped in the Valley of [14] Shaveh. This is the Vale of the King, the Valley of Beth-haccherem. Melchizedek, the king of Salem, brought out [15] food and drink for Abram and for all the men who were with him. He was a priest of God Most High, and he blessed [16] Abram and said, "Blessed be Abram by God Most High, the Lord of heaven and earth! Blessed be God Most High, [17] who has delivered your enemies into your hand." And he gave him a tithe from all the goods of the king of Elam and his confederates. (1QapGen ar XXII, 12-17)[32]

Several issues in this account deserve consideration. For one, it is clear that the author of the *Genesis Apocryphon* understands Salem as Jerusalem, as explicated in line 13. Also, in this retelling the author seeks to smooth the disjunction of the Genesis account between Abram's meetings with Melchizedek and the king of Sodom. Here the king of Sodom journeyed to Salem with the intent of meeting the patriarch, who was in the (presumably nearby) Valley of Shaveh.[33] This differs from Gen 14:17, where the king goes to the valley itself. This adaptation implies that in *Genesis Apocryphon* the kings of Sodom and Salem met in Salem and then together traveled to meet Abram in the valley. This inference is supported by the smooth transition in 1QapGen ar XXII, 18 introducing the meeting of the king

---

extant copy of *Genesis Apocryphon* is the autograph, as proposed by Roland de Vaux, review of J. A. Fitzmyer, *The Genesis Apocryphon of Qumran Cave I: A Commentary*, *RB* 74 (1967): 100-02, esp. 101.

[31] Fitzmyer, "Genesis Apocryphon," 1:303. See also his discussion in *Genesis Apocryphon*, 16-25.

[32] The translation is that of Fitzmyer, *Genesis Apocryphon*, 109. His italics, indicating where the Aramaic very closely follows the Hebrew of the Gen 14 account, (see Fitzmyer, *Genesis Apocryphon*, 38), have not been retained.

[33] Several ancient writers located the Valley of Shaveh near Jerusalem. See Astour, "Shaveh, Valley of," 5:1168.

of Sodom and the patriarch: 'Then [באדין] the king of Sodom approached Abram . . .'

Another issue worth noting is Melchidek's initial act toward Abram. Melchizedek presents 'food and drink' (מאכל ומשתה), something less specific than the 'bread and wine' (לֶחֶם וָיָיִן) of Gen 14:18. He gives it not just to Abram but also to his troops.

Finally, while not explicitly named, it is strongly implied that Abram is the figure who pays the tithe of Gen 14:20. This is evident because the bounty from which the tithe was drawn is explicitly identified as 'all the flocks of the king of Elam and his confederates.' The king of Elam is identified as the leader of the enemy coalition in both Gen 14:17 and 1QapGen ar XXI.

In the hands of the author of *Genesis Apocryphon*, the event loses its mysterious aura through these additions to the story. Why Abram first met Melchizedek rather than the king of Sodom is partially explained—the kings presumably visited him together. This adaptation serves to make Melchizedek's introduction much less dramatic than his sudden appearance in Gen 14:18. What appears in Genesis to be a sacral encounter becomes something like a dinner on the grounds for the victorious troops; presence of wine is still explicit, but the bread becomes generic fare. Though still priest of God Most High, Melchizedek is a hospitable king-priest but not quite the mysterious figure he is in Gen 14 or Heb 7. The account in *Genesis Apocryphon* betrays no dependence on Ps 110:4.

2.2. *Jubilees*

As one would expect in a text of rewritten Scripture like *Jubilees*, Abram's encounter with Melchizedek is addressed.[34] Unfortunately, however, the extant text is defective in this section, leaving only the following:

> When he had armed his household servants . . . for Abram and his descendants the tithe of the firstfruits for the Lord. The Lord made it an

[34] See the previous chapter for introductory information on *Jubilees*.

> eternal ordinance that they should give it to the priests who serve before him for them to possess it forever. (*Jub.* 13:25)[35]

Regrettably, Melchizedek's name is now missing from most extant manuscripts of *Jubilees*. It seems certain, however, that the book originally narrated his encounter with Abram. This is evidenced by the fact that just after the lacuna in *Jub.* 13:25—where one would expect to find mention of Abram's encounter with the mysterious priest in a book so dependent on the narrative of Genesis—the issue of tithing is discussed (*Jub.* 13:25-27). Here one finds a digression on the divine origins of the tithe to support the priests of Israel, followed by an unimaginative paraphrase of Abram's meeting with the king of Sodom. Thus it seems a safe assumption that *Jubilees* originally contained an account of Abram's tithe to Melchizedek, and this deed prompted *Jubilees*' subsequent discussion of the tithe as the LORD's provision for priests.

Some scholars have suggested that the account of their meeting has been excised from *Jubilees*, perhaps with the intent of dampening speculation on the mysterious priest-king.[36] Others, however, argue that the omission is due to scribal error. James VanderKam agrees with scholars who suppose that haplography, or the accidental omission of a phrase because it began with similar letters as a subsequent phrase in the passage, has occurred. He argues that this most likely occurred in the transmission of Hebrew texts of *Jubilees* before the book was translated into Ethiopic, not in the Ethiopic manuscript tradition itself. VanderKam notes, however, that several minor Ethiopic manuscripts do contain some mention of Melchizedek (even if only in marginal notations), and on their basis he reconstructs *Jub.* 13:25 as follows (with the reconstructed words in brackets):

> When he had armed his household servants, [Abram went and killed Chedorlaomer. Upon returning, he took a tithe of everything and gave it to Melchizedek. This tithe was] for Abram and his descendants the tithe of the firstfruits for the Lord. The Lord made it an eternal ordinance that

[35] The translation given here is adapted from the restored translation of VanderKam, *Book of Jubilees* (1989), 1:82, 2:81-82.

[36] See, for example, Kugel, *Traditions*, 293; E. Tisserant, "Fragments syriaques du Livre des Jubilés," *RB* 30 (1921): 55-86, 206-32, esp. 215; and A. Caquot, "Le Livre des Jubilés, Melkisedeq et les dîmes," *JJS* 33 (1982): 257-64, esp. 261-64.

they should give it to the priests who serve before him for them to possess it forever.[37]

Assuming VanderKam's reconstruction is appropriate, *Jubilees* appears to affirm that Abram encountered Melchizedek, a priestly figure, and paid tithes to the latter. A striking feature is that the author of *Jubilees* associates tithes paid to Melchizedek with those later paid to support Levitical priests, basing the latter practice on the former. Nothing implies that the author of *Jubilees* saw discontinuity between the two priestly traditions. All of this differs much from the interpretation of this encounter in Hebrews, where Abraham's tithe to Melchizedek serves as a symbol of the superiority of Melchizedek's priesthood to that of the Levites (Heb 7:4-10).

2.3. *Pseudo-Eupolemus*

Seven Greek fragments attributed to Eupolemus are preserved in Eusebius, *Praep. ev.*, Book 9, and Eusebius indicates his dependency for these passages on Alexander Polyhistor, *Concerning the Jews*. Two of the fragments, albeit in different forms, also were preserved in Clement of Alexandria, *Stromata*; Clement too cites his dependence on Alexander Polyhistor. This Eupolemus was a second-century B.C.E. Jewish historian of a priestly family who was sent as an ambassador to Rome by Judas Maccabeus (1 Macc 8:17; 2 Macc 4:11; Josephus, *J.W.* 12.415-16).[38]

Of the seven fragments preserved by Eusebius, only five are attributed to Eupolemus by most modern scholars. The other two, including one narrating the Melchizedek event of Gen 14, have been widely deemed as pseudonymous because of their Samaritan tendencies since identified as such by Jacob Freudenthal in the late 19th century.[39] Freudenthal's identification of one of these fragments—the

[37] VanderKam, *Book of Jubilees* (1989), 1:82, 2:81-82. See also VanderKam, *Book of Jubilees* (2001), 49.

[38] Carl R. Holladay, "Eupolemus," *ABD* 2:671-72, esp. 2:671.

[39] For an introduction, critical text, and translation of these two fragments, see Carl R. Holladay, "Pseudo-Eupolemus (Anonymous)," in *Fragments from Hellenistic Jewish Authors* (Vol. 1: Historians; Chico, Calif.: Scholars Press, 1983), 157-87. See also Carl R. Holladay, "Eupolemus, Pseudo-," *ABD* 2:672-73; and Jacob Freudenthal, "Ein ungenannter samaritanischer Geschichtschreiber," in *Alexander Polyhistor und*

one in question here—as pseudonymous has been opposed by Robert Doran, and Nikolaus Walter has argued that the second is a composite text whose authorship is impossible to determine.[40] Neither recent argument has found a consensus.

Pseudo-Eupolemus' reference to Melchizedek is preserved in Eusebius, *Praep. ev.* 9.17.5-6:

> [5] When the ambassadors approached him [Abraham], requesting that he might release the prisoners in exchange for money, he did not choose to take advantage of those who had been unfortunate enough to lose. Instead, after he had obtained food for his young men, he returned the booty. He was also received as a guest by the city at the temple Argarizin, which is interpreted 'mountain of the Most High.' [6] He also received gifts from Melchizedek who was a priest of God and a king as well.[41]

This brief account clearly is derived from Gen 14, yet its conformity to the source on two matters is questionable. Melchizedek, identified as a ruler and priest, is associated with Argarizin, reflecting the Aramaic for Mt. Gerizim. It is unclear if this is an alternate tradition about the identity of Melchizedek's city or, as is more likely, if the author understands Salem to be located in Samaria.[42] Centuries later Jerome and Aetheria (both late fourth century C.E.) would make the latter identification, but such is not claimed in the Samaritan Pentateuch or the *Samaritan Targum*.[43]

Also unclear is the nature of the gifts which Abraham (not Abram as in Gen 14) receives from Melchizedek. The Greek word used here, δώρον, could be used in the LXX to translate various Hebrew terms denoting gifts, including both food (seven times for לֶחֶם) and money.[44] It most often was used in the LXX in sacrificial contexts, especially to

die von ihm erhaltenen Reste judäischer und samaritanischer Geschichtswerke (Hellenistische Studien 1-2; Breslau: Skutsch, 1875), 82-103, 207-08, 223-25.

[40] See Robert Doran, "Pseudo-Eupolemus," *OTP* 2:873-79; and Nikolaus Walter, "Pseudo-Eupolemus (Samaritanischer Anonymus)," in *Jüdische Schriften aus hellenistisch-römischer Zeit* (vol. 1, pt. 2; ed. W. G. Kümmel; Gütersloh: G. Mohn, 1976), 137-43.

[41] The translation of Pseudo-Eupolemus is that of Holladay, *Fragments*, 173.

[42] James L. Kugel, *The Bible as It Was* (Cambridge, Mass: Belknap, 1997), 160, argues that this author understood Salem as a Samaritan site on the basis of Gen 33:18 LXX ("Salem, the city of Shechem") and *Jub.* 30:1 ("Salem, to the east of Shechem"). See also the note above concerning Freudenthal and the perceived Samaritan tendencies of this text.

[43] McNamara, "Melchizedek," 9-10.

[44] See further Gerhard Schneider, δώρον, *EDNT* 1:365.

translate the broad sacrificial term קָרְבָּן, though numerous non-cultic uses of the term also are found.[45] Doran is correct to note that the gifts may be the bread and wine of Gen 14:18, presumably understood as for Abraham only.[46] It is unlikely that Pseudo-Eupolemus means here a group meal (like that of *Genesis Apocryphon*) because Abraham is already credited a few lines earlier by Pseudo-Eupolemus with holding back some of the spoils to nourish his servants.

One cannot be certain, however, about the identification Doran proposes, and the possibility remains that Pseudo-Eupolemus means Abraham received a financial gift rather than nourishment. In Gen 14:18-20 two exchanges are recorded, those of the bread and wine and of the tithe; as noted above, the Hebrew is vague as to who pays whom, though the overwhelming tradition is that Abraham pays Melchizedek. The Greek is clear in Pseudo-Eupolemus, though, that Melchizedek gives *something* to Abraham. As mentioned above, δῶρον frequently was used in the LXX for financial gifts. Though Abraham's generosity in the bartering of the prisoners already implied his lack of interest in financial gain, the most natural reading of the text nevertheless is that Abraham, 'treated as a guest,' received material gifts, not something of purely religious significance. Since ancient temples were storehouses of material wealth, one need not assume that the location of this exchange in the temple at Argarizin (Mt. Gerizim) rules out identification of the gifts as tangible wealth. Similarly, one should remember that Melchizedek, both priest and king, certainly would be understood as possessing fiscal authority over the temple.

Even if Pseudo-Eupolemus means that Abraham received a lucrative reward, this does not mean he intentionally played on the ambiguity of Gen 14:20 concerning who pays whom. The remainder of his discussion of Abraham is constituted of legends and expansions rather than precise biblical exegesis, and one may give this author too much credit for biblical fidelity if such a nuanced reading of Gen

[45] It is never used to translate the Hebrew מַעֲשֵׂר ("tithe"), nor is a tithe necessarily implied in Pseudo-Eupolemus, even though tithes in the HB could be given to those in need (widows, orphans, sojourners; Deut 14:28-29; 26:12). See J. Christian Wilson, "Tithe," *ABD* 6:579-80. Comparisons involving LXX usage are valid even if Samaritan authorship of the fragment is accepted; according to Holladay, "the fragments reflect clear dependence on the LXX." See Holladay, "Eupolemus, Pseudo," 2:672-73.

[46] Doran, "Pseudo-Eupolemus," 2:880 n. o.

14:20 is perceived here.[47] Pseudo-Eupolemus's account bears no evidence of use of Ps 110:4 and bears only faint resemblances to Heb 7.

2.4. *Josephus*

Josephus mentions Melchizedek on two occasions in his works. In both cases he presents the king-priest as a historical figure relevant to his retelling of Jewish history. He includes etymologies of the names Salem and Melchizedek that are similar to those found in Heb 7.

2.4.1. *Jewish War 6.438*

Josephus alludes to Melchizedek in his *Jewish War* when he briefly recounts previous occasions on which Jerusalem had been subdued by foreign armies. Melchizedek is not explicitly named, but it is clear that he is the subject of Josephus' discussion:

> Its original founder was a Canaanite chief, called in the native tongue 'Righteous King'; for such indeed he was. In virtue thereof [διὰ τοῦτο] he was the first to officiate as priest of God and, being the first to build the temple, gave the city, previously called Solyma, the name of Jerusalem.[48]

Several interesting issues arise in this passage. First, Josephus understands the name 'Melchizedek' to mean 'righteous king,' an etymology for the name which he shares with Philo (see below).[49] Though this translation differs from the rendering 'king of righteousness' in Heb 7:2, both efforts demonstrate an eagerness to

[47] Note the comments of Holladay in "Eupolemus, Pseudo-," 2:672-73: "The fragments reflect clear dependence on the LXX and possible use of the MT. They are especially characterized, however, by the inclusion of nonbiblical traditions, both haggadic . . . and pagan mythological traditions drawn from Babylonian and Greek sources."

[48] Josephus, *J. W.* 6.438 (Thackeray, LCL).

[49] Melchizedek's name is interpreted as 'the righteous king' (Aramaic מלכא צדיקא) in *Targum Pseudo-Jonathan* (seventh-ninth centuries C.E.) on Gen 14:18, but note the comments of McNamara: "the change is probably intentional: the identification of Melchisedek with Shem has been so thoroughly made that he has lost his identity and name." See McNamara, "Melchizedek," 3, 8.

extrapolate the significance of certain names in the Second Temple period.

Second, Josephus implies that Melchizedek's position as 'righteous king' qualified him to be the first priest before God. It is, however, unclear if it is Melchizedek's *righteousness* or his status as *king*—in this particular city—that makes him priest. To restate the latter, does Josephus view Jerusalem as a sacred city which must by nature have a priesthood, thus Melchizedek fills the role based on his status as king, not because of his personal qualities? Perhaps the most natural reading, however, is that he attained his priesthood due to his righteousness.

Third, and closely related to the previous point, Melchizedek is identified as the *first* priest of God. Is this deduced from Josephus' idea that Melchizedek was founder of this sacred city (implying that Jerusalem as the holy city naturally has a priest), or does it derive from his status as righteous, as king, or as a righteous king? Stepping away from the immediate context, might Josephus actually have based this observation on the fact that Melchizedek is the first priest mentioned in Scripture? (See also the discussion below on Josephus, *Ant.* 1.179-81.) The latter of these three options seems most likely. Similarly, the author of Hebrews never declares Melchizedek to the be first priest, but this is implied because he puts great stress in Heb 7 on—and clearly argues on the basis of—Melchizedek's encounter with the ancient progenitor of the Levitical priests.

Fourth, Josephus says that Melchizedek built the first temple in the city. This is striking because Josephus implies that it was Melchizedek's temple that was destroyed by the Babylonians. In *J.W.* 6.437, Josephus dates this destruction 1468 years, six months after the foundation of the temple. This clearly associates the foundation of the temple with Melchizedek rather than Solomon, who is not mentioned in this context. Indeed, Josephus later writes that the temple was razed 477 years, six months after the time of *David* (*J.W.* 6.439). Josephus clearly sees continuity in the temples of Jerusalem. Rather than describing a series of temples in the city, he writes of the span of time between its initial foundation and destruction by the Romans, dating it as 2168 years (*J.W.* 6.441).

Presumably Josephus was not bothered that a Canaanite is credited with the establishment of Israel's temple. Instead, he seems more interested in appealing to the antiquarian tastes of his Roman readership.

Fifth, Melchizedek is credited as both founder of Solyma and the person who later changed the city's name to Jerusalem (Ἱεροσόλυμα). It is unclear if Melchizedek actively changed the city's name or if the name was transformed in common parlance because of the presence of the temple (ἱερόν, cf. Ἱεροσόλυμα).

Sixth, Josephus recognizes that Melchizedek is a Canaanite and later notes that David expelled the Canaanites from Jerusalem. As noted above, however, he does not explain how a Canaanite could be the first priest of Israel's deity. Like his Second Temple period contemporaries, he is very restrained on this particular issue, which may strike modern interpreters as odd since ancient interpreters normally were quite concerned to explicate (and domesticate) passages of Scripture with similarly surprising implications.

As noted above, Josephus here draws upon the Gen 14 account but does not seem to utilize Ps 110:4. Josephus shares with the author of Hebrews an interest in the etymology of the name 'Melchizedek,' and both authors may recognize Melchizedek as God's first priest.

2.4.2. *Antiquities 1.179-81*

As one would expect in *Antiquities*, here Josephus mentions Melchizedek in the course of his rewriting of the biblical narrative. Josephus' retelling of Melchizedek's encounter with Abraham is generally faithful to Gen 14 but also incorporates some additional elements present in other Second Temple recountings.

> [179] So Abraham, having rescued the Sodomite prisoners, previously captured by the Assyrians, including his kinsman Lot, returned in peace. The king of the Sodomites met him at a place which they call the "royal plain." [180] There he was received by the king of Solyma, Melchisedek; this name means "righteous king," and such was he by common consent, insomuch that for this reason he was moreover made priest of God; Solyma was in fact the place afterwards called Hierosolyma. [181] Now this Melchisedek hospitably entertained Abraham's army, providing abundantly for all their needs, and in the course of the feast he began to extol Abraham and to bless God for having delivered his enemies into his hand. Abraham then offered him the tithe of the spoil, and he accepted the gift.[50]

[50] Josephus, *Ant.* 1.179-81 (Thackeray, LCL).

Again several matters deserve attention. Josephus demonstrates an attempt to smooth the disjunctions in Gen 14:18, 21 between Abraham's encounters with the king of Sodom and Melchizedek, but he does not do so to the extent that the author of *Genesis Apocryphon* does. Here Josephus has both kings meet the patriarch at the 'royal plain,' and the transition from Abraham's interaction with Melchizedek to his conversation with the king of Sodom (*Ant.* 1.182) is more graceful than the disjointed narration of Gen 14:21.

As in *Jewish War*, Melchizedek's name is understood to mean 'righteous king,' and this again is cited as the reason he also serves as priest. Here Josephus puts additional stress on the public recognition of Melchizedek's righteousness. The reason for this is unclear. One might infer that the connection between righteousness and the priesthood leads to God's selection of him as priest in *Jewish War*, and here too his righteousness seems to be the reason he also is priest.

Josephus again identifies Solyma with Jerusalem.[51] As in *Genesis Apocryphon*, Josephus transforms Melchizedek's bread and wine of Gen 14 into provisions for Abraham's entire army. Finally, Josephus makes it explicit that Abraham paid the tithe to Melchizedek.

2.4.3. *Synthesis*

Two things about Josephus' accounts are most striking. First, in both *Jewish War* and *Antiquities*, Josephus puts great stress on the etymology of the name Melchizedek as 'righteous king.' Philo will understand the name similarly, but he will use this meaning as an opportunity to allegorize (see below). For Josephus, the meaning of the name is an insight into Melchizedek's character. Hebrews also presents a similar etymology of the name 'Melchizedek.'

Second, one finds several additional details when Josephus discusses the story in *Antiquities* as opposed to *Jewish War*. This in itself is not surprising since Melchizedek is evoked in very different contexts in the two works, which themselves were written over a

[51] The LCL translations of *Jewish War* and *Antiquities* are both by Thackarey, but he translated Ἱεροσόλυμα as 'Jerusalem' in the former and as 'Hierosolyma' in the latter.

decade apart.[52] It is interesting, though, that Josephus in *Antiquities* shares two details with *Genesis Apocryphon*. One would expect ancient biblical interpreters to smooth off the rough edges of Gen 14 in regard to the relationship between Abraham's meeting with Melchizedek and the king of Sodom, and both Josephus and the author of *Genesis Apocryphon* do this. Less obvious, though, is the motivation for transforming the bread and wine into provisions for Abraham's entire army, especially since the patriarch provides for them in Gen 14:24. Among extant Second Temple treatments of this story, only Josephus, the author of *Genesis Apocryphon*, and Philo propose a mass meal, and only the first two seek to explain more smoothly the meetings of the patriarch with the two kings. In light of both of these correspondences, perhaps one might argue that Josephus was familiar with the version of the story recorded in the *Genesis Apocryphon*. Again, though, Josephus shows no reliance on Ps 110:4.

2.5. *Philo of Alexandria*

Philo discusses Melchizedek in three of his works and for three different purposes. As one would expect from this author, he finds fertile opportunities to allegorize with the Gen 14 passage and Melchizedek's name.

2.5.1. *On the Life of Abraham 235*

Melchizedek's name is not mentioned in this rewritten account of Abraham's defeat of the allied kings and rescue of Lot, but clearly it is his encounter with the patriarch that is discussed. Great editorial liberties are taken as Philo includes numerous details about the divine nature of Abraham's victory, and this expansive quality is also evident in his account of Melchizedek's encounter with the patriarch:

[52] Dating Josephus' texts is difficult, especially *Jewish War*. Books 1-6 likely were finished by 79 C.E., and they presumably had some relationship to an earlier version, likely in Aramaic. Book 7 likely was a much later addition and perhaps dates to the 90s. *Antiquities* dates to the early 90s. See Louis H. Feldman, "Josephus," *ABD* 3:981-98; and Steve Mason, "Josephus: Value for New Testament Study," *DNTB* 596-600.

> When the high priest of the most high God saw him [Abraham] approaching with his trophies, leader and army alike unhurt, for he had lost none of his own company, he was astonished by the feat, and, thinking, as indeed was natural, that such success was not won without God's directing care and help to their arms, he stretched his hands to heaven and honoured him with prayers on his behalf and offered sacrifices of thanksgiving for the victory and feasted handsomely those who had taken part in the contest, rejoicing and sharing their gladness as though the success were his own, and so indeed it was, for "the belongings of friends are held in common," as the proverb says, and this is far more true of the belongings of the good whose one end is to be well-pleasing to God.[53]

Several things may be noted here. Melchizedek, though unnamed, nevertheless is identified as the 'high priest'—not just 'priest'—in the service of the 'most high God' (ὁ μέγας ἱερεὺς τοῦ μεγίστου θεοῦ). Also, whereas in Gen 14 Melchizedek goes out to meet Abraham, here Melchizedek sees Abraham approaching with his troops, all unharmed, and determines that God must be responsible for this military success. This functions as the rationale for Melchizedek's subsequent actions toward Abraham. It perhaps is based on Melchizedek's words in Gen 14:20, where God is blessed for giving Abram the victory over his foes.

Melchizedek, seemingly functioning as a priest of Abraham's God, spontaneously offers prayers and sacrifices in thankfulness for Abraham's victory. This is a significant adaptation of Gen 14, where Melchizedek simply pronounces a blessing on Abraham. Also, Melchizedek provides a feast for Abraham's entourage. This clearly is an expansion of the Genesis account, but such an motif was also noted above as present in *Genesis Apocryphon* and Josephus. Philo uses this opportunity to allegorize the situation into a comment on friendship. Philo's treatment of the encounter between Melchizedek and Abraham clearly is selective; he says nothing about Abraham's response to Melchizedek and/or the tithe.

In conclusion, Philo takes liberties with the Gen 14 story and uses it for his allegorical purposes to expound on friendship. Both Philo's discussion of Melchizedek's response to Abraham and the rationale for this are unprecedented in extant sources, but he shares with other Second Temple period authors the interpretation that Melchizedek fed

[53] Philo, *Abr.* 235 (Colson, LCL).

Abraham's entire entourage. No ties between Philo's account and Heb 7 are manifest, nor is dependence on Ps 110:4 evident.

2.5.2. *On the Preliminary Studies 99*

Philo mentions Melchizedek briefly while discussing tithes, an element in a broader discussion on the significance of the number ten.

> It was this feeling which prompted the Man of Practice [Jacob] when he vowed thus, "Of all that thou givest me, I will give a tenth to thee"; which prompted the oracle that follows the blessing given to the victor by Melchisedek the holder of that priesthood, whose tradition he had learned from none other but himself. For "he gave him," it runs, "a tenth from all"; from the things of sense, right use of sense; from the things of speech, good speaking; from the things of thought, good thinking.[54]

Whereas Philo ignored the tithe in the previous passage, here it is the *raison d'être* for mentioning Melchizedek. As in *Jubilees*, the author uses this encounter as an opportunity to discuss the Jewish practice of tithing. Though Heb 7 also focuses on tithe in this encounter, the author of Hebrews stresses the discontinuity between the priesthood of Melchizedek and Israel's later Levitical priesthood, to whom the tithe was paid in actual practice. This differs from the perspective of Philo and the author of *Jubilees*, both of whom assume continuity between Abraham's tithe to Melchizedek and Israel's tithes to the Levitical priests.

Another significant element here is that Philo sees Melchizedek as having a 'self-taught' priesthood (τὴν αὐτομαθῆ καὶ αὐτοδίδακτον λαχὼν ἱερωσύνην). This, of course, is a high compliment for Philo, who elsewhere discusses Isaac as self-taught (cf. *Ios*. 1).[55] Underlying this assertion, however, seems to be the assumption that Melchizedek was the first priest, an idea known elsewhere in Second Temple interpretations of the passage; as discussed above, Josephus explicitly makes this claim. In a sense, so does the author of Hebrews, though there the timeline is stressed differently. Chronologically Hebrews

[54] Philo, *Congr*. 99 (Colson, LCL).

[55] One might be tempted to see here a possible parallel to Hebrews' description of Melchizedek as lacking parentage, i.e. Philo presents Melchizedek as 'self-taught' because he too knows a tradition about Melchizedek's lack of ancestry. Arguing against this, however, is Philo's presentation of Isaac as 'self-taught' while clearly knowing his relationship to Abraham.

does see Melchizedek's priesthood as predating the Levitical priesthood and setting the pattern for Jesus' later priesthood. Hebrews, however, stresses the temporal restraints of the Levitical system and contrasts it with Jesus' new—not resumed—priesthood like Melchizedek's. This supports observations that the Melchizedek discussion in Hebrews is only a tool, not an end, in the author's presentation of Jesus priesthood.

So, clearly Philo draws here on Gen 14, and his comments resemble some elements found in other Second Temple Jewish discussions and in Hebrews. No use of Ps 110:4 is evident.

2.5.3. *On the Embassy to Gaius 3.79-82*

In the course of his allegorical interpretation of Gen 3:14, Philo raises Melchizedek as an example to contrast with evildoers.

> [79] Melchizedek, too, has God made both king of peace, for that is the meaning of "Salem," and His own priest. He has not fashioned beforehand any deed of his, but produces him to begin with as such a king, peaceable and worthy of His own priesthood. For he is entitled "the righteous king," and a "king" is a thing at enmity with a despot, the one being the author of laws, the other of lawlessness. [80] So mind, the despot, decrees for both soul and body harsh and hurtful decrees working grievous woes, conduct, I mean, such as wickedness prompts, and free indulgence of the passions. But the king in the first place resorts to persuasion rather than decrees, and in the next place issues directions such as to enable a vessel, the living being I mean, to make life's voyage successfully, piloted by the good pilot, who is right principle. [81] Let the despot's title therefore be ruler of war, the king's prince of peace, of Salem, and let him offer to the soul food full of joy and gladness; for he brings bread and wine, things which Ammonites and Moabites refused to supply to the seeing one, on which account they are excluded from the divine congregation and assembly. These characters, Ammonites deriving their nature from sense-perception their mother, and Moabites deriving theirs from mind their father, who hold that all things owe their coherence to these two things, mind and sense-perception, and take no thought of God, "shall not enter," saith Moses, "into the congregation of the Lord, because they did not meet us with bread and water" when we came out from the passions of Egypt. [82] But let Melchizedek instead of water offer wine, and give to souls strong drink, that they may be seized by a divine intoxication, more sober than sobriety itself. For he is a priest, even Reason, having as his portion Him that is, and all his thoughts of God are high and vast and sublime: for he is the priest of the

> Most High, not that there is any other not Most High—for God being One "is in heaven above and on earth beneath, and there is none beside Him"—but to conceive of God not in low earthbound ways but in lofty terms, such as transcend all other greatness and all else that is free from matter, calls up in us a picture of the Most High.[56]

Though clearly Philo has other agendas here than just recounting the narrative of Gen 14, several elements of this story can nevertheless be discerned.

Salem is interpreted as 'peace,' and Melchizedek is said to be both 'king of peace' and God's priest. The author of Hebrews also identifies Melchizedek as 'king of peace' (Heb 7:2) based on an etymology of Salem.

Philo appears to address Melchizedek's lack of background in *Leg.* 3.79: "He [God] has not fashioned beforehand any deed of his, but produces him to begin with as such a king, peaceable and worthy of His own priesthood." Presumably this is derived by means of an argument from Scripture's silence on Melchizedek's origins. If so, this is paralleled in Heb 7:3, which assumes that Melchizedek is eternal and without genealogy. Commentators on Hebrews recognize two possible sources for this thinking for the NT author, the silence of Genesis about Melchizedek's past and future, and the statement in Ps 110:4 that the one like Melchizedek would be a priest forever. While knowledge of Ps 110 is foundational and explicit in Hebrews, it is not evident in Philo, nor is it requisite for his comments here.

Without specifying it as an etymology, Philo notes that Melchizedek is called 'the righteous king.' Philo uses this as an opportunity to contrast despots and kings, which allegorically are understood to represent the mind, the former prone toward evil and commands detrimental to one's body and soul, the latter using persuasion and producing a successful life.[57] The author of Hebrews

[56] Philo, *Leg.* 3.79-82 (Whitaker, LCL).

[57] Note the words of James R. Davila, *Liturgical Works* (ECDSS; Grand Rapids: Eerdmans, 2000), 165: "Philo of Alexandria treats Melchizedek as a high priest representing Logos or Reason, a peaceable and righteous king who is contrasted with the tyrant Mind, the Ruler of War, which leads the organism into wickedness and excessive indulgence of the passions. . . . Philo seems to be at pains to distinguish Melchizedek from the warrior angel we find in 11Q13, but his association of him with the demiurgic and divine Logos may mean that Philo accepted Melchizedek's divine status." For discussion of 11Q13 (11QMelchizedek), see below.

also plays on the supposed etymology of the name Melchizedek and calls him 'king of righteousness' (Heb 7:20).

Philo initially relates Melchizedek's presentation of bread and wine to Abraham as a function of his kingship, not his priesthood. This action is contrasted with the later refusal of the Ammonites and Moabites to offer food and water to the Israelites during the exodus wanderings. Philo then contrasts the wine offered by Melchizedek with the water withheld by Israel's enemies and allegorizes the effects of the wine as 'a divine intoxication, more sober than sobriety itself.' Melchizedek's function as priest is now stressed, and he is identified with Reason or the Logos.

Melchizedek's deity, God Most High, clearly is understood as Abraham's deity. Philo dismisses any hint of a multiplicity of gods, and he understands the title as stressing God's transcendence.

Overall, this passage is striking because it has several parallels with the discussion of Melchizedek in Heb 7. As noted above, etymologies for Melchizedek's name and city are offered by both Philo and the author of Hebrews, though they differ on the meaning of Melchizedek's name. It was also noted that Philo may extrapolate significance for Melchizedek based on the silence of Genesis on the figure. Hebrews does a similar thing, though there both the silence of Genesis and the voice of Ps 110 are factors.

Perhaps most striking, though, is Philo's correlation of Melchizedek with the Logos, whom Philo sees as a mediating figure between God and humanity. Philo's Logos is Judaism's personification of Wisdom in Greek philosophical clothes, and (as seen in chapter 1 of this study) the author of Hebrews frequently draws on Wisdom motifs to explain the identity of the Son in Heb 1. It has been asserted that the author of Hebrews posits Jesus as the divine Son in order to present him as the heavenly high priest, so in this sense one might conclude that the author of Hebrews establishes Jesus' priesthood by drawing on Wisdom motifs. This, though, is convoluted and does not allow one to claim, for example, that the author of Hebrews adapted this motif from Philo's correlation of the priest Melchizedek with the Logos. A better conclusion from this observation is that the author of Hebrews was a writer immersed in the various intellectual currents of his era.

3. Melchizedek in the Texts of the Qumran Community

Melchizedek appears in several texts found among the Dead Sea Scrolls, both in texts composed in the community or shared with wider Judaism. One example of the latter, the *Genesis Apocryphon*, was discussed above, as its portrait of Melchizedek differs significantly from that otherwise found in the Qumran texts. In the other texts discovered there, Melchizedek is a heavenly figure rather than an earthly king-priest. Unfortunately the texts discussed below tend to be in poor states of preservation. Nevertheless, important conclusions can be drawn about his significance in that community.

3.1. *Songs of the Sabbath Sacrifice*

The name 'Melchizedek' is a proposed reading in three small fragments from the cave 4 and 11 manuscripts of *Songs of the Sabbath Sacrifice*.[58] This text is represented at Qumran by several scrolls from Cave 4 (4Q400-407) along with 11Q17. The Cave 4 copies date to the first century B.C.E. and are in widely-varying states of preservation.[59] The other manuscript, 11Q17, preserves portions of ten columns, and its significant overlapping contents with 4Q405 indicate that those two manuscripts represent the same version of the text; it is written in an "inconsistent hand" and dates to "the first half or the first third of the 1st century CE."[60] As for the date of composition of the *Songs of the Sabbath Sacrifice*, Carol Newsom proposes a date no later than 100 B.C.E.; understanding the text as a pre-Qumran composition that was appropriated by the sect and influenced its own compositions, she notes that the origins of the text could lie "sometime in the second century BCE . . . although there is no evidence to preclude an earlier date."[61] Newsom bases her theory of pre-Qumran origins on the text's

---

[58] For the texts, see Carol A. Newsom, DJD XI, 173-401 and plates XIV-XXXI; and Florentino García Martínez, Eibert J. C. Tigchelaar, and Adam S. van der Woude, DJD XXIII, 259-304 and plates XXX-XXXIV, LIII. See also James H. Charlesworth and Carol A. Newsom, eds., PTSDSSP 4b; this edition also includes discussion of Mas1k.

[59] Charlesworth and Newsom, PTSDSSP 4b, 1-2.

[60] García Martínez, Tigchelaar, and van der Woude, DJD XXIII, 260-67, esp. 263-64.

[61] Carol Newsom, "Songs of the Sabbath Sacrifice," *EDSS* 2.887-89, esp. 2.887.

geographical distribution (a copy, Mas1K, also was found at Masada), internal evidence, and the probability that certain texts written at the community (*Berakhot*[a-b] [4Q286-287] and *Songs of the Sage*[a-b] [4Q510-511]) show dependence on it.[62]

As the title implies, these texts are songs to accompany thirteen Sabbath offerings, and the officiants are angels with priestly roles. The songs chiefly describe the glories of God and the heavenly sanctuary. Relatively little text has survived concerning the nature of the sacrifices themselves. What is extant on the subject is in 11Q13 IX, 4; though the text is quite fragmentary, burnt offerings are implied by the mention of aroma (ריח).

A צדק element is clearly preserved in two lines of 4Q401, leading some scholars to propose both as references to Melchizedek. In both cases, however, the readings are far from certain because of the lack of extant contextual material.

Newsom reads מלכי]צדק כוהן בעד[ת אל, 'Melchi]zedek, priest in the assemb[ly of God,' in 4Q401 11 3, and this reading is also supported by James Davila.[63] If this is correct, it is very significant in light of the context of *Songs of the Sabbath Sacrifice*—Melchizedek, a human priest in the Hebrew Bible (clearly so in the narrative of Gen 14, presumably so in Ps 110), is here presented as priest in a text "largely concerned with invoking and describing the praise of angelic priests in the heavenly temple."[64] Melchizedek then would be a heavenly, angelic priest in the service of God.

Newsom notes that it would be the only place in the text where an angel is named, and use of the singular כוהן itself is unusual in *Songs of the Sabbath Sacrifice*. Newsom restores the name 'Melchizedek' on the basis of a possible parallel with 11QMelch II, 10, where the phrase בעדת אל appears and Melchizedek is presented as the subject (and first occurrence of אלוהים) of Ps 82:1.[65] Davila further notes that this section of 4Q401 appears to be part of the fifth song, "which describes an eschatological 'war in heaven.'"[66] If Davila's interpretation here is correct, Melchizedek is mentioned here in a *context* similar to that of

---

[62] Newsom, "Songs," 2.887.

[63] Newsom, DJD XI, 205; Davila, *Liturgical Works*, 162; see also García Martínez, Tigchelaar, and van der Woude, DJD XXIII, 270.

[64] Newsom, "Songs," 2.887.

[65] Newsom, DJD XI, 205. See further discussion of 11QMelch II, 10 below.

[66] Davila, *Liturgical Works*, 162; cf. 223.

11QMelchizedek, a text discussed in detail below, though admittedly no militaristic language in reference to Melchizedek has survived in 4Q401 itself.

Davila finds another reference to Melchizedek in 4Q401 22 3, though Newsom is less convinced. Three partial lines and only 21 letters remain; the extant text of line three is]כי צדק[.[67] The phrase מלו ידיהם, 'they fill their hands,' is likely in line 2, and Davila finds parallels in biblical passages discussing priestly installation ceremonies (Exod 28:41; Lev 8:33; Judg 17:5, 12; cf. *T.Moses* 10:2). In light of this, he proposes that this fragment preserves discussion of the priestly installation of Melchizedek and other angelic priests.[68] Newsom is more cautious, preferring to read the extant צדק as 'righteousness' rather than an element in Melchizedek's name (which in the reconstructions above, as in 11QMelchizedek, is written as two words). Nevertheless she comments that "in view of the reference to consecration of priests in the preceding line, it is tempting to restore the name of Melchizedek here."[69]

The letters למלכ (the כ is less certain) appear on 11Q17 3 II, 7. Davila and the editors of the text in DJD XXIII (García Martínez, Tigchelaar, and van der Woude) find here a passage from song 8, otherwise composed of 4Q403 1 II, 21 and 4Q405 8-9 5-6.[70] According to this reconstruction, the phrase ראשי נשיאי כהונות פ[לא למלכ]י צדק, 'the chiefs of the princes of the wonderful priesthoods of Melchizedek' (DJD), appears in a song that invokes the praises of heavenly priests serving in the heavenly sanctuary. The striking feature is that Melchizedek would stand at the head of the heavenly priesthood, which is reminiscent of 'the order of Melchizedek' in Ps 110:4. Both the DJD editors and Davila admit that other readings are possible, however, and Newsom rejects mention of Melchizedek here.[71]

---

[67] Newsom, DJD XI, 213.

[68] Davila, *Liturgical Works*, 162-63.

[69] Newsom, DJD XI, 213. See also Charlesworth and Newsom, PTSDSSP 4b, 38 n. 46.

[70] Davila, *Liturgical Works*, 132-33; García Martínez, Tigchelaar, and van der Woude, DJD XXIII, 266, 269-70.

[71] Newsom, DJD XI, 205, limits references to Melchizedek (or any named angel) in the Sabbath songs to the aforementioned 4Q401 11 3. See also Davila, *Liturgical Works*, 133; and García Martínez, Tigchelaar, and van der Woude, DJD XXIII, 270: "in view of the context, למלכ]י צדק is very attractive."

In summary, though lacunae abound, at least one passage—and possibly more—in the *Songs of the Sabbath Sacrifice* appears to identify Melchizedek as an angelic priest serving in God's heavenly temple court; the context *may* be a discussion of eschatological warfare. Another passage may identify Melchizedek as head of an angelic priesthood (with possible overtones of Ps 110). This differs significantly from other Second Temple period understandings of Melchizedek surveyed thus far, but its perspective is similar to that of other Qumran texts that mention the figure.

3.2. *Visions of Amram*

This Aramaic text from the second century B.C.E. is preserved in fragments of six (perhaps seven) Cave 4 manuscripts, 4Q543-549, the most significant of which for this study is 4Q544 (4Q Visions of Amram^{b} ar).[72] It takes the form of a testament and recounts a vision of its namesake, the grandson of Levi.[73] Amram dreams that two watchers are fighting over him, one evil and the other good; he inquires about their identities and powers. Though no letters of Melchizedek's name are preserved, Józef Milik and most subsequent scholars have proposed that he indeed was mentioned in the text in 4Q544 3 IV, 2-3 based on a parallel with 4Q544 2 III, 13:[74]

> 4Q544 2 III, 13
> ואנון תלתה שמהתה בליעל ושר חשוכה]ומלכי רשע
> [And these are his three names: Belial, Prince of Darkness],
> and Melchireša‘

> 4Q544 3 IV, 2-3
> לי תלתה שמהן[די לי ואנון מיכאל ושר נהורא ומלכי צדק]
> [My] three names [are Michael, Prince of Light, and Melchizedek][75]

---

[72] The DJD edition is that of Émile Puech, DJD XXXI, 283-405 and plates XVI-XXII.

[73] Kobelski, *Melchizedek*, 24-25. On the dating, see also Michael E. Stone, "Amram," *EDSS* 1:23-24.

[74] Milik, "4Q Visions de 'Amram et une citation d'Origène," *RB* 79 (1972): 77-97, esp. 85-86, and now also Puech, DJD XXXI, 328-29; Kobelski, *Melchizedek*, 36; and Émile Puech, *La Croyance des Esséniens en la Vie Future: Immortalité, Résurrection, Vie Éternelle?* (*EBib* n.s. 21; Paris: Gabalda, 1993), 536.

[75] The text and line numbers are those of DJD; Milik cited the texts as 4Q544 3 2 and 4Q544 2 3. The translation is that of Kobelski, *Melchizedek*, 28.

As is evident, both lists of names are heavily based on reconstructions, and scholars have proposed the particular names based on conceptual parallels with 1QM and 11QMelch.[76] The one name present in the text is מלכי רשע, Melchireša' ('my king is wicked'), and the extant text indicates that three names are to be listed. The passages do seem to be parallel opposites, and admittedly מלכי צדק seems to be a likely restoration.

If the reconstruction of this very fragmentary text is correct, Melchizedek is identified as (or with) the angel Michael and the 'Prince of Light.' Michael often appears in Qumran texts as the opponent of Belial and is invoked in the war between the sons of light and the sons of darkness in 1QM, a text that may also describe Michael as 'Prince of Light' in 1QM XIII, 10-11.[77] Melchizedek then would be an angelic opponent of Belial in the eschatological war on behalf of God's people. This also appears to be his role in 11QMelchizedek, to which attention now turns.

3.3. *11QMelchizedek*

This manuscript, 11QMelchizedek (11Q13), was discovered in 1956 and was first published by Adam S. van der Woude in 1965.[78]

---

[76] For explanations of the reconstructions, see Milik, "4Q Visions," 85-86, and Kobelski, *Melchizedek*, 33, 36.

[77] For a survey of Michael traditions in the Dead Sea Scrolls, see Erik W. Larson, "Michael," *EDSS* 1:546-48. Larsen asserts that some Gnostic texts identify Michael with Melchizedek. This is not explicit in the texts, though they do correlate Melchizedek and Christ. See Birger A. Pearson, "Melchizedek in Early Judaism, Christianity, and Gnosticism," in *Biblical Figures Outside the Bible* (ed. Michael E. Stone and Theodore A. Bergren; Harrisburg, Penn.: Trinity, 1998), 176-202, and Horton, *Melchizedek Tradition*, 131-51. Two medieval rabbinic texts identify Michael with Melchizedek, a point sometimes raised in support of reconstructing a similar correlation in 4Q544; see van der Woude, "Melchisedek," 370-71; and de Jonge and van der Woude, "11Q Melchizedek," 305. Horton wisely cautions against this, stating that "the medieval evidence . . . cannot be taken seriously in the form in which De Jonge and Van der Woude [*sic*] present it" and that "there is no more justification for quoting short [rabbinic] texts out of context . . . than there is for similar quotations from Christian writers" (*Melchizedek Tradition*, 81-82).

[78] Van der Woude, "Melchisedek," 354-73. The text was published (reflecting minor changes from the *editio princeps*) with an English translation by de Jonge and van der Woude, "11Q Melchizedek," 301-26. (See the previous note for fuller information.) Van der Woude's *editio princeps* also served as the base text in Joseph Fitzmyer's article "Further Light."

Subsequent major editions have been published by J. T. Milik; Paul J. Kobelski; Émile Puech; and finally in DJD by Florentino García Martínez, Eibert J. C. Tigchelaar, and van der Woude.[79]

Portions of at least three columns are extant, though only col. II is preserved substantially. García Martínez, Tigchelaar, and van der Woude find among the textual remains 10 fragments in 15 pieces.[80] This presentation differs slightly from that of van der Woude's *editio princeps* (and his subsequent article on the text with de Jonge), where he examined 13 fragments, though Kobelski notes that van der Woude's photo of the fragments included an unidentified fourteenth fragment.[81] Puech, following van der Woude's earlier study, also cites 13 fragments.[82] The discrepancy is explained in part by the decision of the DJD editors to reclassify adjoining fragments as such, thus necessitating a new numbering system for the fragments.[83]

As noted above, scholars recognize extant portions of three columns. Of these, col. I is represented by only a few fortuitously-placed letters. Portions of three letters remain from a supralinear notation that continued vertically into the margin between cols. I and II; traces of at least 11 letters are evident in the vertical portion. Though significantly more remains of col. III, rather little can be deduced from its fragmentary contents. Only the first few words in each line are preserved intact, and it is unclear whether several of the remaining fragments of the manuscript preserve portions of col. III or subsequent columns.[84] As for col. II, no complete lines remain, but enough material has survived to allow significant reconstruction of this

---

[79] Milik, "*Milkî-ṣedeq*"; Kobelski, *Melchizedek*, 3-23; Émile Puech, "Notes sur le manuscrit de XIQMelkîsédeq," *RevQ* 12 (1987): 483-513; and García Martínez, Tigchelaar, and van der Woude, DJD XXIII, 221-41, Pl. XXVII. A later edition with a very brief introduction is J. J. M. Roberts, PTSDSSP 4b, 264-73.

[80] García Martínez, Tigchelaar, and van der Woude, DJD XXIII, 221-22. In addition, an eleventh fragment (with minimal extant text) appears in both the DJD transcription and plate, and in a later publication the presence of this eleventh fragment is further acknowledged. See García Martínez, "Las tradiciones," 72.

[81] Kobelski, *Melchizedek*, 3 n. 2. This tiny fragment is included among those recognized in the DJD edition.

[82] Puech, "Notes," 485.

[83] See the chart of García Martínez, Tigchelaar, and van der Woude, DJD XXIII, 222.

[84] For differing views on the placement of fragments 5-11 (according to the DJD numbering, which differs from that first proposed by van der Woude), compare the arrangements presented in García Martínez, Tigchelaar, and van der Woude, DJD XXIII; Milik, "*Milkî-ṣedeq*"; and Puech, "Notes."

section of the document. The column includes 25 lines of text in various states of preservation.[85]

Drawing on Frank Moore Cross's widely-accepted paleographical classifications, van der Woude argued in the *editio princeps* that the hand was Herodian and the manuscript should be dated to the first half of the first century C.E.[86] Milik, also drawing on the work of Cross, argued instead for a first-century B.C.E. date for the manuscript, more specifically 75-50 B.C.E., and van der Woude and his fellow DJD editors express support for this option.[87] As for the original composition of the Melchizedek text, Milik argued that it was part of a longer 'Pesher on the Periods' that was written by the *Maître de Justice* himself and thus must be dated c. 120 B.C.E.[88] Puech opts for a similar date (second half of the second century B.C.E.) for two reasons: he identifies the anointed messenger of 11Q13 II, 18 (והמבשר הואה משיח הרוח) as the Teacher of Righteousness, and he proposes that the author was prompted (actually, Puech more forcefully credits the author with *engouement*, 'infatuation') to present Melchizedek as a heavenly priest and eschatological liberator at this time in response to the Hasmonean appropriation of Melchizedek's title כֹּהֵן לְאֵל עֶלְיוֹן from Gen 14:18.[89]

Despite its fragmentary condition, this text attracted much attention shortly after its initial publication—and prompted bold claims about its applicability to the interpretation of Hebrews—because it presents Melchizedek in an eschatological context that has priestly, prophetic, and judgment themes.[90] As indicated below, however, the extant

---

[85] Van der Woude had indicated 26 lines in his *editio princeps* ("Melchisedek," 358; also in de Jonge and van der Woude, "11Q Melchizedek," 302; and accepted by Fitzmyer, "Further Light," 247). Subsequently most scholars have preferred to read the traces of three letters that van der Woude considered as evidence for his line 22 as part of the following line, as in the DJD edition van der Woude recently coauthored. Jean Carmignac also proposed 26 lines but with no traces extant for the 22nd line; see his "Le document," 351.

[86] Van der Woude, "Melchisedek," 357. See Frank M. Cross, Jr., "The Development of the Jewish Scripts," in *The Bible and the Ancient Near East* (ed. G. Ernest Wright; Garden City, N.Y.: Doubleday, 1961; repr., Garden City, N.Y.: Anchor, 1965), 133-202 (repr., 170-264) for his classic paleographical study.

[87] Milik, "*Milkî-ṣedeq*," 97, followed by García Martínez, Tigchelaar, and van der Woude, DJD XXIII, 223. For a brief defense of dating the manuscript to 50-25 B.C.E., see Kobelski, *Melchizedek*, 3.

[88] Milik, "*Milkî-ṣedeq*," 126.

[89] Puech, "Notes," 509-10.

[90] See the discussion above in chapter 3.

portions of 11QMelchizedek—like the other Dead Sea Scrolls texts that (possibly) mention Melchizedek surveyed above—do not overtly draw upon the explicit references to the figure in Gen 14:18-20 or Ps 110:4, passages central to the argument in Hebrews. Equally clear, though, is that the authors of Qumran that mention (or may mention) Melchizedek have a well-developed understanding of the figure with biblical roots; this understanding seems to have been derived in some manner from Ps 110:4, whereas other Second Temple Jewish authors who mentioned Melchizedek (Josephus, Philo, etc.) did so in the context of his encounter with Abram in Gen 14:18-20.

As noted above, most readers (ancient and modern) seem to have understood Ps 110:4 as addressed to someone receiving a eternal priesthood *like* that of Melchizedek apart from the Levitical order, though Flusser argues that the ambiguity of the Hebrew statement may have allowed it to be read in antiquity as directed *to* Melchizedek himself. This direct address, according to Flusser, also provides a better rationale for the assertion in Heb 7:3 that Melchizedek is eternal than does the silence about Melchizedek's origins and destiny in Gen 14.[91] Because the author of 11QMelchizedek read Ps 110:4 as stating that Melchizedek possessed an eternal priesthood, he must also be the figure addressed elsewhere in the psalm as enthroned at God's right hand (Ps 110:1), having dominion over his enemies (Ps 110:1-2), and bringing judgment (Ps 110:5-6). This judgment theme then prompted the author to read Ps 82, with its similar emphasis, as also about Melchizedek.[92] As is demonstrated below, Melchizedek seems clearly to be understood as אלוהים in Ps 82 in 11Q13 II, 10, and the text relates this final judgment with periods of Jubilee, sabbatical legislation, and the Day of Atonement. This pastiche of themes is justifiable: according to Lev 25:8-10, Jubilees (with the accompanying restoration of land and liberty) began on the Day of Atonement, and a significant feature of Gen 14 is Abram's return of persons and property in the context of his encounter with Melchizedek.[93] As VanderKam notes, "it seems that the writer of 11QMelch used a series of biblical

[91] Flusser, "Melchizedek," 26-27. Flusser is followed by VanderKam, "Sabbatical Chronologies," 173-76; and Kugel, *The Bible as It Was*, 149-62.

[92] Flusser, "Melchizedek," 27; and VanderKam, "Sabbatical Chronologies," 174.

[93] VanderKam, "Sabbatical Chronologies," 175.

passages and themes that allowed him to connect Melchizedek, the day of atonement, and sabbatical and jubilee periods."[94]

Similarly, García Martínez also finds biblical justification for the presentation of Melchizedek in this text. First, García Martínez is careful to note that while the author of 11QMelchizedek certainly seems to envision a heavenly status for Melchizedek, he never refers to the protagonist as an angel. This for García Martínez is proof that the author is developing his portrait of Melchizedek from biblical roots, as the texts there presenting the figure as a king and priest actually inhibit the author from using angelic language for Melchizedek.[95] Instead, these twin roles for Melchizedek in the biblical text determine the presentation of the figure in 11QMelchizedek. A king in both Gen 14 and Ps 110, Melchizedek likewise is presented in the Qumran text as one exercising authority over other heavenly beings and over his lot of humanity, and he also has juridical functions.[96] Similarly, the biblical presentation of Melchizedek as priest seems reflected in his connection with the eschatological Day of Atonement.[97]

García Martínez goes further, however, and identifies Melchizedek in the text as a messianic figure. The term משיח is not extant in 11QMelchizedek, yet Melchizedek is presented as fulfilling functions consistent with messianic figures, including his role in final judgment, effecting eschatological atonement, destruction of the armies of Belial in the eschatological battle, restoration of peace, and bringing salvation for those of his 'lot.'[98] In addition, while never said to be 'anointed' in the extant sections of 11QMelchizedek, the figure nevertheless held two offices—kingship and priesthood—that are associated with anointing in the Hebrew Scriptures.[99] Melchizedek thus is a heavenly messianic figure; similar figures in pre-Christian Jewish texts are also found in the *Parables of Enoch* (*1 Enoch* 37-71) and *4 Ezra*.[100]

Below are the Hebrew text and English translation of col. II from the DJD edition. For reasons to be addressed below, the DJD

---

[94] VanderKam, "Sabbatical Chronologies," 176.
[95] García Martínez, "Las tradiciones," 74.
[96] García Martínez, "Las tradiciones," 74.
[97] García Martínez, "Las tradiciones," 74-75.
[98] García Martínez, "Las tradiciones," 75.
[99] García Martínez, "Las tradiciones," 77.
[100] García Martínez, "Las tradiciones," 76-77, though he is careful to note that because of the uncertain dating for these texts, the Christian conception of a heavenly messianic figure may have influenced them.

translation has been adapted, with by renderings of **אלוהים** in bold print and renderings of **אל** in bold italics:

top margin?

1 [ ] ◦◦ ◦◦◦◦ מׄ◦◦ עׄלׄ[

2 [ ]לׄ וׄאׄשׄר אמר בשנת היובל [הזואת תשובו איש אל אחוזתו ועליו אמר וז]ה

3 [דבר השמטה] שמוט כול בעל משה יד אשר ישה[ברעהו לוא יגוש את רעהו ואת אחיו כיא קרא]שמטה

4 לׄאׄ[ל פשרו]לׄאׄחׄרית הימים על השבויים אשר[ ]ואשׄר

5 מׄוׄריׄהמה הׄחׄבאׄו וסׄתׄרׄ[ו] ומנחלת מלכי צדק כיׄ[א]◦◦◦◦ וׄהמה נחׄלׄ[ת מלכי צ]דק אשר

6 ישיבמה אליהמה וקרא להמה דרור לעזוב להמהׄ[משא]כׄול עוונותיהמה ו[כן יהי]הׄ הׄדבר הזה

7 בׄשׄבׄוׄעׄ היובל הׄראישׄון אחׄרׄ תׄשׄ[עה ה]יובלים ויׄ[ום הכפ]וׄרים ה[וא]ה סׄ[וף ה]הׄ[יו]בל העשירי

8 לכפר בו על כול בני [אור ו]אׄנש[י]גׄורל מל[כי]צדק[ ]◦ם עליׄ[המ]ה הת[ ]לפׄ[י]כׄ[ול עש]ותמה כיא

9 הואה הקׄץׄ לׄשנת הרצון למלכי צדׄק וׄלצׄבׄ[איו ע]םׄ קדושי אל לממׄשׄלת משפט כאשר כתוב

10 עליו בשיריׄ דויד אשר אמר אלוהים [נ]צׄב בעׄ[דת אל]בׄקורב אלוהים ישפוט ועׄליו אׄמׄ[ר ו]עׄליׄ[ה]

11 למרום שובה אל ידין עמים ואשר א[מר עד מתי ת]שפוטו עוול ופני רשע[י]ם תש[או ס]לה

12 פשרו על בליעל ועל רׄוחׄי גורלו אש[ר]◦ים בסוׄ[רמ]הׄ מחׄוקי אל ל[הרשיע]

13 ומלכי צׄדק יקום נקׄםׄ משפׄטׄי א[ל וביום ההואה יצי]לׄ[מה מיד]בׄליעל ומיד כול רׄ[וחי גורלו]

14 ובעזרו כול אלי [הצדק וה]וׄאה א[שר]כׄול בני אל והפ[

15 הזואת הואה יום הׄ[שלום א]שר אמׄרׄ[ביד ישע]יה הנביא אשר אמר[מה]נׄאוו

16 על הרים רגל[י] מבש[ר מ]שמיע שלום מב[שר טוב משמיע ישוע]הׄ [א]וׄמר לציון [מלך]אׄלוהיך

17 פׄשרו ההרׄיׄם[המה] הׄנׄביאיׄ[ם]המה א[ ]◦מׄ[ ] לכול ◦◦[

18 והמבשר הו[אה [מׄשיח הרוׄ[ח] כׄאשר אמר דנׄ[יאל עליו עד משיח נגיד שבועים שבעה ומבשר]

19 טוׄבׄ משמי[ע ישועה [הואה הכׄתוב עליו אשר]

20 לנחׄ[ם] ה[אבלים פשרו [ל[ה]שׄכילמׄה בכול קצי הע[ולם

21 באׄמת למׄ] [מׄה א]

22 ◦◦] [ר הוסרה מבליעל ותשׄ[וב [נׄקׄ]

23] [במשפט[י] אל כאשר כׄתוב עליו] אומר לצי[ון מלך אלוהיך [צי]ון ה[יאה]

24 [עדת כול בני הצדק המה [מקימ[י] הברית הסרים מלכת [בד]רׄךׄ העם ואל[ו]היךׄ הׄואה

25] מלכי צדק אשר יצי[ל[מה מי[ד בליעל ואשר אמר והעברתמה שו[פר ב]כׄולׄ [א]רׄץ

bottom margin

1. [ ] [

2. [ ] and as for what he said: 'In [this] year of jubilee [each of you shall return to his property', concerning it he said: 'And th]is is

3. [the manner of the remission:] every creditor shall remit what he has lent [his neighbour. He shall not press his neighbour or his brother for it has been proclaimed] a remission

4. of ***Go[d'***. Its interpretation] for the final days concerns the captives, who [ ] and whose

5. teachers have been hidden and kept secret, and from the inheritance of Melchizedek, fo[r] and they are the inheritan[ce of Melchize]dek who

6. will make them return. And liberty shall be proclaimed to them, to free them from [the debt of] all their iniquities. And this [wil]l [happen]

7. in the first week of the jubilee (that occurs) after [the] ni[ne] jubilees. And the D[ay of Atone]ment i[s] the e[nd of] the tenth [ju]bilee,

8. in which atonement shall be made for all the sons of [light and for] the men [of] the lot of Mel[chi]sedek[ ] over [th]em [ ] accor[ding to] a[ll] their [doing]s, for

9. it is the time for the year of grace of Melchizedek and of [his] arm[ies, the nati]on [of] the holy ones of ***God***, of the administration of justice, as is written

10. about him in the songs of David, who said: '**Elohim** shall [st]and in the ass[embly of ***God***]; in the midst of the **gods** he shall judge'. And about him he sa[id: 'And] above [it,]

11. to the heights, return: ***God*** shall judge the nations'. And as for what he s[aid: 'How long will you] judge unjustly, and be par[tial] to the wick[e]d. [Se]lah',

12. the interpretation of it concerns Belial and the spirits of his lot wh[o], in [the]ir tur[ning] away from ***God***'s commandments to [commit evil].

13. And Melchizedek will carry out the vengeance of ***Go[d]***'s judgements [and on that day he will f]r[ee them from the hand of] Belial and from the hand of all the s[pirits of his lot.]

14. And all the ***gods*** [of justice] are to his help; [and h]e is (the one) wh[o] all the sons of ***God***, and he will [

15. This [ ] is the day of the [peace ab]out which he said [through Isa]iah the prophet who said: ['How] beautiful

16. upon (the) mountains are the feet [of] the messen[ger who an]nounces peace, the mes[senger of good who announces salvati]on, [sa]ying to Zion: your **God** [is king'].

17. Its interpretation: the mountains [are] the prophet[s]; they [ ] every [ ]

18. And the messenger i[s] the anointed of the spir[it], as Dan[iel] said [about him: 'Until an anointed, a prince, it is seven weeks'. And the messenger of]

19. good who announ[ces salvation] is the one about whom it is written [

20. 'To comfo[rt] the [afflicted', its interpretation:] to [in]struct them in all the ages of the w[orld

21. in truth [ ] [

22. [ ] has turned away from Belial and shall retu[rn to] [[101]

23. [ ] in the judgement[s of] ***God***, as is written about him: '[saying to Zi]on: your **God** is king'. [Zi]on i[s]

24. [the congregation of all the sons of justice, who] establish the covenant, who avoid walking [on the p]ath of the people. And 'your **G[o]d**' is

---

[101] Either two or three letters are present in the untranslated portion at the end of this line. Kobelski reconstructs מלכי] צדק[and thus a reference to Melchizedek, which seems fitting in light of lines 23-25 (*Melchizedek*, 6, 22). Others instead read נק[; see García Martínez, Tigchelaar, and van der Woude, DJD XXIII, 225; and Puech, "Notes," 489.

25. [Melchizedek who will fr]ee [them from the han]d of Belial. And as for what he said: 'And you shall blow the ho[rn in] all the [l]and (of)[102]

As is evident from the translation, the text essentially is a midrash—or perhaps a thematic pesher—providing an eschatological interpretation of several passages of Scripture.[103] Clearly the author engages in a pesher style of interpretation, but the approach also has a midrashic nature, as represented in the following schematic outline:

line 2 Lev 25:13, interpreted by Deut 15:2
lines 2-4 Deut 15:2
lines 4-9 pesher on Deut 15:2 (with Isa 61:1)[104]

[102] García Martínez, Tigchelaar, and van der Woude, DJD XXIII, 229-30.

[103] Classification of 11QMelchizedek as a midrash dates back to its original publication by van der Woude, "Melchisedek," 357. Jean Carmignac argued that 11QMelchizedek is a thematic pesher ("*péshèr* «discontinue» ou «thématique»") because it focuses on a single subject, the deliverance of God's people from Belial. Such pesherim may draw on related passages from a number of different texts, whereas other Qumran pesharim deal with a variety of subjects arising while interpreting long passages from a particular book of Scripture. See Carmignac, "Le document," 360-62. Timothy Lim agrees and notes, "If the sub-genre of 'thematic pesher' describes any text at all, it would be 11QMelch, since there is a prominent theme in the text." See Timothy Lim, *Pesharim* (Companion to the Qumran Scrolls 3; London: Sheffield, 2002), 53. On 11QMelchizedek as thematic pesher, see also García Martínez, "Las tradiciones," 72; and Xeravits, *King, Priest, Prophet*, 69-70. See Anders Aschim, "The Genre of 11QMelchizedek," in *Qumran Between the Old and New Testaments* (ed. Frederick H. Cryer and Thomas L. Thompson; JSOTSup 290; Copenhagen International Seminar 6; Sheffield: Sheffield, 1998), 17-31, for criticism of this classification; he instead favors (following Fitzmyer) the suggestion that the text is a pesher on Lev 25.

[104] The significance of Isa 61 for interpretation of 11QMelchizedek was highlighted by Merrill P. Miller. While recognizing that 11QMelchizedek is not a pesher on Isa 61:1-2 *per se*, he nevertheless sees it "behind the unfolding pesher material . . . as if it were telescoped in those verses." See his article "The Function of Isa 61:1-2 in 11Q Melchizedek," *JBL* 88 (1969): 467-69, esp. 469.

The DJD editors note that "the preserved text of the column uses an expression from Isa 61:1-3 six times, but nowhere does it quote even a complete hemistich . . . Apparently, Isa 61:1-3 is a key passage that was considered to be commonly known" (García Martínez, Tigchelaar, and van der Woude, DJD XXIII, 230). The six expressions are in lines 4, 6, 9, 13, 18, and 20. The editors note that a quotation of several words may be reconstructed in the lacuna of line 4 but consider it "very uncertain." When discussing line 19, they note that the introductory formula used to introduce other quotations is never used for Isa 61:1-3 in the extant text (García Martínez, Tigchelaar, and van der Woude, DJD XXIII, 232). Others, including Milik, Puech, and Kobelski, prefer to view these as quotations of Isa 61. In line 19 the phrase הואה הכתוב עליו אשר appears to be a citation formula but is followed by a large lacuna. Milik proposes to fill the lacuna with language from Isa 61:3 ("*Milkî-ṣedeq,*" 98, 108-09), but note the caution of Kobelski: "I hesitate to follow Milik, however, because it seems that 11QMelch never introduces citations of Isaiah 61 by elaborate

line 10 Ps 82:1, in conjunction with
lines 10-11 Ps 7:8-9 and
line 11 Ps 82:2
lines 12-14 pesher on Pss 82:1; 7:8-9; and 82:2 (with Isa 61:3)[105]

lines 15-16 Isa 52:7[106]
lines 17-25 pesher on Isa 52:7, incorporating Dan 9:25 and Lev 25:9 (with Isa 61:2-3)[107]

Attention now turns to two major issues concerning the presentation of Melchizedek in this text—author's use of the terms אל and אלוהים, and the functions of Melchizedek described in the text.

3.3.1. *Use of the Terms* אל *and* אלוהים

The first step is to examine how the author of 11QMelchizedek uses the words אל and אלוהים. Translations of these terms were indicated above, but further analysis is appropriate:

3.3.1.1. Uses of אל

line 4—In a quotation of Deut 15:2 concerning the remission of debts, אל clearly is God. This reading differs from that of the MT of Deut 15:2, where יהוה appears rather than אל. Unfortunately Qumran

---

introductory formulas, but rather alludes to this portion of Isaiah in interpreting other scriptural quotations" (*Melchizedek*, 22).

Brooke stresses the importance of Isa 61 for the text and argues that its use here in connection with the Day of Atonement theme and Lev 25 is influenced by Jewish lectionary practices. See his *Exegesis at Qumran*, 319-23.

Puech finds an allusion to Ezek 2:7 in the first two words of line 5, which he transcribes as מורידהמה מחבאי ("Notes," 488, 493). This section of the manuscript is poorly preserved, however, and transcriptions vary widely; Puech himself later presented a different reading (*La Croyance*, 523).

Kobelski posits quotations of phrases from Lev 25:10 in line 6 and Lev 25:9 in line 7 (*Melchizedek*, 8, 14-15), as do Puech ("Notes," 490) and Milik (line 7 only; "*Milkî-ṣedeq*," 103-04).

[105] Cf. García Martínez, Tigchelaar, and van der Woude, DJD XXIII, 230; Milik, "*Milkî-ṣedeq,*" 106; and Puech, "Notes," 497-98.

[106] In line 15 Kobelski restores יום ה]ישועה and understands the term as drawn from Isa 49:8 (*Melchizedek*, 6, 20). Most scholars instead read יום ה]שלום. See, for example, García Martínez, Tigchelaar, and van der Woude, DJD XXIII, 232; Puech, "Notes," 488; and Milik, "*Milkî-ṣedeq*," 98.

[107] Again see García Martínez, Tigchelaar, and van der Woude, DJD XXIII, 232; Milik, "*Milkî-ṣedeq,*" 108-09; and Puech, "Notes," 500.

manuscripts which include Deut 15:2 are missing this last word of the verse.[108]

line 9—God would seem to be the אל in the phrase 'the holy ones of God.' As presented in the DJD edition, this phrase appears to be part of an appositive further identifying the army of Melchizedek.[109]

line 10—A quotation of Ps 82:1 refers to God as אל in the phrase 'assembly of God.'

line 11—A quotation of Ps 7:9 discusses God (אל) and his act of judgment. As was the cases above in line 4, the reading in 11QMelchizedek (אל ידין עמים) has a different name for God than the MT, which has יהוה. Unfortunately this verse has not survived in a Qumran psalter.

line 12—God (אל) is the source of the commandments that are rejected by 'Belial and the spirits of his lot,' who are the 'wicked' of Ps 82:2 as quoted in line 11.

line 13—Here אל refers to God as the authority behind judgment, in accord with Ps 7:9 (quoted in line 11). Note that in line 13 it is Melchizedek who administers the judgments of אל (cf. line 10, where אלוהים is said to judge in the assembly of אל).

line 14—The plural of אל appears in the phrase אלי [הצדק].[110] Editors of 11QMelchizedek uniformly read אלי without hesitation. In PAM 43.979, the top stroke of the proposed ל is missing, though the shape of the lower stroke indeed appears consistent with a ל.[111]

This plural form of אל rather than אלוהים is surprising because the latter normally is used in passages where the plural of the former would be possible.[112] The DJD editors propose that the author may here

[108] Overall the differences between the biblical text cited in 11QMelchizedek and the MT are minor, though the quotation of Lev 25:9 in 11Q13 II, 25 may diverge from this trend. See García Martínez, Tigchelaar, and van der Woude, DJD XXIII, 223.

[109] See Kobelski, *Melchizedek*, 5, for a rather different reading of the poorly-preserved middle section of the line. The key phrase 'the holy ones of God,' however, is not in question.

[110] Others, including Kobelski (*Melchizedek*, 19) and de Jonge and van der Woude ("11Q Melchizedek," 302) read אלי [מרומים], 'gods of the heights,' but the term supplied in the lacuna is not the significant issue for this discussion. Van der Woude's rendering in the *editio princeps* was אלי עולמים ("Melchisedek," 358).

[111] This photo was accessed electronically on Timothy H. Lim and Philip S. Alexander, eds., *The Dead Sea Scrolls Electronic Reference Library* (vol. 1). CD-ROM. Oxford University Press and Brill, 1997; and Emanuel Tov, ed., *The Dead Sea Scrolls Electronic Library, Revised Edition 2006*. CD-ROM. Brill, 2006.

[112] See Frank Moore Cross, "אֵל 'ēl," *TDOT* 1:242-61, esp. 254-55, for a brief survey of the few plural uses of אֵל in the MT.

be influenced by the reading אילי הצדק in Isa 61:3; there the phrase clearly is 'trees of righteousness' (NRSV 'oaks of righteousness').[113] Assuming the standard transcription of this phrase is correct, use here of the plural of אל appears to preserve the distinction between the singular אל as God, and אלוהים (which one would expect where the plural of אל occurs) as Melchizedek in 11QMelchizedek. Thus the appearance here of אלי seems deliberate and unusual. This distinction, however, was not maintained in line 10; as discussed below, there אלוהים is used in its plural sense for the divine council in its second appearance in a quotation of Ps 82:1.

line 14—This second use of אל in the line appears in the phrase בני אל ('sons of God'). Here אל clearly is God; presumably the 'sons of God' are the humans who benefit from deliverance rather than heavenly figures who provide it, as one might expect to find אלוהים if the latter were intended (see below). Elsewhere in the column such humans are called 'captives' (line 4; cf. line 13, 'he [Melchizedek] will free them from the hand of Belial and from the hand of all the spirits of his lot,' and line 25, 'Melchizedek who will free them from the hand of Belial'); 'sons of light' (line 8); 'the lot of Melchizedek' (also line 8); 'afflicted' (line 20); and 'the congregation of all the sons of justice' (line 24).

line 23—The משפטי אל ('judgments of God') are exercised by the agent Melchizedek on God's behalf (as in line 13). Here אל clearly is God.

3.3.1.2. Uses of אלוהים

line 10—The author quotes Ps 82:1, where אלוהים (MT אֱלֹהִים) appears in both clauses: אֱלֹהִים נִצָּב בַּעֲדַת־אֵל בְּקֶרֶב אֱלֹהִים יִשְׁפֹּט. In Ps 82:1 the first use of אלוהים clearly is for God. The second אלוהים is in reference to a council of heavenly beings, and it is paralleled in the first clause which presents God as אֱלֹהִים standing בַּעֲדַת־אֵל ('in the assembly of God').

The meaning of אלוהים in 11QMelchizedek, however, is not necessarily the same as that of the author of Ps 82:1. Interpretation of the first use of אלוהים in this line is complicated by the uncertain antecedent of עליו, which begins the line and prompts the midrashic quotation of Ps 82:1. Fitzmyer (later followed by Carmignac) proposed

[113] García Martínez, Tigchelaar, and van der Woude, DJD XXIII, 232.

that עליו may be read as 'about it' with reference to the action of judgment mentioned in the ensuing quotation.[114] Most scholars, though, read 'about him,' and this interpretation is preferable.[115] The antecedent of 'him' is Melchizedek in line 9; Melchizedek should also be understood as the אלוהים of line 10 (for the first appearance of the term) and thus the agent of God's judgment.

line 10—The second occurrence of אלוהים is to be understood as referring to a heavenly council, as in the original context of Ps 82:1. This departs, though, from the use noted above in line 14 of the plural of אל for this meaning. Perhaps this can be attributed to a hesitancy of the author of 11QMelchizedek to change the wording of biblical quotations (though note the absence of יהוה in the quotations above); אלוהים is used for the council in line 10 because it is the word used in the psalm, but the author is free in line 14 to exercise his lexical preference in his interpretative comments and there uses the plural of אל instead in the phrase אלי הצדק (see also above).

The members of this heavenly court, which receives elaboration in lines 10-14, may include 'Belial and the spirits of his lot' (line 12) who have oppressed humanity, or Melchizedek may be chiding other אלוהים who have allowed Belial to undertake his program.[116]

lines 16, 23, 24—In line 16, the extant text is a quotation of Isaiah 52:7 displaying only minor variants in comparison with the MT, and relevant portions of this quotation are repeated in the course of the pesher in lines 23-24. The most significant part of the quotation is the proclamation by a messenger that מלך אלוהיך ('your God is king') and the subsequent identification of this אלוהים in line 25.

Determining the identity of אלוהים here is one of the more vexing issues in 11QMelchizedek. For this reason, the translation of lines 23-25 is repeated here, with occurrences of אלוהים indicated in bold print:

> 23. [ ] in the judgement[s of] God, as is written about him: '[saying to Zi]on: your God is king'. [Zi]on i[s]

---

[114] Fitzmyer, "Further Light," 261, credits the idea to Patrick Skehan. Carmignac's position is much more extreme than Fitzmyer's, as the former denies that 11QMelchizedek ever presents Melchizedek as a heavenly figure. Instead, he identifies Melchizedek with the Teacher of Righteousness. See Carmignac, "Le document," 353, 365-67.

[115] See, for example, García Martínez, Tigchelaar, and van der Woude, DJD XXIII, 229; and Horton, *Melchizedek Tradition*, 74.

[116] Kobelski, *Melchizedek*, 62. Kobelski prefers the former, as does van der Woude, "Melchisedek," 365.

> 24. [the congregation of all the sons of justice, who] establish the covenant, who avoid walking [on the p]ath of the people. And 'your G[o]d' is
>
> 25. [Melchizedek who will fr]ee [them from the han]d of Belial. And as for what he said: 'And you shall blow the ho[rn in] all the [l]and (of)

Obviously the major complicating factor is that only about half of each line is extant. Particularly unfortunate is the absence of the first few words of line 25, where the identity of אלוהיך is revealed. The present reading is reconstructed based on a similar (but also reconstructed) reading in line 13, itself proposed in light of passages like 4QpPs[a] (4Q171) 3-10 IV, 21.[117] Below are the relevant phrases in 11Q13 II, 13 and 25, with extant letters in bold print:[118]

line 13: יצי]**ל**[מה מיד]**בליעל ומיד כול ר**[וחי גורלו][119]

line 25: מלכי צדק אשר יצי]ל[מה מי]**ד בליעל**

Notice that in both lines only the ל of the key word יצילמה ('he will free them') is preserved, and even this is questionable for line 13.[120] (Despite differences of opinion on the reading of line 13, the reading proposed above for line 25 has wide acceptance.)[121] The word, however, is proposed based on use of the term in other Qumran texts as noted above. Furthermore, in both lines the full wording of the phrase translated 'from the hand of Belial' is lacking in the extant text,

---

[117] García Martínez, Tigchelaar, and van der Woude, DJD XXIII, 232.

[118] The transcription is from García Martínez, Tigchelaar, and van der Woude, DJD XXIII, 225-26. A similar, but slightly different, reading for the key phrase of line 13 is preferred by Puech, *La Croyance*, 523: וינצי]ל[ו מיד]בליעל. As indicated in a subsequent note, several scholars offer quite different readings in place of this phrase.

[119] Melchizedek as subject is extant earlier in the line.

[120] Milik and Kobelski reject the ל that figures so prominently in the reconstructions of DJD and Puech. Milik prefers instead to read יגור]מה מיד]בליעל in line 13 ("*Milkî-ṣedeq*," 98). Similarly, Kobelski sees ויעזור לכול בני אור מיד] בליעל (*Melchizedek*, 6). Admittedly the physical evidence of the disputed ל is miniscule; the DJD transcription marks the letter with an open circle, and in van der Woude's two earlier publications of the text no attempt was made to fill the sizable lacuna in the middle of line 13 before **מיד ב]ליעל** (note the different location of the bracket in the two earlier transcriptions). See van der Woude, "Melchisedek," 358; and de Jonge and van der Woude, "11Q Melchizedek," 302.

[121] Van der Woude did not attempt to reconstruct this key phrase of line 25 (=line 26 in some older transcriptions) in his first two publications of the text. See van der Woude, "Melchisedek," 358; and de Jonge and van der Woude, "11Q Melchizedek," 302. The DJD transcription of the phrase is identical to that of Milik, Puech, and Kobelski; see Milik, "*Milkî-ṣedeq*," 98; Puech, *La Croyance*, 524; and Kobelski, *Melchizedek*, 6.

though the presence of בליעל followed by the parallel phrase [ומיד כול ר[וחי גורלו in line 13 makes the readings in both lines quite likely.

Though one certainly must argue with caution when studying reconstructed texts, it seems clear that again the author of 11QMelchizedek is identifying Melchizedek with אלוהים. Two elements of Isa 52:7 are treated in the extant portions of the pesher interpretation of this verse, the identity of 'Zion' and the referent of the phrase מלך אלוהיך. As noted above, 'Zion' is interpreted as the members of the faithful community. Presumably these are the same persons who earlier in the column were called 'the men of the lot of Melchizedek' (11Q13 II, 8), and here they are to be freed from the 'hand of Belial' (11Q13 II, 25). This is precisely Melchizedek's task in 11Q13 II, 13, so context demands that he also is the one called מלך אלוהיך from Isa 52:7. If that were not enough, the similarity of the name מלכי צדק with the phrase מלך אלוהיך would also be enough to imply this identification in a pesher interpretation, especially if those whom he is to free are indeed called בני צדק as reconstructed by the DJD editors in 11Q13 II, 24.[122]

Several observations can be noted from this lexical survey. First, the author of 11QMelchizedek reserves use of the singular אל to refer to God, which is not surprising, and on two occasions אל may have been substituted for יהוה in biblical quotations. The plural form of אל is once used in reference to other heavenly beings, but use of the singular is always consistent.

Second, the author may quote Scripture in which אלוהים means God, though he may not always interpret the term as such. That his own preference is to call God אל is evident in his interpretative comments, yet the author certainly does not avoid using quotations of Scripture that used אלוהים instead, nor does he edit the quotations themselves. Also, the author is content not to edit biblical quotations that use אלוהים in reference to other heavenly beings.

Third, the author prefers to use אלוהים in reference to Melchizedek. This occurs even when his interpretation of the term differs from the

[122] García Martínez, Tigchelaar, and van der Woude, DJD XXIII, 233, assuming an allusion to עיר הצדק in Isa 1:26.

literal meaning of the biblical text he interprets.[123] This is demonstrated in line 10 and in lines 24-25. This term can be applied in the Hebrew Bible to heavenly figures other than the God of Israel, and use of this term for Melchizedek certainly implies some sort of heavenly status for the figure.[124]

The third of these observations leads to the major questions that demand consideration if one seeks to relate 11QMelchizedek to the presentation of Melchizedek in Hebrews. Namely, who (or what) actually is Melchizedek in this text, what does he do, and what is his relationship to God?

3.3.2. *The Role of Melchizedek*

Melchizedek appears in 11QMelchizedek as the figure carrying out both God's deliverance and judgment. Deliverance is the theme at the beginning and end of col. II. The author understands history as consisting of ten Jubilee units concluding with an eschatological Day of Atonement (line 7).[125] In lines 2-9, Melchizedek acts to deliver the 'captives' (line 4), presumably the same persons as 'the inheritance of

---

[123] Admittedly such a statement is fraught with peril and bias, as the author of 11QMelchizedek no doubt claimed to understand the 'real' meaning of the text he interprets.

[124] Kevin Sullivan notes that Melchizedek has an "exalted status" in 11Q-Melchizedek, but he rejects attempts to correlate the presentation of Melchizedek in this text with information about the figure in other Qumran texts. Sullivan rejects identifications of Melchizedek with Michael argued on the basis of attribution to the figures of similar functions, but he does not mention the evidence surveyed above from *Songs of the Sabbath Sacrifice* and *Vision of Amram*. See Kevin P. Sullivan, *Wrestling with Angels: A Study of the Relationship between Angels and Humans in Ancient Jewish Literature and the New Testament* (AGJU 55; Leiden: Brill, 2004), 96-98.

[125] See Kobelski, *Melchizedek*, 49-50, for a brief survey of other Second Temple Jewish literature in which time is divided into Jubilees or weeks of years. The division of time into Jubilee periods in 11QMelchizedek differs from that in the book of *Jubilees* as the latter envisions many more Jubilee periods; *Jubilees* narrates events into a fiftieth Jubilee period, which spans only the time from creation to the early exodus period, and an unspecified number of future Jubilees are envisioned (*Jub.* 50:4-6).

VanderKam implies that a connection between the Day of Atonement and Jubilee years may already be present in Lev 25:9, where a trumpet call on the tenth day of the seventh month (i.e., the Day of Atonement) announces the beginning of a Jubilee year. See his article "Yom Kippur," in *EDSS* 2:1001-03, esp. 2:1002. See also the brief survey of the significance of Lev 25 and Isa 61 for 11QMelchizedek in VanderKam, "Sabbatical Chronologies," 169-72.

Melchizedek' (line 5); he proclaims liberty to them and frees them 'from the debt of all their iniquities' (line 6). This last phrase has cultic overtones, and the next line mentions the Day of Atonement. Melchizedek appears to be the agent executing God's pronouncement (lines 3-4). Melchizedek announces liberty in the first week of the tenth Jubilee (line 6), but it is unclear if liberation actually occurs at that time or if this is a proleptic announcement of liberation that occurs in conjunction with the eschatological Day of Atonement at the end of the tenth Jubilee, when 'atonement shall be made for all the sons of light and for the men of the lot of Melchizedek' (line 8; presumably these are two terms for the same group of persons).[126] This Day of Atonement appears to be the 'year of grace of Melchizedek' (line 9). Melchizedek is the active figure thus far in the passage. Since he is presented as a priest in Gen 14; Ps 110:4; and the *Songs of the Sabbath Sacrifice*, it seems clear that the author of 11QMelchizedek envisions him as the high priest conducting this eschatological Day of Atonement sacrifice.[127] Line 9 also speaks 'of the administration of justice,' thus introducing the theme of judgment. The extant text of line 8 implies that the righteous benefit from this judgment ('according to all their doings').

This mention of judgment smoothes the transition to the quotations of Ps 82:1; Ps 7:8-9; and Ps 82:2 in lines 10-11. Here the emphasis clearly is on God's judgment of the wicked (with overtones of theodicy in the Ps 82:2 quotation). As is evident in the discussion above of uses of אל and אלוהים, both words appear frequently in these lines and their subsequent interpretation in lines 12-14. The overall

[126] Xeravits notes that "the 'tenth jubilee' in the historical view of several writings of the late biblical and intertestamental literature—some of which were known and revered also at Qumran—denotes the last age before the closing of the present aion." See Xeravits, *King, Priest, Prophet*, 72.

[127] See a similar suggestion in Kobelski, *Melchizedek*, 57-59, though his understanding of Melchizedek as priest is based in part on a very different rendering of II, 5 than that adopted in DJD. See Kobelski, *Melchizedek*, 5, 13, for his transcription and textual notes. Unfortunately it seems impossible to verify either Kobelski's or the DJD reading of the first several words of line 5 using the photographs of the text in DJD XXIII or those available in the two electronic editions noted above. Van der Woude proposed לכפר in a lacuna in 11QMelch II, 6, which would make the priestly action of Melchizedek explicit ("Melchisedek," 358; also de Jonge and van der Woude, "11Q Melchizedek," 302) and was followed by Fitzmyer, "Further Light," 259. The reading in DJD agrees with that of Kobelski, *Melchizedek*, 5. For a rejection of the identification of Melchizedek as priest in 11QMelchizedek, see Laub, *Bekenntnis*, 39. See also an overview of the issue in Aschim, "Melchizedek and Jesus," 139-40.

impression is that Melchizedek is an angelic אלוהים in the heavenly court of אל who administers justice (with the aid of other members of the heavenly court, line 14 'all the gods of justice are to his help') on behalf of אל against Belial and those of his lot.[128]

Deliverance is again stressed in lines 15-25. The major text under consideration is Isa 52:7, where a messenger announces peace and salvation and speaks of the kingship of the אלוהים of Zion. The messenger is identified with the prince anointed by the Spirit from Dan 9:25; perhaps the identity of this messenger was further clarified in lines 21-22, but few words remain there. Perhaps also the messenger was correlated with the figure who blows the horn (presumably to announce the Day of Atonement, as in Lev 25:9) in line 25, but the subsequent text has not survived. Admittedly Melchizedek seems to have a role in proclamation in the early lines of the column, leading some scholars to identify him as the messenger.[129] Presumably, though, the messenger is not Melchizedek. Melchizedek instead is the אלוהים in lines 24-25 whom the messenger announces.

In summary, 11QMelchizedek presents Melchizedek as a heavenly, eschatological figure in the service of God. He will delivers the righteous on God's behalf and will execute judgment on Belial and his lot. Also, Melchizedek will make atonement for those of his own lot. This presentation of Melchizedek as a figure at war with Belial is consistent with that of *Visions of Amram*, and the portrait of Melchizedek as a heavenly priest corresponds with that found in *Songs of the Sabbath Sacrifice*.

The interpretation espoused here is much indebted to the positions originally articulated by van der Woude and de Jonge in their early publication of the text. The first significant objections to this reading were voiced by Milik, who agreed that Melchizedek is to be identified with אלוהים but proposed a different relationship between this figure

---

[128] For similar interpretations, see Kobelski, *Melchizedek*, 72; and Aschim, "Melchizedek and Jesus," 132-35. Others reject this identification. For the view that Melchizedek is the messiah, perhaps even Davidic, see Paul Rainbow, "Melchizedek as a Messiah at Qumran," *BBR* 7 (1997): 179-94; for Melchizedek as Yahweh, see Manzi, *Melchizedek*.

[129] For Melchizedek as herald, see Miller, "Function," 468-69. Milik ("*Milkî-ṣedeq*," 126) and Puech ("Notes," 509-10) argue that the messenger is the Teacher of Righteousness himself. De Jonge and van der Woude, followed by Kobelski, understand the messenger as the eschatological prophet of 1QS IX, 11 and 4Q175 5-8. See de Jonge and van der Woude, "11Q Melchizedek," 306-08; and Kobelski, *Melchizedek*, 61-62.

and God. For Milik, Melchizedek was not in the service of God but instead was a hypostasis of God: "Il est en réalité une hypostase de Dieu, autrement dit le Dieu transcendant lorsqu'il agit dans le monde, Dieu lui-même sous la forme visible où il apparaît aux hommes, et non pas un ange créé distinct de Dieu (*Ex* 23:20)."[130] Milik asserts that the Qumran sect read the phrase על דברתי of Ps 110:4 as 'according to *my* order' and thus found God associating himself with Melchizedek. Likewise, he identified the several 'angel of Yahweh' passages in the 'Octateuque' (particularly citing examples in Genesis, Exodus, and Judges) as an expression of the same phenomenon.[131] Few have followed Milik's proposal, and it falters because of the careful distinctions in 11QMelchizedek between usage of אל and אלוהים and the presentation (as in 11Q13 II, 9-14) of Melchizedek in the service of God but as the righteous counterpart and opponent to Belial (again, echoing the portrait of Melchizedek in *Visions of Amram*).

More recent challenges to the interpretation first established by van der Woude and de Jonge have been even more stark. Paul Rainbow rejects the notion that Melchizedek is a heavenly figure in any sense. Instead, he asserts that Melchizedek is the Davidic messiah.[132] Rainbow calls into question textual reconstructions that correlate Melchizedek with the term אלוהים in 11Q13; connect Melchizedek with an angelic liturgy in *Songs of the Sabbath Sacrifice* (specifically in 4Q401); and understand Melchireša' as a name for the non-human evil figure in *Visions of Amram*.[133] Questions about reconstructions are certainly legitimate, though Rainbow rejects the scholarly consensus on all three accounts. More troublesome is Rainbow's discussion of the meaning of אלוהים in 11QMelchizedek. His first tactic is to deny that its attribution to Melchizedek makes him a heavenly figure, arguing instead that kings can bear the term in the Hebrew Bible.[134] Yet his further argumentation is built on the idea that Melchizedek cannot be אלוהים in 11QMelchizedek because Melchizedek cannot be

[130] Milik, "*Milkî-ṣedeq*," 125.
[131] Milik, "*Milkî-ṣedeq*," 125.
[132] Rainbow presents his article as a developed defense of a suggestion made earlier by Carmignac, Anders Hultgård, and Flusser, none of whom "has argued the case at length." See Rainbow, "Melchizedek as a Messiah," 181, n. 6.
[133] Rainbow, "Melchizedek as a Messiah," 182-85.
[134] Rainbow, "Melchizedek as a Messiah," 182.

God; no flexibility is allowed for אלוהים to be a heavenly figure *other* than God.[135]

Having dismissed all of the Qumran textual evidence for a heavenly Melchizedek, Rainbow conveniently is left with little more than a Melchizedek who carries out God's judgment; this role is appropriate for a Davidic messiah, a figure frequently anticipated in Qumran texts.[136] (Similarly, Rainbow argues that Melchizedek's closest analogy in 1QM is the mortal 'Prince of the battle,' not Michael; his direct antagonist is Gog, not Belial.[137]) Everything said about Melchizedek in 11QMelchizedek can be drawn from Gen 14 or especially Ps 110; the latter is about a Davidic figure, and other texts utilized in 11QMelchizedek are interpreted as Davidic in the NT and rabbinic literature.[138] Even discussion of the 'inheritance' or 'lot' of Melchizedek in 11QMelchizedek indicates his Davidic identity. Since in the Hebrew Bible humans typically have the former and the latter involves property, Rainbow makes an acontextual leap to conclude that 11QMelchizedek says Melchizedek is to inherit the land of Canaan. Rainbow asserts that "this makes sense if Melchizedek is the king and benefactor of the whole people of Israel," i.e., the Davidic messiah.[139]

The numerous problems with Rainbow's thesis should be evident in the description above, and it (like Milik's hypostasis reading) has found few supporters. More formidable is the proposal of Manzi, who argues that 'Melchizedek' is a descriptive title for Yahweh.[140] In one sense Manzi's argument was anticipated by Gareth Cockerill, who also developed the idea that the meaning of the name 'Melchizedek' was the key to understanding 11QMelchizedek. Cockerill assumed that since the author of Hebrews, Philo, and Josephus all knew similar etymological interpretations of the name 'Melchizedek' as 'king of righteousness,' that must also explain how the author of 11QMelchizedek understood the term.[141] Cockerill found further evidence for this in the scribal practice of writing the name as two

---

135 Rainbow, "Melchizedek as a Messiah," 182-83.
136 Rainbow, "Melchizedek as a Messiah," 183.
137 Rainbow, "Melchizedek as a Messiah," 186.
138 Rainbow, "Melchizedek as a Messiah," 184, 189-90.
139 Rainbow, "Melchizedek as a Messiah," 191-92.
140 Manzi, *Melchisedek e l'angelologia*. See further below.
141 Gareth Lee Cockerill, "Melchizedek or 'King of Righteousness,'" *EvQ* 63:4 (1991): 305-12, esp. 307-08.

distinct words in 11QMelchizedek, whereas it was written as one word in texts (like the *Genesis Apocryphon*) that clearly presented Melchizedek as an individual figure.[142] Ultimately Cockerill understood 'king of righteousness' in 11QMelchizedek to be a descriptive title for the archangel Michael. He denied any connection between 11QMelchizedek and the Melchizedek traditions of Gen 14, Ps 110, and Hebrews, but he admitted that use of the *title* מלכי צדק for Michael in 11QMelchizedek likely paved the way for later rabbinic assimilation of the *figures* Melchizedek and Michael.[143]

The fatal flaw in Cockerill's argument is his assumption that a Hebraist like the author of 11QMelchizedek would find the meaning 'king of righteousness' in מלכי צדק. Rather, as noted above, the Hebrew more accurately is translated as 'my king is Sedeq' (or even 'my king is righteous'). The rendering 'king *of* righteousness' is a popular etymology cited by Greek-speaking Jews who otherwise evidence little knowledge of Hebrew (Philo; author of Hebrews) or else freely augmented their paraphrases of Scripture for a Greek-reading audience with traditional materials (Josephus, his claim for textual fidelity in *Ant.* 1.5 notwithstanding).[144] Cockerill's thesis demands that one presume that the author of 11QMelchizedek, competent to compose in Hebrew, would nevertheless ignore the plain-sense meaning of a key term in his own text and language, instead introducing a specious etymological interpretation of the Hebrew—popular among Greek speakers—into his Hebrew text.

Manzi likewise argues for a symbolic meaning for מלכי צדק (as 'king of justice'), but his case is more nuanced, with the thesis that understandings of the figure Melchizedek evolved over time at Qumran in trajectories that ultimately have scant connection with use of the figure in Hebrews. At the root of Qumran's conceptual development lay the understanding of Melchizedek as a mortal priest-king, as found in Gen 14 and in the *Genesis Apocryphon*. At this stage Manzi finds nothing celestial about the presentation of Melchizedek, an evaluation consistent with the discussion earlier in this chapter of those two texts. Manzi then proposes, however, that this portrait of the

[142] Cockerill, "Melchizedek or 'King of Righteousness,'" 308.
[143] Cockerill, "Melchizedek or 'King of Righteousness,'" 314.
[144] On Josephus' utilization of Hebrew, Aramaic, and Greek texts of Scripture for Antiquities, see Feldman, "Josephus," 3:985-88. On Philo, see Gregory E. Sterling, "Philo," *DNTB* 789-93, esp. 789.

human Melchizedek is transformed at Qumran through a process of "angelificazione," or reinterpretation toward an angelic understanding of the figure under the influence of Ps 110:4.[145] From there, three symbolic approaches to the figure develop. *Visions of Amram* emphasized his princely role by correlating him with the angel Michael as the protagonist against Belial. Though Melchizedek is not addressed in priestly terms in this text, the seed is sown for this development: Aaron is set apart as priest and told he will be called מלאך אל, 'the angel of God.'[146] Melchizedek and this angelic Aaron image next are assimilated in *Songs of the Sabbath Sacrifice*, which now emphasizes Melchizedek's celestial, angelic priesthood rather than a princely role.[147] Through this process of "angelificazione," Melchizedek becomes so identified as a mediating salvific figure—particularly as the deliverer of *Visions of Amram*—that his name becomes synonymous with the function and can even be used to describe the activity of Yahweh:

> È chiaro, però, che il Malkî ṣedeq angelico così delineato assurge a figura simbolica di mediatore salvifico, in grado di esprimere l'intervento sensibile di JHWH *ad extra*, salvaguardandone l'assoluta trascendenza. Un intento simile soggiace probabilmente anche a 11QMelch, in cui si parla di JHWH senza nominare il tetragramma sacro, ma ricorrendo al titolo di "Re di Giustizia". Dio viene così descritto attraverso l'apparato simbolico dell'apocalittica, oltre che mediante una serie di citazioni veterotestamentarie. Le caratteristiche fondamentali sia di JHWH in 11QMelch sia del mediatore salvifico di 4Q'Amram[b] sono la regalità e la giustizia. Già espresso dal nome מלכי צדק, esse lasciano intravvedere un motivo etimologico alla base della scelta di questo appellativo non solo per un arcangelo (4Q'Amram[b] e 4Q**401** 11 1-3) ma anche per JHWH (11QMelch).[148]

Manzi's examination, unlike those of Milik and Rainbow, is a monograph treatment, described by one reviewer as "a rigorous piece of work."[149] Yet its argument is open to similar criticisms as those directed to the theories of Milik and Cockerill above. Granting that

---

[145] Manzi, *Melchizedek e l'angelologia*, 102-03.

[146] Manzi, *Melchizedek e l'angelologia*, 103, citing 4Q543 3 1 (=DJD 5Q543 2ab II, 4) and 4Q545 1 17-18 (=DJD 4Q545 1a I, 17-18).

[147] Manzi, *Melchizedek e l'angelologia*, 103.

[148] Manzi, *Melchizedek e l'angelologia*, 102.

[149] George J. Brooke, review of Franco Manzi, *Melchizedek e l'angelologia nell'Epistola agli Ebrei e a Qumran*, *CBQ* 60 (1998): 770-71, esp. 770. See also Bernas, review of Manzi, *Melchizedek e l'angelologia*, 368-70.

Manzi essentially is correct that the understanding of Melchizedek evolved at Qumran, still one faces the difficulty of understanding Melchizedek and God as the *same* figure in 11QMelchizedek. Instead, the point of the text seems to be that Melchizedek actually is the person carrying out—on God's behalf—those things ascribed to God in the passages of Scripture cited; if God indeed is acting directly, one would question the need for a pesher explanation of the obvious.

Similarly, the idea that the author of 11QMelchizedek would understand מלכי צדק as 'king of justice' remains problematic. Manzi does advance the discussion beyond that of Cockerill—whereas the latter relied solely on the useage of the phrase in Josephus, Philo, and Hebrews as evidence for its application to 11QMelchizedek, Manzi seeks to justify his position on grammatical grounds, appealing to Paul Joüon's discussion of the *ḥireq compaginis* and substantatives in construct state.[150] Joüon indeed cites מַלְכִּי־צֶדֶק as an example of the latter, but he does so inconsistently and without explanation; the term is glossed as 'king of justice,' but the suggested translation for the key phrase of Ps 110:4 is 'after the manner of M[elchizedek].' Furthermore, Manzi recognizes that 'Melchizedek' is a theophoric Canaanite name in Gen 14, but he asserts that the name was so rich with etymological meaning that the author of 11QMelchizedek was free to appropriate that and felt no compulsion to rework the spelling of the term.[151] Not clear, however, is an explanation for why someone writing in a community with such speculation on Melchizedek already evidenced would risk confusing the angelic priest-king of other texts with Yahweh in 11QMelchizedek. In the end, Manzi's thesis raises more questions than it explains, and the more traditional view articulated above remains preferable.

Having discussed Second Temple Jewish texts relating to a priestly messiah and Melchizedek in these last two chapters, a consideration of the influence of these texts on Hebrews' presentation of Jesus is now appropriate.

---

[150] Manzi, *Melchizedek e l'angelologia*, 51, n. 100; Paul Joüon, *A Grammar of Biblical Hebrew* (trans. and rev. T. Muraoka; 2 vols.; Rome: Pontifical Biblical Institute, 1993), 282 (§93 l-m).

[151] Manzi, *Melchizedek e l'angelologia*, 52.

CHAPTER FIVE

THE PRIESTLY CHRISTOLOGY OF HEBREWS AND QUMRAN TRADITIONS

The first chapter of this study concluded with a summary of Hebrews' presentation of Jesus as the priestly messiah. Though not of priestly lineage, he becomes priest by God's affirmation and oath because he also is the divine Son. He is prepared for this priestly service by his earthly sufferings through which—along with his common origins in God—he develops solidarity with the people. He serves as priest offering the ultimate, final sacrifice for the sins of his people and is that sacrifice himself. Modeled on the Day of Atonement ritual, Jesus' sacrificial act includes his presentation of the blood of his sacrifice for his entrance into the heavenly sanctuary. There he makes eternal intercession for his people, and he is seated in glory at the right hand of the Father.

The nature of Jesus' priesthood is very significant. His priesthood is greater than the Levitical priesthood because his is like Melchizedek's, which in turn was shown superior to the Levitical order when Abraham paid tithes to him. Furthermore, Jesus' priesthood is eternal, his atoning sacrifice is final and all-sufficient, and his sanctuary is true and abiding.

Clearly several elements impact this presentation of Jesus. Most obvious are the pastoral needs of the people, whose faith the author sees as endangered through persecution, apathy, or a combination thereof. The author's theological creativity and pastoral sensitivity are beyond question. He writes to them about a priest who suffered yet endured, who prepared their way to heaven and intercedes there for them, but he also raises the specter of a dire fate for those who would renounce their faith in the midst of their difficulties.

No doubt the Christian *kerygma* of Jesus as the Son of God who died on behalf of the people also lies behind this presentation. Likewise, the conception of a heavenly sanctuary with an angelic liturgy was commonplace in Second Temple Judaism and early

Christianity, and this also is reflected in Hebrews. As noted in the first chapter, the author freely uses Platonic vocabulary to express a traditional Jewish understanding of the relationship between the heavenly and earthly sanctuaries.

The author's exegetical skills certainly play a major role in the presentation of Jesus as priest. He justifies Jesus' status as priest on the basis of his exegesis of Ps 2:7; Ps 110:1; and Ps 110:4. The begotten Davidic Son of Ps 2:7 is the enthroned 'lord' addressed by God in Ps 110:1. This enthroned Son is also granted an eternal priesthood like that of Melchizedek by divine decree in Ps 110:4. Jesus, the Son, is also Jesus, the priest.

Why, though, does the author of Hebrews present Jesus as a priest, and why is Melchizedek utilized as he is? Could the pastoral situation have only been addressed with a priestly motif? Did a prior tradition—of which we have no certain record—circulate in earliest Christianity of Jesus as priest? Does this motif result *solely* from the author's exegetical prowess? Why would one propose the need for a messianic priest? Might the author have appropriated and adapted Jewish traditions about heavenly, messianic priestly figures and found impetus in them to present Jesus as the priestly messiah?

As noted in chapter 3 above, the discovery of the Qumran texts—both those discussing a priestly messiah and an angelic Melchizedek—prompted flurries of interest in the possible relationship of those traditions with Hebrews' presentation of Jesus. As also noted, such enthusiasm was relatively short-lived, as rebuttals quickly questioned theories that the recipients of Hebrews were formerly Essenes or that Melchizedek the eschatological warrior was also Melchizedek the priest who blessed Abraham. Viewed from hindsight, one easily can admit that several early proponents of Qumran-Hebrews ties zealously claimed too much. Recently, however, Anders Aschim has argued that the examination (specifically concerning Melchizedek) should be reopened, and the conclusions reached here also affirm that need.[1]

Likewise, Charlotte Hempel and John Poirier have sounded recent calls that the Qumran materials should no longer be treated as representative of (in the words of Hempel) "a small group on the

---

[1] Aschim, "Melchizedek and Jesus," 145-47.

fringes of late Second Temple society."[2] If, for example, such diverse ancient writers as Pliny the Elder could discuss the Qumran sect and Josephus and Philo could praise the virtues of the distinctive practices of Essenes with reasonable accuracy, might that not also imply that theological tenets of the Qumran community and their fellow Essenes could be known and even shared to an extent in wider Judaism and early Christianity?

Admittedly no textual dependence of Hebrews on a Qumran document can be produced. What can be considered, though, are hints of shared views in the Qumran texts and Hebrews. What follows is a narrative analysis of the theology expressed by the author of Hebrews, then further discussion of these shared views on priestly messianism and Melchizedek evident in Hebrews and the Qumran texts.

1. A Narrative Theology of Hebrews

The author of Hebrews expresses a theological understanding of Jesus as divine yet Davidic Son and messianic priest. The Son is truly divine with all the prerogatives that such status entails (Heb 1:1-14). While previous generations spoke of the Wisdom of God, the author utilizes such language to describe the Son, who is the figure active in Creation, bearing the image of God, and sustaining the world even from the beginning (Heb 1:1-3). He has been appointed priest (5:5-6), but his divine mission of self-sacrifice on behalf of humanity was his ultimate, eschatological act of making atonement on behalf of his people (1:3; 10:14). In the process he brought the ultimate revelation of God and God's purposes (1:2).

God ordained an earthly tabernacle for Israel, modeled on the heavenly sanctuary (8:5), and presumably the earthly Levitical priesthood for Israel was modeled on the heavenly angelic liturgical service. Like his Jewish contemporaries and prophetic forerunners, the author of Hebrews assumes the presence of a heavenly sanctuary and cultus staffed by courses of angels (1:6, 14). God has been intimately

[2] Charlotte Hempel, "Qumran Communities: Beyond the Fringes of Second Temple Society," in *The Scrolls and the Scriptures: Qumran Fifty Years After* (ed. S. Porter and C. Evans; JSPSup 26; Sheffield: Sheffield, 1997), 43-53, esp. 43; and John C. Poirier, "The Endtime Return of Elijah and Moses at Qumran," *DSD* 10 (2003): 221-42.

involved on behalf of his people and guiding their destiny. God's deliverance of the people from captivity in Egypt and call for them to journey to Canaan is an earthly type of God's plan to free the faithful people from sin so that they can journey in faith toward God's eschatological rest (3:7-4:13). Moses led Israel and interceded for it, but only under the leadership of Joshua did the people complete their journey. Likewise, the Levitical priests interceded for God's people during their appointed time, but ultimately it would be Jesus (the play on names in Greek perhaps not coincidental) who made the ultimate sacrifice and led God's children to glory.

God always intended to show that the heavenly and spiritual things were the true things with the earthly things only copies. Indeed, God foreshadowed the eventual coming of the Son, the ultimate high priest, even before the establishment of the Levitical priesthood. Melchizedek, the priest-king of Salem, was made to be like Jesus, the divine priest-king (7:3). Melchizedek appeared in Gen 14 in an angelophany and demonstrated his priestly precedence over the future Levitical line in his sacral encounter with the patriarch Abraham (7:4-10). Like his Jewish contemporaries at Qumran, the author conceives of a supernatural Melchizedek, a heavenly figure in God's service (7:3). But this Melchizedek is no rival to the divine Son.

When Jesus later came as the great high priest, he appeared to humans as one like and 'according to the order of' Melchizedek (7:15-17 and elsewhere). From the heavenly perspective, though, actually the opposite was true: even as exalted an agent of God as Melchizedek was inferior to the divine Son. Though divine, the Son showed solidarity with God's people (2:5-18) and was prepared ('made perfect') to be their compassionate high priest by suffering and experiencing all aspects of the human condition short of commission of sin (4:14-5:10). Thus Jesus' toils in life are given great meaning for his salvific mission.

Like Melchizedek, Jesus is a priest outside of and superior to the Levitical line (7:11-19). Jesus as priest offers the sacrifice that was anticipated by the Levitical offerings but which is ultimate, final, and need not be repeated. Doing so, he made final, once-for-all atonement in the real, heavenly sanctuary (9:11-14).

The recipients of the letter have confessed the basics of the Christian gospel—Jesus came from God, died on their behalf, and returned to the Father—and have experienced the Holy Spirit (2:1-4).

They have not matured in their faith, however, and are in danger of abandoning their confession of faith in the midst of hardships and persecution (5:11-6:8 and elsewhere). The author writes with pastoral concerns, intending both to encourage and warn his readers. Though feeling abandoned in their difficulties, the author assures them that the divine Son himself is their sympathetic, merciful high priest who has made that final, once-for-all atonement for them and who is in the direct presence of God Almighty interceding for them. This comforting image is described alternately by stating that Jesus is seated at God's right hand in power (1:3; 8:1-2) or that he entered the Most Holy Place of the heavenly sanctuary (6:13-20). Intertwined with these words of comfort, however, are dire warnings of their precarious situation. The readers stand in danger of abandoning their confession and, like Israelites of the exodus generation, of forfeiting their opportunity to reach their destination appointed by God (3:7-4:13). Only those who remain faithful despite their obstacles and inability to comprehend what lies in store for them will enter God's presence, yet Jesus and the faithful Hebrews of generations past have provided examples of the faithfulness necessary to reach this goal (11:1-12:17).

The author appeals to his readers by means of a sophisticated rhetorical argument utilizing *synkrisis*, comparing Jesus systematically to major figures and elements of Judaism in order to demonstrate his superiority even to such God-ordained things. The series of comparisons unfolds systematically: Jesus is superior to the angels who delivered the law (1:1-14; cf. 2:2), his message is more significant even than that law (2:1-4), he is superior to Moses who received and taught the law (3:1-6), superior to the priests who mediated for Israel under that law (7:11-28), and as part of a greater covenant offers a superior sacrifice to theirs in a sanctuary greater than theirs (9:11-10:28). Those faithful to this Jesus receive their just reward and 'rest.' But those who turn away after having experienced God and the Holy Spirit because of Jesus' atoning work are left without hope, as no other means of atonement is possible (6:4-8). Confident that his readers have not reached this dire point, he urges them on toward faithfulness (6:9-12).

2. Comparison with Qumran Traditions

Several points in Hebrews' thought intersect with ideas also known from the Qumran texts. The cosmology is similar, but that could be said of numerous Second Temple Jewish texts. More substantial are the presentation of a heavenly priest who makes eschatological atonement and the understanding of Melchizedek as a heavenly figure. Though the correspondences are not exact—nor should they be expected to be since Hebrews focuses on a particular person in Jesus as the messiah—they are similar enough to indicate shared views. In fact, the Qumran texts (including *Jubilees* and *Aramaic Levi*) are the *only* extant texts from Second Temple Judaism that discuss an eschatological priest and a heavenly Melchizedek.

2.1. *Hebrews and the Priestly Messianism of Qumran*

The priestly messianic traditions at Qumran and possible antecedent traditions that laid the exegetical groundwork for Qumran's sacerdotal expectations were addressed above in chapter 3. In several texts from the Dead Sea Scrolls, a priestly figure appears and occasionally bears the title משיח. Admittedly the activities of the priestly figure are not always clear in the extant texts, but tasks described include making atonement, instructing in the law, blessing and exhorting in eschatological warfare (along with cursing Belial and his lot), and presiding at an eschatological banquet. One also notes that the messianic priest may be treated with deference by the Davidic or royal messiah.

When and why the Qumran community developed an expectation for a messianic priest remain topics of scholarly investigation, as do considerations of whether the community had or demanded uniform thought on messianic expectations. Surprising, though, is the relative lack of exegetical justification for the expectation of the messianic priest in the extant texts, especially in light of the several proof-texts used to articulate royal messianic expectations. This disparity has prompted scholars to seek exegetical justification for the priestly expectation in other materials known to the Qumran sect, and traditions of Levi's reception of an eternal priesthood are a fruitful source. *Jubilees*, *Aramaic Levi*, and the (admittedly later) *Testament of*

Levi present Levi as receiving an eternal priesthood from God because of his religious zeal, a motif derived from midrashic readings of several passages from the Hebrew Bible that relate priesthood and righteous vengeance on sinners. As addressed in chapter 3, a cogent argument can be made that the Qumran community saw this Levi tradition as providing the scriptural foundation for their position.

These texts have been examined with the purpose of reevaluating whether there is a relationship between the priestly messianism of Qumran and the priestly Christology of Hebrews. A common objection to this proposal is that the priestly messiah of Qumran was one of several expected figures, not the single messiah as Jesus clearly is identified in Hebrews. This obviously is true, and most scholars do indeed assert that the Qumran texts evidence a number of messianic expectations. So too, though, do texts in the broader realm of Second Temple Judaism. Most scholars today are convinced that no *one* messianic expectation defined Second Temple Judaism, though hopes of a Davidic figure were most widely held.

The author of Hebrews describes a Davidic messiah and a priestly messiah, though naturally because of his commitment that *Jesus* is the messiah, these offices are combined in the same figure. One should only expect that someone convinced that Jesus was the messiah would not identify multiple messianic figures. Yet while no scholar seriously questions whether the Christian identification of Jesus as a Davidic messiah has roots in broader Second Temple Jewish messianic expectations (even though such expectations overall are varied), most scholars deny that Second Temple Jewish presentations of a priestly messiah might also influence the thought of Hebrews.

One must consider whether presentations of Jesus in Hebrews and the priestly messiah of Qumran are actually similar. In both a priestly figure is discussed in the context of a Davidic figure, though the priestly and Davidic figures are synonymous in Hebrews. Both present priests appointed to their eschatological duty by God's divine decree; compare Jesus in Heb 5:5-6 and Levi's commission from God in the various Levi priestly texts. Both present priests offering an eschatological sacrifice of atonement: Jesus offers his ultimate sacrifice in Hebrews after his incarnation, and Qumran's messianic priest makes atonement in the eschaton. Furthermore, even the angelic priest-warrior Melchizedek is associated with the eschatological Day of Atonement in 11QMelchizedek. Admittedly Jesus' sacrificial activity in Hebrews is not understood as occurring in the eschaton in the same way as in the Qumran texts, i.e., at the climactic end when God breaks into history and dramatically changes the world order, yet even in Hebrews Jesus' appearance in the world is dated to the 'last days' (Heb 1:2; in contrast, the Levitical system is said to be 'passing away'). Thus the theme of a priestly service—even described as heavenly—at the decisive point in history binds these traditions.

The suggestion naturally arises that Hebrews' emphasis on the superiority of Jesus' priesthood over the Levitical line may imply knowledge of eschatological Levitical or Aaronic priestly traditions like those at Qumran. In recent years most major commentators on Hebrews have rejected the older notion that the author was writing to encourage Jewish Christians not to revert to Judaism or refuse to separate from it because of an emotional and psychological longing for the comfort of a physical sacrificial cult. As noted above and in chapter 1, a better way to read the comparisons of Jesus and various elements of Judaism in Hebrews is to recognize the rhetorical method of *synkrisis*. Might the author also have intended a gentle polemic of clarification against ideas that a *Levitical priest* would have an enduring role in the heavenly sanctuary? Drawnel's study of the *Aramaic Levi Document* was motivated by a similar suggestion; he questions whether the combination of royal and priestly motifs for Levi prompted a different explanation in Hebrews:

> The author of the Letter to the Hebrews demotes Levi from his priestly and royal position by affirming that, in the person of Abraham, Levi has already paid the tithe to Melchizedek, the royal priestly without genealogy and a typological forerunner of Christ's priesthood (*Hebrews* 7). By introducing Melchizedek and the tithe motif into the discussion concerning the installation of a non-Levitical priesthood, *Hebrews* 7 appears to react against the vision of Levitical royal priesthood depicted in the *Aramaic Levi Document*.[3]

The line of thought proposed in the present study initially was drafted without knowledge of Drawnel's similar suggestion. While it is tempting to assent to his argument that a combination of royal and priestly roles for Levi lay behind Hebrews' alternate presentation of

[3] Drawnel, *Aramaic Wisdom Text*, 14. Compare Drawnel, *Aramaic Wisdom Text*, 307-09; and Greenfield, Stone, and Eshel, *Aramaic Levi Document*, 184-88 on the royal language of Gen 49:10 applied to Kohath. On Drawnel's motivation for undertaking his study, see *Aramaic Wisdom Text*, xiii.

Melchizedek, Drawnel's thesis was rejected above in chapter 3 in favor of the idea that the author of the *Aramaic Levi Document* was co-opting royal dynastic language in order to describe the priesthood entrusted to Levi and his descendents. Also, one would be obliged to consider carefully whether the author wrote chiefly to revise the theological tenets of the readers and if his own presentation of Jesus was driven by polemic against the Levitical priesthood.

The first of these would be very difficult to support from the text of Hebrews. One would be required to demonstrate that the author of Hebrews feared his readers espoused what he considered to be a defective understanding of the heavenly priesthood. In other words, one would have to prove that the author was writing to challenge his readers' intellectual commitments more so than to rally them to faithful obedience. Since the repeated call in the book is to firm commitment and faithfulness, not for the recipients to alter their doctrinal commitments, arguing for such a position is unwise.

It is a very different matter, though, to consider the likelihood that the author of Hebrews was himself somehow influenced by such conceptions. Naturally one cannot claim to know the thoughts of an ancient author, but the survey above has highlighted several similarities between the discussion of a priestly messiah and Hebrews' priestly Christology. Certainly differences are also evident, but it is reasonable in light of the positive correspondences to assert that the author's conception of Jesus as a heavenly priest was prompted at least in part by an intellectual context in which a priest called משיח was expected and the priestly endowment of Levi in the Hebrew Scriptures was understood in heavenly terms. Jesus is *not* the 'messiah of Aaron' of Qumran or the Levi of *Jubilees* and *ALD*, but those conceptions—along with the broader heavenly temple cult supposed in Jewish apocalyptic texts—provided a precedent for the author of Hebrews to conceive of Jesus similarly as a priest making atonement and eternal intercession in the heavenly sanctuary.

2.2. *Hebrews and the Melchizedek Traditions of Qumran*

Much more can be said with confidence about the relationship between Hebrews and the Melchizedek traditions at Qumran. As indicated in chapter 1, interpretation of Heb 7:3 lies at the heart of this consideration, and one must also reconcile the portrayals of Melchizedek as an angelic, eschatological warrior figure at Qumran with that of the priest who encountered Abraham in Hebrews.

It has long been traditional to compare presentations of Melchizedek in 11QMelchizedek and in Hebrews with the point that the figures vary greatly. Melchizedek in Hebrews is a priest who encountered Abraham and received tithes, whereas Melchizedek at Qumran is a heavenly figure bringing eschatological judgment. The most that is allowed typically is that the portrait of Melchizedek in 11QMelchizedek bears more similarities to Hebrews' presentation of *Jesus* than to the latter's discussion of Melchizedek.[4]

It is only appropriate to concede that certain differences do exist. Qumran's presentation of the angelic Melchizedek had two emphases—he is a heavenly priest, as likely is the case in the *Songs of the Sabbath Sacrifice* and is strongly implied by the atonement themes of 11QMelchizedek, and he is an eschatological warrior akin to the archangel Michael in the latter text and in 4Q Visions of Amram[b] ar. Clearly the judgment activity is absent from Hebrews' portrayal of Melchizedek, but neither is that an emphasis for Hebrews' presentation of Jesus.[5] Interesting, though, is that other early Christian texts (including Revelation and Jude) could maintain a role (even militaristic) for the archangel Michael—with whom Melchizedek was assimilated at Qumran and later in Jewish tradition—alongside their obvious understanding of Jesus as the ultimate envoy of God.[6] Similarly, the author of Hebrews may share *certain* aspects of Melchizedek's presentation at Qumran without accepting their portrait in toto.

Arguments to the contrary overlook the complex presentations of Melchizedek in both Hebrews and the Qumran texts. On the one hand, while Melchizedek could be understood at Qumran as an angelic

---

[4] See, for example, the comparisons offered by Horton, *Melchizedek Tradition*, 167; and Kobelski, *Melchizedek*, 128.

[5] See, however, Aschim, "Melchizedek and Jesus," 140-43, who argues that Jesus is presented as a holy warrior in Heb 2:10-18. On Melchizedek as liberator in other texts, see Anders Aschim, "Melchizedek the Liberator: An Early Interpretation of Genesis 14?" in *Society of Biblical Literature 1996 Seminar Papers* (Atlanta: Scholars Press, 1996), 243-58.

[6] See Duane F. Watson, "Michael," *ABD* 4:811. See also James R. Davila, "Melchizedek, Michael, and War in Heaven," in *Society of Biblical Literature 1996 Seminar Papers* (Atlanta: Scholars Press, 1996), 259-72.

figure, one must not ignore the presence of more mundane portraits of Melchizedek in other texts the Qumran community prized, including the *Genesis Apocryphon* and *Jubilees* (presuming their copies predated thc haplography that plagued later manuscripts).[7] One is correct to note a distinction between texts composed at Qumran and simply read there, but *Jubilees* was esteemed at Qumran on a level comparable with Scripture.[8] As demonstrated above in chapter 4, both of these texts have relatively tame retellings of Gen 14. Thus at Qumran one could find very different discussions of Melchizedek, not a monolithic conception.

Likewise, the author of Hebrews can discuss the Melchizedek who encountered Abraham, yet in Heb 7:3 he can describe him as an eternal—presumably angelic—figure, a position espoused in chapter 1 above. As Kobelski argues, this must be recognized as the clear intent of the author's statements about Melchizedek's lack of parentage, genealogy, beginning or end of life, and eternal priesthood. Shortly thereafter in Heb 7:15-17 the similarity between Jesus and Melchizedek is restated: Jesus, κατὰ τὴν ὁμοιότητα Μελχισέδεκ, is priest because of 'the power of an indestructible life.' This correspondence goes beyond the mere lack of a Levitical genealogy, as Horton contends. Melchizedek is a heavenly figure in Hebrews; presumably the author understands Melchizedek's appearance to Abraham as an angelophany, a phenomenon that certainly would not be foreign to the Abraham narratives in Genesis.

One might question whether the author of Hebrews would dare evoke a conception of Melchizedek like that in 11QMelchizedek for comparison with Jesus in light of his emphasis in Heb 1 on the Son's superiority over the angels. For many scholars this is the major impediment to recognizing the common elements of Hebrews' and Qumran's ideas about Melchizedek, and some even assert that *any* knowledge of Qumran's understanding of Melchizedek would have caused the author of Hebrews to avoid use of the character altogether.[9]

Such scholars frequently point to the insistence in Heb 1 of Jesus' superiority over the angels as the chief factor demanding this schism of

[7] Unfortunately the relevant passage is not extant in the Qumran manuscripts of *Jubilees*.

[8] Note the evaluation of VanderKam and Flint, *Meaning*, 199: "*Jubilees* was most likely viewed as Scripture by the Qumran community."

[9] So, for example, Horton, *Melchizedek Tradition*, 169.

thought. The argument of Heb 1, however, may be construed as a point in favor of—not as an impediment against—the idea that Hebrews drew on prior traditions of Melchizedek as an angel. Most scholars of Hebrews today have abandoned older arguments that the author criticizes the recipients' propensity to worship angels, so that removes the assumption that the theory of an angelic Melchizedek would cause theological confusion for the readers. Instead, Heb 1 can be read as a clear assertion of the priority of the eternal Son, the one bearing the glory and essence of the Father and who is superior to the angels in every way, thus making it safe to compare Jesus to an angel (without again stressing the latter's subjugation) later in the epistle.

As noted above and earlier in chapter 1, the author of Hebrews has a traditional Jewish understanding of the relationship between the heavenly and earthy sanctuaries—the latter is modeled on the former—yet discusses this using the language of Middle Platonism. Such thought also seems evident in his discussion of the relationship between Jesus and Melchizedek. The author can explain Jesus' priestly status as being like that of Melchizedek and does so on numerous occasions; this functions well to document an authorized priestly line outside the Levitical tribe. About Jesus, the author can write that he 'resembles [κατὰ τὴν ὁμοιότητα] Melchizedek' (Heb 7:15), but just verses earlier he can state that Melchizedek 'was made to resemble [ἀφωμοιωμένος] the Son of God' (Heb 7:3).

A maximal reading of these comments might support the idea that the author of Hebrews was thinking of the relationship of Jesus and Melchizedek in terms akin to his conception of the sanctuaries, but with one further component. The eternal, divine Son was the model, and the angelic Melchizedek was the copy who encountered Abraham and established a non-Levitical priestly precedent in ancient Israel. This in turn prepared the way for the incarnate Son—both the model for Melchizedek yet now also resembling him—to be comprehended as priest.

Thus conceptions of an otherworldly Melchizedek actually aid—rather than hinder—Hebrews' presentation of Jesus as the heavenly high priest. Transferal of certain heavenly prerogatives from Melchizedek to Jesus is natural given the Christian conviction that Jesus is the ultimate agent of God, but (as demonstrated in chapter 4 above) Qumran's presentation of a heavenly Melchizedek certainly has more points of contact with Hebrews' conception of Melchizedek than do other Second Temple Jewish discussions of the figure. Of the latter, the closest similarities could be seen in the thought of Philo, but only when he allegorized Melchizedek toward an image of the Logos, whose similarities with the Wisdom motifs that lie behind description of the Son in Heb 1 were discussed in chapter 4.

In the end, it is fitting that the author of Hebrews evoked the angelic Melchizedek to further his explanation of Jesus' priesthood, so the epistle and the Qumran literature exhibit shared views.

3. Conclusion

Hebrews' presentation of Jesus as priest finds its closest parallels at Qumran. One need not assent to the extreme positions of earlier proponents of the view in order to recognize that Hebrews and the Qumran texts share a conception of a heavenly Melchizedek and that the conception of Levi's eternal priesthood paved the way for Hebrews' Christological reflections on Jesus as priest. No assertion need be made that the author or recipients of Hebrews were former Essenes or that particular Qumran texts were quoted by the author of the epistle; nor may such claims be substantiated. Instead, two elements contributing to Hebrews' presentation of Jesus as priest—the notion of a heavenly priesthood and an angelic understanding of Melchizedek—are best paralleled in ideas found in the Dead Sea Scrolls.

BIBLIOGRAPHY

1. Discoveries in the Judaean Desert

Barthélemy, D., and J. T. Milik, eds. *Qumran Cave 1*. Discoveries in the Judaean Desert I. Oxford: Clarendon, 1955.

Baillet, M., J. T. Milik, and R. de Vaux, eds. *Les 'petites grottes' de Qumrân*. 2 vols. Discoveries in the Judaean Desert of Jordan III. Oxford: Clarendon, 1962.

Allegro, John M., with A. A. Anderson, eds. *Qumran Cave 4.I (4Q158-4Q186)*. Discoveries in the Judaean Desert of Jordan V. Oxford: Clarendon, 1968.

Baillet, M., ed. *Qumrân grotte 4.III (4Q482-4Q520)*. Discoveries in the Judaean Desert VII. Oxford: Clarendon, 1982.

Skehan, Patrick W., Eugene Ulrich, and Judith E. Sanderson, eds. *Qumran Cave 4.IV: Palaeo-Hebrew and Greek Biblical Manuscripts*. Discoveries in the Judaean Desert IX. Oxford: Clarendon, 1992.

Eshel, Ester, et al., in consultation with J. VanderKam and M. Brady. *Qumran Cave 4.VI: Poetical and Liturgical Texts, Part 1*. Discoveries in the Judaean Desert XI. Oxford: Clarendon, 1998.

Baumgarten, Joseph M., ed. *Qumran Cave 4.XIII: The Damascus Document (4Q266-273)*. Discoveries in the Judaean Desert XVIII. Oxford: Clarendon, 1996.

Broshi. Magen, et al., in consultation with J. VanderKam. *Qumran Cave 4.XIV: Parabiblical Texts, Part 2*. Discoveries in the Judaean Desert XIX. Oxford: Clarendon, 1995.

Brooke. George J., et al., in consultation with J. Vanderkam. *Qumran Cave 4.XVII: Parabiblical Texts, Part 3*. Discoveries in the Judaean Desert XXII. Oxford: Clarendon, 1996.

García Martínez, Florentino, Eibert J. C. Tigchelaar, and Adam S. van der Woude, eds. *Manuscripts from Qumran Cave 11 (11Q2-18, 11Q20-30)*. Discoveries in the Judaean Desert XXIII. Oxford: Clarendon, 1997.

Alexander, Philip S., and Geza Vermes, eds. *Qumran Cave 4.XIX: 4QSerekh Ha-Yaḥad and Two Related Texts*. Discoveries in the Judaean Desert XXVI. Oxford: Clarendon, 1998.

Gropp, Douglas M., ed. *Wadi Daliyeh II: The Samaria Papyri for Wadi Daliyeh*; Schuller, Eileen, et al., in consultation with James VanderKam and Monica Brady. *Qumran Cave 4.XXVIII: Miscellanea, Part 2*. Discoveries in the Judaean Desert XXVIII. Oxford: Clarendon, 2001.

Puech, Émile, ed. *Qumrân Grotte 4.XXII: Textes Araméens Première Partie 4Q529-549*. Discoveries in the Judaean Desert XXXI. Oxford: Clarendon, 2001.

Pfann, Stephen J.. ed. *Qumran Cave 4.XXVI: Cryptic Texts*; Alexander, Philip S., et al., in consultation with J. VanderKam and M. Brady. *Miscellanea, Part 1*. Discoveries in the Judaean Desert XXXVI. Oxford: Clarendon, 2000.

2. Princeton Theological Seminary Dead Sea Scrolls Project

Charlesworth, James H., et al., eds. *The Dead Sea Scrolls: Hebrew, Aramaic, and Greek Texts with English Translations.* Vol. 1, Rule of the Community and Related Documents. Louisville: Westminster John Knox, 1994.

Charlesworth, James H., et al., eds. *The Dead Sea Scrolls: Hebrew, Aramaic, and Greek Texts with English Translations.* Vol. 2, Damascus Document, War Scroll, and Related Documents. Louisville: Westminster John Knox, 1994.

Charlesworth, James H., and Carol A. Newsom, eds. *The Dead Sea Scrolls: Hebrew, Aramaic, and Greek Texts with English Translations*. Vol. 4B, Angelic Liturgy: Songs of the Sabbath Sacrifice. Louisville: Westminster John Knox, 1999.

Charlesworth, James H., and Henry W. Reitz, eds. *The Dead Sea Scrolls: Hebrew, Aramaic, and Greek Texts with English Translations*. Vol. 6B, Pesharim, Other Commentaries, and Related Documents. Louisville: Westminster John Knox, 2002.

3. Electronic Editions of the Dead Sea Scrolls

Lim, Timothy H., and Philip S. Alexander, eds. *The Dead Sea Scrolls Electronic Reference Library* (vol. 1). CD-ROM. Oxford University Press and Brill, 1997.

Tov, Emanuel, ed. *The Dead Sea Scrolls Electronic Library, Revised Edition 2006*. CD-ROM. Brill, 2006.

4. General Bibliography

Aalen, Sverre. "'Reign' and 'House' in the Kingdom of God in the Gospels." *New Testament Studies* 8 (1962): 215-40.

Abegg, Martin G., Jr. "The Messiah at Qumran: Are We Still Seeing Double?" *Dead Sea Discoveries* 2 (1995): 125-44.

——. "1QSb and the Elusive High Priest." Pages 3-13 in *Emanuel: Studies in Hebrew Bible, Septuagint, and Dead Sea Scrolls in Honor of Emanuel Tov.* Edited by S. M. Paul, R. A. Kraft, L. H. Schiffman, and W. W. Fields. Leiden: Brill, 2003.

——. "Who Ascended to Heaven? 4Q491, 4Q427, and the Teacher of Righteousness." Pages 61-73 in *Eschatology, Messianism, and the Dead Sea Scrolls*. Edited by C. A. Evans and P. W. Flint. Studies in the Dead Sea Scrolls and Related Literature 1. Grand Rapids: Eerdmans, 1997.

Abegg, Martin, Jr., Peter Flint, and Eugene Ulrich. *The Dead Sea Scrolls Bible*. New York: Harper San Francisco, 1999.

Aitken, Ellen Bradshaw. "Portraying the Temple in Stone and Text: The Arch of Titus and the Epistle to the Hebrews." Pages 131-48 in *Hebrews: Contemporary Methods, New Insights*. Edited by G. Gelardini. Biblical Interpretation Series 75. Leiden: Brill, 2005.

Alexander, Philip S. "The Redaction-History of Serekh ha-Yaḥad: A Proposal." *Revue de Qumran* 17 (1996): 437-57.

Allegro, John M. "Fragments of a Qumran Scroll of Eschatological Midrašim." *Journal of Biblical Literature* 77 (1958): 350-54.

——. "Further Messianic References in Qumran Literature." *Journal of Biblical Literature* 75 (1956): 174-87.

Allen, Leslie C. *Psalms 101-50, Revised.* Word Biblical Commentary 21. Nashville: Nelson, 2002.

Anderson, Francis I. "Enoch, Second Book of." Pages 516-22 in vol. 2 of *The Anchor Bible Dictionary*. Edited by D. N. Freedman. 6 vols. New York: Doubleday, 1992.

Aschim, Anders. "The Genre of 11QMelchizedek." Pages 17-31 in *Qumran Between the Old and New Testaments*. Edited by F. H. Cryer and T. L. Thompson. Journal for the Study of the Old Testament: Supplement Series 290. Copenhagen International Seminar 6. Sheffield: Sheffield, 1998.

——. "Melchizedek and Jesus: 11QMelchizedek and the Epistle to the Hebrews." Pages 128-47 in *The Jewish Roots of Christological Monotheism: Papers from the St. Andrews Conference on the Historical Origins of the Worship of Jesus*. Edited by C. C. Newman, J. R. Davila, and G. S. Lewis. Supplements to the Journal for the Study of Judaism 63. Leiden: Brill, 1999.

——. "Melchizedek the Liberator: An Early Interpretation of Genesis 14?" Pages 243-58 in *Society of Biblical Literature 1996 Seminar Papers*. Atlanta: Scholars Press, 1996.

Astour, Michael C. "Shaveh, Valley of." Page 1168 in vol. 5 of *The Anchor Bible Dictionary*. Edited by D. N. Freedman. 6 vols. New York: Doubleday, 1992.

Attridge, Harold W. *The Epistle to the Hebrews*. Hermeneia. Philadelphia: Fortress, 1989.

——. "The Epistle to the Hebrews and the Scrolls." Pages 315-42 in vol. 2 of *When Judaism and Christianity Began: Essays in Memory of Anthony J. Saldarini*. Edited by A. J. Avery-Peck, D. Harrington, and J. Neusner. 2 vols. Supplements to the Journal for the Study of Judaism 85. Leiden: Brill, 2004.

Aune, David E. *The Westminster Dictionary of New Testament and Early Christian Literature and Rhetoric*. Louisville: Westminster John Knox, 2003.

——. "Heracles and Christ: Heracles Imagery in the Christology of Early Christianity." Pages 3-19 in *Greeks, Romans, and Christians: Essays in Honor of Abraham J. Malherbe*. Edited by D. L. Balch, E. Ferguson, and W. A. Meeks. Minneapolis, Fortress, 1990.

Avigad, Nahman, and Yigael Yadin. *A Genesis Apocryphon: A Scroll from the Wilderness of Judaea: Description and Contents of the Scroll, Facsimiles, Transcription and Translation of Columns II, XIX-XXII*. Jerusalem: Magnes, 1956.

Balz, Horst, and Gerhard Schneider, eds. *Exegetical Dictionary of the New Testament*. 3 vols. Grand Rapids: Eerdmans, 1990-93.

Barbel, Joseph. *Christos Angelos*. 2nd ed. Theophaneia 3. Bonn: Peter Hanstein, 1964.

Barrett, C. K. "The Eschatology of the Epistle to the Hebrews," Pages 363-93 in *The Background of the New Testament and Its Eschatology*. Edited by W. D. Davies and D. Daube. Cambridge: Cambridge University Press, 1956.

Batdorf, Irvin W. "Hebrews and Qumran: Old Methods and New Directions." Pages 16-35 in *Festschrift to Honor F. Wilbur Gingrich*. Edited by E. H. Barth and R. E. Cocroft. Leiden: Brill, 1972.

Baumgarten, Joseph M. "Damascus Document." Pages 166-70 in vol. 1 of *Encyclopedia of the Dead Sea Scrolls*. Edited by L. H. Schiffman and J. C. VanderKam. 2 vols. Oxford: Oxford University Press, 2000.

Baxter, Wayne. "1QSB: Old Divisions Made New." *Revue de Qumran* 21 (2004): 615-29.

Becker, Joachim. *Messianic Expectation in the Old Testament*. Philadelphia: Fortress, 1980.

Bernas, Casimir. Review of F. Manzi, *Melchisedek e l'angelologia nell'Epistola agli Ebrei e a Qumran. Review of Biblical Literature*, February 15, 1999. Cited February 2, 2005. Online: http://www.bookreviews.org/pdf/2724_1918.pdf.

Biblia Hebraica Stuttgartensia. Edited by K. Elliger and W. Rudoph. 4th ed. Stuttgart: Deutsche Bibelgesellschaft, 1990.

Blackman, E. C. *Biblical Interpretation*. London: Independent Press, 1957.

Bodinger, Martin. "L'Énigme de Melkisédeq." *Revue de l'histoire des religions* 211 (1994): 297-333.

Boling, Robert G. "Deborah." Pages 113-14 in vol. 2 of *The Anchor Bible Dictionary*. Edited by D. N. Freedman. 6 vols. New York: Doubleday, 1992.

Booij, Th. "Psalm CX: 'Rule in the Midst of Your Foes!'" *Vetus Testamentum* 41 (1991): 396-407.

Botterweck, G. Johannes, et al., eds. *Theological Dictionary of the Old Testament*. Grand Rapids: Eerdmans, 1974-.

Böttrich, Christfried. "The Melchizedek Story of 2 (Slavonic) Enoch: A Reaction to A. Orlov." *Journal for the Study of Judaism* 32 (2001): 445-70.

Bousset, *Kyrios Christos: A History of the Belief in Christ from the Beginnings of Christianity to Irenaeus*. Translated by J. E. Steely. Nashville: Abingdon, 1970.

——. *Die Religion des Judentums im Späthellenistischen Zeitalter*. 4th ed. Tübingen: Mohr Siebeck, 1966.

Braun, Herbert. *An die Hebräer*. Handbuch zum Neuen Testament 14. Tübingen: Mohr, 1984.

——. *Qumran und das Neue Testamant*. 2 vols. Tübingen: Mohr Siebeck, 1966.

Brooke, George J. "Catena." Pages 121-22 in vol. 1 of *Encyclopedia of the Dead Sea Scrolls*. Edited by L. H. Schiffman and J. C. VanderKam. 2 vols. Oxford: Oxford University Press, 2000.

——. *Exegesis at Qumran: 4QFlorilegium in Its Jewish Context*. Journal of the Study of the Old Testament: Supplement Series 29. Sheffield: JSOT, 1985.

——. "Florilegium." Pages 297-98 in vol. 1 of *Encyclopedia of the Dead Sea Scrolls*. Edited by L. H. Schiffman and J. C. VanderKam. 2 vols. Oxford: Oxford University Press, 2000.

——. Review of Franco Manzi, *Melchizedek e l'angelologia nell'Epistola agli Ebrei e a Qumran. Catholic Biblical Quarterly* 60 (1998): 770-71.

Broshi, Magen. *The Damascus Document Reconsidered*. Jerusalem: Israel Exploration Society, 1992.

Brown, Raymond E. *An Introduction to the New Testament*. Anchor Bible Reference Library. New York: Doubleday, 1997.

——. "J. Starcky's Theory of Qumran Messianic Development." *Catholic Biblical Quarterly* 28 (1966): 51-57.

Brown, Raymond E., and John P. Meier, *Antioch and Rome: New Testament Cradles of Catholic Christianity*. New York: Paulist, 1983.

Bruce, F. F. *The Epistle to the Hebrews*. Rev. ed. New International Commentary on the New Testament. Grand Rapids: Eerdmans, 1990.

——. "'To the Hebrews': A Document of Roman Christianity?" *ANRW* 25.4:3496-3521. Part 2, *Principat*, 25.4. Edited by W. Haase. New York: de Gruyter, 1987.

——. "'To the Hebrews' or 'To the Essenes'?" *New Testament Studies* 9 (1962-63): 217-32.

Buchanan, George Wesley. *To the Hebrews*. Anchor Bible 36. Garden City, N.Y.: Doubleday, 1972.

Bühner, J. A. *Der Gesandte und sein Weg im 4.Evangelium: Die kultur- und religionsgeschichtlichen Grundlagen der johanneischen Sendungs-christologie sowie ihre traditionsgeschichtliche Entwicklung*. Wissenschaftliche Untersuchungen zum Neuen Testament 2/2. Tübingen: Mohr Siebeck, 1977.

Bultmann, Rudolf. *Theology of the New Testament*. Translated by K. Grobel. 2 vols. New York, Scribner's, 1951-55.

Burrows, Millar, ed. *The Dead Sea Scrolls of St. Mark's Monastery, Volume II, Fascicle 2: Plates and Transcription of the Manual of Discipline*. New Haven: American Schools of Oriental Research, 1951.

Caquot, Andre. "Le Livre des Jubilés, Melkisedeq et les dîmes." *Journal of Jewish Studies* 33 (1982): 257-64.

——. "Le messianisme Qumrànien." Pages 231-47 in *Qumrân: Sa piété, sa théologie et son milieu*. Edited by M. Delcor. Bibliotheca ephemeridum theologicarum lovaniensium 46. Paris-Gembloux: Duculot/Leuven University Press, 1978.

Carmignac, Jean. "Le document de Qumrân sur Melkisédeq." *Revue de Qumran* 7 (1970): 343-78.

Chadwick, H. "St. Paul and Philo of Alexandria." *Bulletin of the John Rylands Library* 48 (1965-66): 286-307.

Charles, R. H. "The Book of Jubilees." Pages 1-82 in vol. 2 of *The Apocrypha and Pseudepigrapha of the Old Testament*. Edited by R. H. Charles. 2 vols. Oxford: Clarendon, 1913.

——. *The Book of Jubilees or the Little Genesis*. London: A. & C. Black, 1902.

——. *The Greek Versions of the Testaments of the Twelve Patriarchs*. Oxford: Oxford University Press, 1908.

Charles, R. H., and A. Cowley. "An Early Source of the Testaments of the Patriarchs." *Jewish Quarterly Review* 19 (1907): 566-83.

Charles, R. H., and C. Rabin, "Jubilees." Pages 1-139 in *The Apocryphal Old Testament*. Edited by H. F. D. Sparks. Oxford: Clarendon, 1984.

Charlesworth, James H. "Challenging the Consensus Communis Regarding Qumran Messianism (1QS, 4QS MSS)." Pages 120-34 in *Qumran-Messianism: Studies on the Messianic Expectations in the Dead Sea Scrolls*. Edited by J. H. Charlesworth, H. Lichtenberger, and G. S. Oegema. Tübingen: Mohr Siebeck, 1998.

——. "From Jewish Messianology to Christian Christology: Some Caveats and Perspectives." Pages 225-64 in *Judaisms and Their Messiahs at the Turn of the Christian Era*. Edited by J. Neusner, W. S. Green, and E. Frerichs. Cambridge: Cambridge University Press, 1987.

——. "From Messianology to Christology: Problems and Prospects." Pages 3-35 in *The Messiah: Developments in Earliest Judaism and Christianity*. Edited by J. H. Charlesworth. Minneapolis: Fortress, 1992.

——, ed. *The Old Testament Pseudepigrapha*. 2 vols. New York: Doubleday, 1983-85.

Clarkson, Mary E. "The Antecedents of the High-Priest Theme in Hebrews." *Australasian Theological Review* 29 (1947): 89-95.

Cockerill, Gareth Lee. "Melchizedek or 'King of Righteousness.'" *Evangelical Quarterly* 63:4 (1991): 305-12.

Cody, Aelred. *Heavenly Sanctuary and Liturgy in the Epistle to the Hebrews*. St. Meinrad, Ind.: Grail, 1960.

Collins, John J. *The Scepter and the Star: The Messiahs of the Dead Sea Scrolls and Other Ancient Literature*. Anchor Bible Reference Library. New York: Doubleday, 1995.

Cook, Stephen L. *Prophecy and Apocalypticism: The Post-Exilic Social Setting*. Minneapolis: Fortress, 1995.

Coppens, Joseph. *Les affinities qumrâniennes de l'Épître aux Hébreux*. Analecta lovaniensia biblica et orientalia 6/1. Louvain: Publications Universitaires, 1962.

Craddock, Fred B. "The Letter to the Hebrews." Pages 1-173 in vol 12 of *The New Interpreter's Bible*. Edited by L. Keck. 12 vols. Nashville: Abingdon, 1998.

Cross, Frank M., Jr. "The Development of the Jewish Scripts." Pages 133-202 in *The Bible and the Ancient Near East*. Edited by G. E. Wright. Garden City, N.Y.: Doubleday, 1961.

Cullmann, Oscar. *The Christology of the New Testament*. Rev. ed. New Testament Library. Philadelphia: Westminster, 1964.

D'Angelo, Mary Rose. *Moses in the Letter to the Hebrews*. Society of Biblical Literature Dissertation Series 42. Missoula, Mont.: Scholars Press, 1979.

Daniélou, Jean. *Les manuscrits de la Mer Morte et les origins du Christianisme*. Paris: Editions de l'Orante, 1957.

Danker, Frederick William, ed. *A Greek-English Lexicon of the New Testament and Other Early Christian Literature*. 3rd ed. Chicago: University of Chicago Press, 2000.

Davies, Philip R. "War of the Sons of Light Against the Sons of Darkness." Pages 965-68 in vol. 2 of *Encyclopedia of the Dead Sea Scrolls*. Edited by L. H. Schiffman and J. C. VanderKam. 2 vols. Oxford: Oxford University Press, 2000.

Davila, James R. *Liturgical Works*. Eerdmans Commentaries on the Dead Sea Scrolls. Grand Rapids: Eerdmans, 2000.

——. "Melchizedek, Michael, and War in Heaven." Pages 259-72 in *Society of Biblical Literature 1996 Seminar Papers*. Atlanta: Scholars Press, 1996.

DeSilva, David A. *Perseverance in Gratitude: A Socio-Rhetorical Commentary on the Epistle "to the Hebrews."* Grand Rapids: Eerdmans, 2000.

Dey, Lala K. K. *The Intermediary World and Patterns of Perfection in Philo and Hebrews*. Society of Biblical Literature Dissertation Series 25. Missoula, Mont.: Scholars Press, 1975.

Dodd, C. H. *The Authority of the Bible*. London: Collins, 1978.

Doran, Robert. "Pseudo-Eupolemus." Pages 873-79 in vol. 2 of *The Old Testament Pseudepigrapha*. Edited by J. H. Charlesworth. 2 vols. New York: Doubleday, 1983-85.

Drawnel, Henryk. *An Aramaic Wisdom Text from Qumran: A New Interpretation of the Levi Document*. Supplements to the Journal for the Study of Judaism 86. Leiden: Brill, 2004.

——. Review of J. Greenfield, M. Stone, and E. Eshel, *The Aramaic Levi Document: Edition, Translation, Commentary*. *Revue biblique* 113 (2006): 127-31.

Driver, S. R. *An Introduction to the Literature of the Old Testament*. New York: Scribner's, 1913. Repr., Cleveland: Meridian, 1956.

Dunn, James D. G. *Christology in the Making: A New Testament Inquiry into the Origins of the Doctrine of the Incarnation*. 2nd ed. Grand Rapids: Eerdmans, 1989.

——. *The Theology of Paul the Apostle*. Grand Rapids: Eerdmans 1998.

Eager, A. "The Hellenistic Elements in the Epistle to the Hebrews." *Hermathena* 11 (1901): 263-87.

Eisenbaum, Pamela M. "Locating Hebrews Within the Literary Landscape of Christian Origins." Pages 213-37 in *Hebrews: Contemporary Methods, New Insights*. Edited by G. Gelardini. Biblical Interpretation Series 75. Leiden: Brill, 2005.

Ellingworth, Paul. *The Epistle to the Hebrews: A Commentary on the Greek Text*. New International Greek Testament Commentary. Grand Rapids: Eerdmans, 1993.

Emerton, J. A. "The Riddle of Genesis XIV." *Vetus Testamentum* 21 (1971): 403-39.

Endres, John C. *Biblical Interpretation in the Book of Jubilees*. Catholic Biblical Quarterly Monograph Series 18. Washington, D. C.: Catholic Biblical Association, 1987.

Eshel, Hanan. "The Historical Background of the Pesher Interpreting Joshua's Curse on the Rebuilder of Jericho." *Revue de Qumran* 15 (1992): 409-20.

Eskola, Timo. *Messiah and Throne: Jewish Merkabah Mysticism and Early Christian Exaltation Discourse*. Wissenschaftliche Untersuchungen zum Neuen Testament 2/142. Tübingen: Mohr Siebeck, 2001.

Evans, Craig A. "Messiahs." Pages 537-42 in vol. 1 of *Encyclopedia of the Dead Sea Scrolls*. Edited by L. H. Schiffman and J. C. VanderKam. 2 vols. Oxford: Oxford University Press, 2000.

——. "Messianic Hopes and Messianic Figures in Late Antiquity." *Journal of Greco-Roman Christianity and Judaism* 3 (2006): 9-40.

Fabry, Heinz-Jozef. "Die Messiaserwartung in den Handschriften von Qumran." Pages 357-84 in *Wisdom and Apocalypticism in the Dead Sea Scrolls and in the Biblical Tradition*. Edited by F. García Martínez. Bibliotheca ephemeridum theologicarum lovaniensium 168. Leuven: Peeters, 2003.

Feld, Helmut. *Der Hebräerbrief*. Erträge der Forschung 228. Darmstadt: Wissenschaftliche Buchgesellschaft, 1985.

——. "Der Hebräerbrief: Literarische Form, religionsgeschichtlicher Hintergrund, theologische Fragen." *ANRW* 25.4:3558-60. Part 2, *Principat*, 25.4. Edited by W. Haase. New York: de Gruyter, 1987.

Feldman, Louis H. "Josephus." Pages 981-98 in vol. 3 of *The Anchor Bible Dictionary*. Edited by D. N. Freedman. 6 vols. New York: Doubleday, 1992.

Filson, Floyd. "The Epistle to the Hebrews." *Journal of Bible and Religion* 22 (1954): 20-26.

Fitzmyer, Joseph A. "'4QTestimonia' and the New Testament." Pages 59-89 in *The Semitic Background of the New Testament*. Grand Rapids: Eerdmans, 1997. Repr. from *Theological Studies* 18 (1957): 513-37.

——. "Further Light on Melchizedek from Qumran Cave 11." Pages 245-67 in *The Semitic Background of the New Testament*. Grand Rapids: Eerdmans, 1997. Repr. from *Journal of Biblical Literature* 86 (1967): 25-41.

——. "Genesis Apocryphon." Pages 302-04 in vol. 1 of *Encyclopedia of the Dead Sea Scrolls*. Edited by L. H. Schiffman and J. C. VanderKam. 2 vols. Oxford: Oxford University Press, 2000.

——. *The Genesis Apocryphon of Qumran Cave I*. 3rd ed. Biblical et orientalia 18B. Rome: Pontifical Biblical Institute, 2004.

——. "Melchizedek in the MT, LXX, and the NT." *Biblica* 81 (2000): 63-69.

——. "'Now This Melchizedek . . .' (Heb 7:1)." Pages 221-43 in *The Semitic Background of the New Testament*. Grand Rapids: Eerdmans, 1997. Repr. from *Catholic Biblical Quarterly* 25 (1963): 305-21.

——. The One Who is to Come. Grand Rapids: *Eerdmans*, 2007.

——. Review of Johannes Zimmermann, *Messianische Texte aus Qumran. Theological Studies* 60 (1999): 750-51.

——. *Romans: A New Translation with Introduction and Commentary*. Anchor Bible 33. New York: Doubleday, 1993.

Flusser, David. "The Dead Sea Sect and Pre-Pauline Christianity." *Scripta hierosolymitana* 4 (1958): 215-66.

——. "Melchizedek and the Son of Man (A preliminary note on a new fragment from Qumran)." *Christian News from Israel* (April 1966): 23-29.

Forbes, Christopher. "Comparison, Self-praise and Irony: Paul's Boasting and the Conventions of Hellenistic Rhetoric." *New Testament Studies* 32 (1986): 1-30.

Fossum, Jarl. *The Name of God and the Angel of the Lord: Samaritan and Jewish Conceptions of Intermediation and the Origin of Gnosticism*. Wissenschaftliche Untersuchungen zum Neuen Testament 2/36. Tübingen: Mohr Siebeck, 1985.

——. "Son of God." Pages 128-37 in vol. 6 of *The Anchor Bible Dictionary*. Edited by D. N. Freedman. 6 vols. New York: Doubleday, 1992.

Freedman, David Noel, ed. *The Anchor Bible Dictionary*. 6 vols. New York: Doubleday, 1992.

Freudenthal, Jacob. "Ein ungenannter samaritanischer Geschichtschreiber." Pages 82-103, 207-08, 223-25 in *Alexander Polyhistor und die von ihm erhaltenen Reste judäischer und samaritanischer Geschichtswerke*. Hellenistische Studien 1-2. Breslau: Skutsch, 1875.

Friedrich, Gerhard. "Beobachtungen zur messianischen Hohenpriestererwartung in den Synoptikern." *Zeitschrift für Theologie und Kirche* (1956): 265-311.

Gammie, John. "Loci of the Melchizedek Tradition of Genesis 14:18-20." *Journal of Biblical Literature* 90 (1971): 385-96.

García Martínez, Florentino. "Las tradiciones sombre Melquisedec en los manuscriptos de Qumrán." *Biblica* 81 (2000): 70-80.

García Martínez, Florentino. "Messianic Hopes in the Qumran Writings." Pages 159-89 in *The People of the Dead Sea Scrolls*. Edited by F. García Martínez and J. Trebolle Barrera. Leiden: Brill, 1995.

García Martínez, Florentino, and Eibert J. C. Tigchelaar, eds. *The Dead Sea Scrolls Study Edition*. 2 vols. Leiden: Brill, 1997-98.

Gelardini, Gabriella. "Hebrews, An Ancient Synagogue Homily for Tisha be-Av: Its Function, Its Basis, Its Theological Interpretation." Pages 107-27 in *Hebrews: Contemporary Methods, New Insights*. Edited by G. Gelardini. Biblical Interpretation Series 75. Leiden: Brill, 2005.

——. *'Verhartet eure Herzen Nicht': Der Hebraer, eine Synagogenhomilie zu Tischa be-Aw*. Biblical Interpretation Series 93. Leiden: Brill, 2007.

Gianotto, Claudio. *Melchisedek e la sua tipologia: Tradizioni giudaiche, cristiane e gnostiche (sec. II a.C.-sec. III d.C.).* Supplementi alla Rivista Biblica 12. Brescia: Paideia Editrice, 1984.

Gieschen, Charles A. *Angelomorphic Christology: Antecedents and Early Evidence.* Arbeiten zur Geschichte des antiken Judentums und des Urchristentums 42. Leiden: Brill, 1998.

——. "The Different Functions of a Similar Melchizedek Tradition in *2 Enoch* and the Epistle to the Hebrews." Pages 364-79 in *Early Christian Interpretation of the Scriptures of Israel.* Edited by C. A. Evans and J. A. Sanders. Journal for the Study of the New Testament: Supplement Series 148. Studies in Scripture in Early Judaism and Christianity 5. Sheffield: Sheffield, 1997.

Gilbert, G. H. "The Greek Element in the Epistle to the Hebrews." *American Journal of Theology* 14 (1910): 521-32.

Ginzberg, L. *An Unknown Jewish Sect.* Moreshet Series 1. New York: Jewish Theological Seminary of America, 1976.

Gnilka, Joachim. "Die Erwartung des messianischen Hohenpriesters in den Schriften von Qumran und im Neuen Testament." *Revue de Qumran* 2 (1960): 395-426.

Gordon, Robert P. *Hebrews.* Readings: A New Biblical Commentary. Sheffield: Sheffield Academic, 2000.

Grabbe, Lester L. *Etymology in Early Jewish Interpretation: The Hebrew Names in Philo.* Brown Judaic Studies 115. Atlanta: Scholars Press, 1988.

Grant, R. M. *The Letter and the Spirit.* London: SPCK, 1957.

Grässer, Erich. *An die Hebräer.* 3 vols. Evangelisch-katholischer Kommentar zum Neuen Testament VII.1-3. Zürich: Benzinger; Neukirchen-Vluyn: Neukirchener Verlag, 1990-97.

——. *Der Glaube im Hebräerbrief.* Marburger Theologische Studien 2. Marburg: Elwert, 1965.

Greenfield, Jonas C., and Elisha Qimron. "The Genesis Apocryphon Col. xii." Pages 70-77 in *Studies in Qumran Aramaic.* Edited by T. Muraoka. Abr-Nahrain: Supplement Series 3. Leuven: Peeters, 1992.

Greenfield, Jonas C., Michael E. Stone, and Esther Eshel. *The Aramaic Levi Document: Edition, Translation, Commentary.* Studia in Veteris Testamenti pseudepigraphica 19. Leiden: Brill, 2004.

Guthrie, George H. *Hebrews.* NIV Application Commentary. Grand Rapids: Zondervan, 1998.

Hagner, Donald A. *Hebrews.* New International Biblical Commentary. Peabody, Mass: Hendrickson, 1990.

Hahn, Ferdinand. *Christologische Hoheitstitel: Ihre Geschichte im frühen Christentum.* 5th ed. Göttingen: Vandenhoeck & Ruprecht, 1995.

Hannah, Darrell D. *Michael and Christ: Michael Traditions and Angel Christology in Early Christianity.* Wissenschaftliche Untersuchungen zum Neuen Testament 2/109. Tübingen: Mohr Siebeck, 1999.

Hatch, William H. P. "The Position of Hebrews in the Canon of the New Testament." *Harvard Theological Review* 29 (1936): 133-51.

Hawthorne, Gerald F., Ralph P. Martin, and Daniel G. Reid, eds. *Dictionary of Paul and His Letters.* Downers Grove, Ill.: Intervarsity, 1993.

Hay, David M. *Glory at the Right Hand: Psalm 110 in Early Christianity.* Society of Biblical Literature Monograph Series 18. Nashville: Abingdon, 1973.

Hayward, Robert. "Shem, Melchizedek, and Concern with Christianity in the Pentateuchal Targumim." Pages 67-80 in *Targumic and Cognate Studies: Essays in Honour of Martin McNamara*. Edited by K. J. Cathcart and M. Maher. Journal for the Study of the Old Testament: Supplement Series 230. Sheffield: Sheffield Academic, 1996.

Hegermann, Harald. *Der Brief an die Hebräer*. Theologischer Handkommentar zum Neuen Testament 16. Berlin: Evangelische Verlagsanstalt, 1988.

Hempel, Charlotte. "Qumran Communities: Beyond the Fringes of Second Temple Society." Pages 43-53 in *The Scrolls and the Scriptures: Qumran Fifty Years After*. Edited by S. Porter and C. Evans. Journal for the Study of the Pseudepigrapha: Supplement Series 26. Sheffield: Sheffield, 1997.

Hengel, Martin. *The Cross of the Son of God*. Translated by J. Bowden. Philadelphia: Fortress, 1976.

——. *Judaism and Hellenism: Studies in their Encounter in Palestine during the Early Hellenistic Period*. Translated by J. Bowden. 2 vols. Philadelphia: Fortress, 1974.

Héring, Jean. *The Epistle to the Hebrews*. London: Epworth, 1970.

Higgins, A. J. B. "The Priestly Messiah." *New Testament Studies* 13 (1966-67): 211-39.

Hock, Ronald F. Hock. "General Introduction to Volume I." Pages 3-60 in *The Chreia in Ancient Rhetoric: Volume I. The Progymnasmata*. Edited by R. F. Hock and E. N. O'Neil. Society of Biblical Literature Texts and Translations 27. Graeco-Roman Religion Series 9. Atlanta: Scholars Press, 1986.

Hofius, Otfried. *Katapausis: Die Vorstellung vom endzeitlichen Ruheort im Hebräerbrief*. Wissenschaftliche Untersuchungen zum Neuen Testament 11. Tübingen: Mohr, 1970.

Holladay, Carl R. "Eupolemus." Pages 671-72 in vol. 2 of *The Anchor Bible Dictionary*. Edited by D. N. Freedman. 6 vols. New York: Doubleday, 1992.

——. "Eupolemus, Pseudo-." Pages 672-73 in vol. 2 of *The Anchor Bible Dictionary*. Edited by D. N. Freedman. 6 vols. New York: Doubleday, 1992.

——. *Fragments from Hellenistic Jewish Authors*. Vol. 1: Historians. Chico, Calif.: Scholars Press, 1983.

Hollander, H. W., and M. de Jonge. *The Testaments of the Twelve Patriarchs: A Commentary*. Studia in Veteris Testamenti pseudepigrapha 8. Leiden: Brill, 1985.

Hooker, Morna. *Jesus and the Servant: The Influence of the Servant Concept of Deutero-Isaiah in the New Testament*. London: SPCK, 1959.

Horgan, Maura P. *Pesharim: Qumran Interpretations of Biblical Books*. Catholic Biblical Quarterly Monograph Series 8. Washington, D.C.: Catholic Biblical Association, 1979.

Horton, Fred L., Jr. *The Melchizedek Tradition: A Critical Examination of the Sources to the Fifth Century A.D. and in the Epistle to the Hebrews*. Society for New Testament Studies Monograph Series 30. Cambridge: Cambridge University Press, 1976.

Howard, George. "Hebrews and the Old Testament Quotations," *Novum Testamentum* 10 (1968): 208-16.

Howard, W. F. *The Fourth Gospel in Recent Criticism and Interpretation*. 4th ed. London: Epworth, 1955.

Hughes, Graham. *Hebrews and Hermeneutics: The Epistle to the Hebrews as a New Testament Example of Biblical Interpretation*. Society for New Testament Studies Monograph Series 36. Cambridge: Cambridge University Press, 1979.

Hughes, Philip Edgcumbe. "The Epistle to the Hebrews." Pages 351-70 in *The New Testament and Its Modern Interpreters*. Edited by Eldon Jay Epp and George W. MacRae. Atlanta: Scholars Press, 1989.

Hurst, L. D. *The Epistle to the Hebrews: Its Background of Thought*. Society for New Testament Studies Monograph Scrics 65. Cambridge: Cambridge University Press, 1990.

Hurtado, Larry. *Lord Jesus Christ: Devotion to Jesus in Earliest Christianity*. Grand Rapids: Eerdmans, 2003.

——. *One God, One Lord: Early Christian Devotion and Ancient Jewish Monotheism*. London: SCM, 1988.

——. "Son of God." Pages 900-06 in *Dictionary of Paul and His Letters*. Edited by G. F. Hawthorne, R. P. Martin, and D. G. Reid. Downers Grove, Ill.: Intervarsity, 1993.

Jeremias, Jörg. *The Book of Amos*. Translated by D. W. Stott. Old Testament Library. Louisville: Westminster John Knox, 1998.

Johnson, Luke Timothy. *Hebrews: A Commentary*. New Testament Library. Louisville: Westminster John Knox, 2006.

Jonge, Marinus de. "Messiah." Pages 777-88 in vol. 4 of *The Anchor Bible Dictionary*. Edited by D. N. Freedman. 6 vols. New York: Doubleday, 1992.

——. "Patriarchs, Testaments of the Twelve." Pages 181-86 in vol. 5 of *The Anchor Bible Dictionary*. Edited by D. N. Freedman. 6 vols. New York: Doubleday, 1992.

——. *Testamenta XII Patriarcharum: Edited According to Cambridge University Library MS Ff I.24 fol. 203a-262b with Short Notes*. Pseudepigrapha Veteris Testamenti Graece 1. Leiden: Brill, 1964.

——. "The Testaments of the Twelve Patriarchs." Pages 505-600 in *The Apocryphal Old Testament*. Edited by H. F. D. Sparks. Oxford: Clarendon, 1984.

Jonge, Marinus de, and Adam S. van der Woude. "11Q Melchizedek and the New Testament." *New Testament Studies* 12 (1965-66): 301-26.

Jonge, Marinus de, in cooperation with H. W. Hollander, J. J. de Jonge, and Th. Korteweg. *The Testaments of the Twelve Patriarchs: A Critical Edition of the Greek Text*. Pseudepigrapha Veteris Testamenti Graece 1/2. Leiden: Brill, 1978.

Josephus. Translated by H. St. J. Thackeray et al. 10 vols. Loeb Classical Library. Cambridge, Mass.: Harvard University Press, 1926-65.

Joüon, Paul. *A Grammar of Biblical Hebrew*. Translated and revised by T. Muraoka. 2 vols. Rome: Pontifical Biblical Institute, 1993.

Karrer, Martin. "The Epistle to the Hebrews and the Septuagint." Pages 335-53 in *Septuagint Research: Issues and Challenges in the Study of the Greek Jewish Scriptures*. Edited by W. Kraus and R. G. Wooden. Society of Biblical Literature Septuagint and Cognate Studies 53. Atlanta: Society of Biblical Literature, 2006.

Käsemann, Ernst. *Jesus Means Freedom*. Philadelphia: Fortress: 1970.

——. *The Wandering People of God*. Translated by R. A. Harrisville and I. L. Sandberg. Minneapolis: Augsburg, 1984. Translation of *Das wandernde Gottesvolk: Eine Untersuchung zum Hebräerbrief*. 2nd ed. Göttingen: Vandenhoeck & Ruprecht, 1957.

Kee, Howard Clark. "Testaments of the Twelve Patriarchs." Pages 775-828 in vol. 1 of *The Old Testament Pseudepigrapha*. Edited by J. H. Charlesworth. 2 vols. New York: Doubleday, 1983-85.

Kennedy, H. A. A. *The Theology of the Epistles*. London: Duckworth, 1919.

Kittel, G., and G. Friedrich, eds. *Theological Dictionary of the New Testament*. Translated by G. W. Bromiley. 10 vols. Grand Rapids: Eerdmans, 1964-1976.

Knibb, Michael A. "Eschatology and Messianism in the Dead Sea Scrolls." Pages 379-402 in vol. 2 of *The Dead Sea Scrolls after Fifty Years: A Comprehensive Assessment*. Edited by P. W. Flint and J. C. VanderKam. 2 vols. Leiden: Brill, 1999.

——. "Rule of the Community." Pages 793-97 in vol. 2 of *Encyclopedia of the Dead Sea Scrolls*. Edited by L. H. Schiffman and J. C. VanderKam. 2 vols. Oxford: Oxford University Press, 2000.

Knohl, Israel. *The Messiah Before Jesus: The Suffering Servant of the Dead Sea Scrolls*. Berkeley: University of California Press, 2000.

Knox, John. *The Humanity and Divinity of Christ*. Cambridge: Cambridge University Press, 1967.

Knox, Wilfred L. "The 'Divine Hero' Christology in the New Testament." *Harvard Theological Review* 41 (1948): 229-49.

Kobelski, Paul J. *Melchizedek and Melchireša'*. Catholic Biblical Quarterly Monograph Series 10. Washington: Catholic Biblical Association of America, 1981.

Koester, Craig R. *The Dwelling of God: The Tabernacle in the Old Testament, Intertestamental Jewish Literature, and the New Testament*. Catholic Biblical Quarterly Monograph Series 2. Washington, D.C.: Catholic Biblical Association, 1989.

——. *Hebrews: A New Translation with Introduction and Commentary*. Anchor Bible 36. New York: Doubleday, 2001.

Koester, Helmut. *History and Literature of Early Christianity*. 2nd ed. Vol. 2 of *Introduction to the New Testament*. New York: de Gruyter, 2000.

Kosmala, Hans. *Hebräer-Essener-Christen*. Studia post-biblica 1. Leiden: Brill, 1959.

Kraus, Hans-Joachim. *Theology of the Psalms*. Minneapolis: Fortress, 1992.

Kruijf, Theo de. "The Priest-King Melchizedek: The Reception of Gen 14,18-20 in Hebrews Mediated by Psalm 110." *Bijdragen: Tijdschrift voor filosofie en theologie* 54 (1993): 393-406.

Kugel, James L. *The Bible as It Was*. Cambridge, Mass: Belknap, 1997.

——. "Levi's Elevation to the Priesthood in Second Temple Writings." *Harvard Theological Review* 86 (1993): 1-64.

——. *Traditions of the Bible: A Guide to the Bible as It Was at the Start of the Common Era*. Cambridge, Mass.: Harvard University Press, 1998.

Kugler, Robert A. *From Patriarch to Priest: The Levi-Priestly Tradition from Aramaic Levi to Testament of Levi*. Society of Biblical Literature Early Judaism and its Literature 9. Atlanta: Scholars Press, 1996.

——. "Priesthood at Qumran." Pages 93-116 in vol. 2 of *The Dead Sea Scrolls after Fifty Years*. Edited by P. W. Flint and J. C. VanderKam. 2 vols. Leiden: Brill, 1999.

——. *The Testaments of the Twelve Patriarchs*. Guides to Apocrypha and Pseudepigrapha. Sheffield: Sheffield, 2001.

Kuhn, Karl Georg. "The Two Messiahs of Aaron and Israel." *New Testament Studies* 1 (1954/55): 168-80.

Kümmel, Werner Georg. *Introduction to the New Testament*. Rev. ed. Translated by H. C. Kee. Nashville: Abingdon, 1975.

Kuss, Otto. *Der Brief an die Hebräer*. Regensburg: Friedrich Pustet, 1966.

Lane, William L. *Hebrews*. 2 vols. Word Biblical Commentary 47A-B. Dallas: Word, 1991.

Larson, Erik W. "Michael." Pages 546-48 in vol. 1 of *Encyclopedia of the Dead Sea Scrolls*. Edited by L. H. Schiffman and J. C. VanderKam. 2 vols. Oxford: Oxford University Press, 2000.

Laub, Franz. *Bekenntnis und Auslegung: Die paränetische Funktion der Christologie im Hebräerbrief*. Biblische Untersuchungen 15. Regensburg: Pustet, 1980.

Licht, Jacob. *The Rule Scroll: A Scroll from the Wilderness of Judaea—1QS, 1QSa, 1QSb: Text, Introduction and Commentary*. Jerusalem: Bialik Institute, 1957. [Hebrew]

Liddell, Henry George, Robert Scott, and Henry Stuart Jones, eds. *A Greek-English Lexicon*. 9th ed. with rev. suppl. Oxford: Clarendon, 1996.

Lim, Timothy H. *Pesharim*. Companion to the Qumran Scrolls 3. London: Sheffield, 2002.

Lincoln, Andrew T. *Hebrews: A Guide*. London: T&T Clark, 2006.

Lindars, Barnabas. *The Theology of the Letter to the Hebrews*. New Testament Theology. Cambridge: Cambridge University Press, 1991.

Liver, J. "The Doctrine of the Two Messiahs in Sectarian Literature in the Time of the Second Commonwealth." *Harvard Theological Review* 52 (1959): 149-85.

Lohse, Eduard. *Märtyrer und Gottesknecht: Untersuchungen zur urchristlichen Verkündigung vom Sühnetod Jesu Christi*. Forschungen zur Religion und Literatur des Alten und Neuen Testaments 46. Göttingen: Vandenhoeck & Ruprecht, 1955.

Longenecker, Richard. *The Christology of Early Jewish Christianity*. London: SCM, 1970.

———. "The Melchizedek Argument of Hebrews: A Study in the Development and Circumstantial Expression of New Testament Thought." Pages 161-85 in *Unity and Diversity in New Testament Theology: Essays in Honor of George E. Ladd*. Edited by R. A. Guelich. Grand Rapids: Eerdmans, 1978.

Lübbe, John. "A Reinterpretation of 4Q Testimonia." *Revue de Qumran* 12 (1986): 187-97.

Lueken, Wilhelm. *Michael: Eine Darstellung und Vergleichung der jüdischen und der morgenländisch-christlichen Tradition vom Erzengel Michael*. Göttingen: Vandenhoeck & Ruprecht, 1898.

Macaskill, Grant. "Enoch, Second Book of." Page 265 in volume 2 of *The New Interpreter's Dictionary of the Bible*. Edited by K. D. Sakenfeld. 5 vols. (projected). Nashville: Abingdon, 2007.

MacKay, Cameron. "The Argument of Hebrews." *Church Quarterly Review* 168 (1967): 325-38.

———. "Why Study Ezekiel 40-48?" *Evangelical Quarterly* 37 (1965): 155-67.

MacRae, George W. "Heavenly Temple and Eschatology in the Letter to the Hebrews." *Semeia* 12 (1978): 179-99.

Magness, Jodi. *Archaeology of Qumran and the Dead Sea Scrolls*. Studies in the Dead Sea Scrolls and Related Literature. Grand Rapids: Eerdmans, 2003.

Manzi, Franco. *Melchisedek e l'angelologia nell'Epistola agli Ebrei e a Qumran*. Analecta biblica 136. Rome: Editrice Pontifico Instituto Biblico, 1997.

Mason, Eric F. "Hebrews 7:3 and the Relationship between Melchizedek and Jesus." *Biblical Research* 50 (2005): 41-62.

Mason, Steve. "Josephus: Value for New Testament Study." Pages 596-600 in *Dictionary of New Testament Background.* Edited by C. A. Evans and S. E. Porter. Downers Grove, Ill.: Intervarsity, 2000.

Maxwell, Kenneth L. "Doctrine and Parenesis in the Epistle to the Hebrews, with Special Reference to Pre-Christian Gnosticism." Ph.D. diss., Yale University, 1953.

McCruden, Kevin. "Christ's Perfection in Hebrews: Divine Beneficence as an Exegetical Key to Hebrews 2:10." *Biblical Research* 47 (2002): 40-62.

McKnight, Edgar, and Christopher Church. *Hebrews-James*. Smyth & Helwys Bible Commentary. Macon, Ga.: Smyth & Helwys, 2004.

McNamara, Martin. "Melchizedek: Gen 14,17-20 in the Targums, in Rabbinic and Early Christian Literature." *Biblica* 81 (2000): 1-31.

McNeile, A. H. *New Testament Teaching in the Light of St. Paul's*. Cambridge: Cambridge University Press, 1923.

Meier, John P. "Structure and Theology in Heb 1,1-14." *Biblica* 66 (1985): 168-89.

——. "Symmetry and Theology in the Old Testament Citations of Heb 1,5-14." *Biblica* 66 (1985): 504-33.

Metso, Sarianna. *The Textual Development of the Qumran Community Rule*. Studies on the Texts of the Desert of Judah 21. Leiden: Brill, 1997.

Metzger, Bruce M. *A Textual Commentary on the Greek New Testament.* 2nd ed. Stuttgart: Deutsche Bibelgesellschaft, 1994.

Michel, Otto. *Der Brief an die Hebräer*. Kritisch-exegetischer Kommentar über das Neue Testament 13. 14th ed. Göttingen: Vandenhoeck & Ruprecht, 1984.

Milik, Józef T. "4Q Visions de 'Amram et une citation d'Origène." *Revue biblique* 79 (1972): 77-97.

——. "*Milkî-sedek* et *Milkî-reša'* dans les anciens écrits juifs et chrétiens." *Journal of Jewish Studies* 23 (1972): 95-144.

——. Review of P. Wernberg-Møller, *The Manual of Discipline Translated and Annotated, with an Introduction. Revue biblique* 67 (1960): 411.

——. "Le testament de Lévi in araméen: Fragment de la grotte 4 de Qumrân." *Revue biblique* 62 (1955): 398-406.

Miller, Merrill P. "The Function of Isa 61:1-2 in 11Q Melchizedek." *Journal of Biblical Literature* 88 (1969): 467-69.

Mitchell, Alan C. *Hebrews*. Sacra pagina. Collegeville, Minn.: Liturgical, 2007.

Moe, Olaf. "Der Gedanke des allgemeinen Priestertums im Hebräerbrief." *Theologische Zeitschrift* 5 (1949): 161-69.

Moffatt, James. *A Critical and Exegetical Commentary on the Epistle to the Hebrews*. International Critical Commentary. Edinburgh: T. & T. Clark, 1924.

Montefiore, Hugh. *The Epistle to the Hebrews*. Black's New Testament Commentary. London: A&C Black, 1964.

Morgenstern, M., E. Qimron, and D. Sivan. "The Hitherto Unpublished Columns of the Genesis Apocryphon." *Abr-Nahrain* 33 (1995): 30-54.

Moule, C. F. D. "Commentaries on the Epistle to the Hebrews." *Theology* 61 (1958): 228-32.

Moulton, J. H., and G. Milligan. *Vocabulary of the Greek New Testament*. London: Hodder & Stoughton, 1930.

Nairne, Alexander. *The Epistle to the Hebrews*. Cambridge: Cambridge University Press, 1917.

Newman, Carey C., James R. Davila, and Gladys S. Lewis, eds. *The Jewish Roots of Christological Monotheism: Papers from the St. Andrews Conference on the Historical Origins of the Worship of Jesus*. Supplements to the Journal for the Study of Judaism 63. Leiden: Brill, 1999.

Newsom, Carol A. "Songs of the Sabbath Sacrifice." Pages 887-89 in vol. 2 of *Encyclopedia of the Dead Sea Scrolls*. Edited by L. H. Schiffman and J. C. VanderKam. 2 vols. Oxford: Oxford University Press, 2000.

——. "Throne." Pages 946-47 in vol. 2 of *Encyclopedia of the Dead Sea Scrolls*. Edited by L. H. Schiffman and J. C. VanderKam. 2 vols. Oxford: Oxford University Press, 2000.

Neyrey, Jerome H. "'Without Beginning of Days or End of Life' (Hebrews 7:3): Topos for a True Deity." *Catholic Biblical Quarterly* 53 (1991): 439-55.

Nitzan, Bilha. "Blessings and Curses." Pages 95-100 in vol. 1 of *Encyclopedia of the Dead Sea Scrolls*. Edited by L. H. Schiffman and J. C. VanderKam. 2 vols. Oxford: Oxford University Press, 2000.

Noth, Martin. *A History of the Pentateuchal Traditions*. Englewood Cliffs, N.J.: Prentice-Hall, 1972. Repr., Atlanta: Scholars Press, 1981.

Novum Testamentum Graece. Edited by B. Aland, K. Aland, J. Karavidopoulos, C. M. Martini, and B. M. Metzger. 27th ed. Stuttgart: Deutsche Bibelgesellschaft, 1993.

Oegema, Gerbern S. *The Anointed and his People: Messianic Expectations from the Maccabees to Bar Kochba*. Journal for the Study of the Pseudepigrapha: Supplement Series 27. Sheffield: Sheffield, 1998. Revised and expanded translation of *Der Gesalbte und sein Volk: Untersuchungen zum Konzeptualisierungsprozeß der messianischen Erwartungen von den Makkabäern bis Bar Koziba*. Göttingen: Vanderhoeck & Ruprecht, 1994.

——. "Messianic Expectations in the Qumran Writings: Theses on the Development." Pages 53-82 in *Qumran-Messianism: Studies on the Messianic Expectations in the Dead Sea Scrolls*. Edited by J. H. Charlesworth, H. Lichtenberger, and G. S. Oegema. Tübingen: Mohr Siebeck, 1998.

Orlov, Andrei. "The Heir of Righteousness and the King of Righteousness: The Priestly Noachic Polemics in 2 Enoch and the Epistle to the Hebrews." *Journal of Theological Studies* 58 (2007): 45-65.

——. "Melchizedek Legend of 2 (Slavonic) Enoch." *Journal for the Study of Judaism* 31 (2000): 23-38.

Pass, H. L., and J. Arendzen. "Fragment of an Aramaic Text of the Testament of Levi." *Jewish Quarterly Review* 12 (1900): 651-61.

Paul, M. J. "The Order of Melchizedek (Ps 110:4 and Heb 7:3)." *Westminster Theological Journal* 49 (1987): 195-211.

Pearson, Birger A. "Melchizedek in Early Judaism, Christianity, and Gnosticism." Pages 176-202 in *Biblical Figures Outside the Bible*. Edited by M. E. Stone and T. A. Bergren. Harrisburg, Penn.: Trinity Press International, 1998.

Peterson, David. *Hebrews and Perfection: An Examination of the Concept of Perfection in the Epistle to the Hebrews*. Society for New Testament Studies Monograph Series 47. Cambridge: Cambridge University Press, 1982.

Petuchowski, Jakob J. "The Controversial Figure of Melchizedek." *Hebrew Union College Annual* 28 (1957): 127-36.

Pfitzner, Victor C. *Hebrews*. Abingdon New Testament Commentaries. Nashville: Abingdon, 1997.

Philo. Translated by F. H. Colson et al. 12 vols. Loeb Classical Library. Cambridge, Mass.: Harvard University Press, 1929-53.
Poirier, John C. "The Endtime Return of Elijah and Moses at Qumran." *Dead Sea Discoveries* 10 (2003): 221-42.
Puech, Émile. *La Croyance des Esséniens en la Vie Future: Immortalité, Résurrection, Vie Éternelle?* Études Bibliques n.s. 21. Paris: Gabalda, 1993.
——. "Fragments d'un apocryphe de Lévi et le personnage eschatologique, 4QTestLévi[c-d] (?) et 4QAJa." Pages 449-501 in *The Madrid Qumran Congress: Proceedings of the International Congress on the Dead Sea Scrolls, Madrid, 18-21 March 1991*. Edited by J. Trebolle Barrera and L. Vegas Montaner. 2 vols. Studies on the Texts of the Desert of Judah 11. Leiden: Brill, 1992.
——. "Notes sur le manuscrit de XIQMelkîsédeq." *Revue de Qumran* 12 (1987): 483-513.

Rad, Gerhard von. *Genesis*. Rev. ed. Old Testament Library. Philadelphia: Westminster, 1972.
Rainbow, Paul. "Melchizedek as a Messiah at Qumran." *Bulletin of Biblical Research* 7 (1997): 179-94.
Rawlinson, A. E. J. *The New Testament Doctrine of Christ*. London: Longmans, Green & Co., 1926.
Riggenbach, Eduard. *Der Brief an die Hebräer*. 3rd ed. Leipzig: Deichert, 1922.
Rissi, Mathias. *Die Theologie des Hebräerbriefs*. Wissenschaftliche Untersuchungen zum Neuen Testament 41. Tübingen: Mohr, 1987.
Robinson, T. H. *The Epistle to the Hebrews*. London: Harper, 1933.
Rowland, Christopher. "A Man Clothed in Linen: Daniel 10.6ff and Jewish Angelology." *Journal for the Study of the New Testament* 24 (1985): 99-110.

Sabourin, Leopold. *Priesthood: A Comparative Study*. Studies in the History of Religions 25. Leiden: Brill, 1973.
Sarna, Nahum. *Genesis*. Jewish Publication Society Torah Commentary. Philadelphia: Jewish Publication Society, 1989.
Schaefer, James R. "The Relationship between Priestly and Servant Messianism in the Epistle to the Hebrews." *Catholic Biblical Quarterly* 30 (1968): 359-85.
Schechter, Solomon. *Documents of Jewish Sectaries, Vol. 1: Fragments of a Zadokite Work*. Cambridge: Cambridge University Press, 1910.
Schenck, Kenneth L. "Philo and the Epistle to the Hebrews: Ronald Williamson's Study after Thirty Years." *Studia philonica* 14 (2002): 112-35.
——. *Understanding the Book of Hebrews: The Story Behind the Sermon*. Louisville: Westminster John Knox, 2003.
Schiffman, Lawrence H. *The Eschatological Community of the Dead Sea Scrolls: A Study of the Rule of the Congregation*. Society of Biblical Literature Monograph Series 38. Atlanta: Scholars Press, 1989.
——. "Messianic Figures and Ideas in the Qumran Scrolls." Pages 116-29 in *The Messiah: Developments in Earliest Judaism and Christianity*. Edited by J. H. Charlesworth. Minneapolis: Fortress, 1992.
——. "Rule of the Congregation." Pages 797-99 in vol. 2 of *Encyclopedia of the Dead Sea Scrolls*. Edited by L. H. Schiffman and J. C. VanderKam. Oxford: Oxford University Press, 2000.
Schiffman, Lawrence H., and James C. VanderKam, eds. *Encyclopedia of the Dead Sea Scrolls*. 2 vols. Oxford: Oxford University Press, 2000.

Schmithals, Walter. *Neues Testament und Gnosis*. Erträge der Forschung 208. Darmstadt: Wissenschaftliche Buchgesellschaft, 1984.

——. *The Theology of the First Christians*. Translated by O. C. Dean, Jr. Louisville: Westminster John Knox, 1997.

Schnelle, Udo. *The History and Theology of the New Testament Writings*. Translated by M. E. Boring. Minneapolis: Fortress, 1998.

Schröger, Friedrich. *Der Verfasser des Hebräerbriefes als Schriftausleger*. Regensburg: Pustet, 1968.

Schulz, David. *Der Brief an die Hebräer*. Breslau: Holäufer, 1818.

Segal, Alan F. *Two Powers in Heaven: Early Rabbinic Reports about Christianity and Gnosticism*. Studies in Judaism in Late Antiquity 25. Leiden: Brill, 1977.

Seid, Timothy W. "Synkrisis in Hebrews 7: The Rhetorical Structure and Strategy." Pages 322-47 in *The Rhetorical Interpretation of Scripture: Essays from the 1996 Malibu Conference*. Edited by S. E. Porter and D. L. Stamps. Journal for the Study of the New Testament: Supplement Series 180. Sheffield: Sheffield, 1999.

Septuaginta. Edited by Alfred Rahlfs. Stuttgart: Deutsche Bibelgesellschaft, 1979.

Slingerland, H. Dixon. *The Testaments of the Twelve Patriarchs: A Critical History of Research*. Society of Biblical Literature Monograph Series 21. Missoula, Mont: Scholars Press, 1977.

Smith, Morton. "Ascent to the Heavens and Deification in 4QM[a]." Pages 181-88 in *Archaeology and History in the Dead Sea Scrolls*. Edited by L. Schiffman. Sheffield: JSOT Press, 1990.

Smith, Robert Houston. "Abram and Melchizedek (Gen 14 18-20)." *Zeitschrift für die alttestamentliche Wissenschaft* 77 (1965): 129-53.

Sparks, H. F. D., ed. *The Apocryphal Old Testament*. Oxford: Clarendon, 1984.

Spicq, Ceslas. *L'Epître aux Hébreux*. 2 vols. Paris: Gabalda, 1952-53.

——. "L'Épître aux Hébreux, Apollos, Jean-Baptiste, les Hellénistes et Qumrân." *Revue de Qumran* 1 (1958-59): 365-90.

——. "L'origine Johannique de la conception du Christ-Prêtre dans l'Épître aux Hébreux." Pages 258-69 in *Aux sources de la tradition chrétienne: Mélanges offerts à Maurice Goguel*. Neuchâtel: Delachaux et Niestlé, 1950.

Starcky, Jean. "Les quatre étapes du messianisme à Qumrân." *Revue biblique* 70 (1963): 481-505.

Stegemann, Hartmut. "Some Remarks to 1QSa, to 1QSb, and to Qumran Messianism." *Revue de Qumran* 17 (1996): 479-505.

Sterling, Gregory E. "Ontology Versus Eschatology: Tensions Between Author and Community in Hebrews." *Studia philonica* 13 (2001): 190-211.

——. "Philo." Pages 789-93 in *Dictionary of New Testament Background*. Edited by C. A. Evans and S. Porter. Downers Grove, Ill: Intervarsity, 2000.

Steudel, Annette. "4QMidrEschat: «A Midrash on Eschatology» (4Q174+4Q177)." Pages 531-41 in vol. 2 of *The Madrid Qumran Congress: Proceedings of the International Congress on the Dead Sea Scrolls, Madrid 18-21 March, 1991*. Edited by J. Trebolle Barrera and L. Vegas Montaner. 2 vols. Studies on the Texts of the Desert of Judah 11. Leiden: Brill, 1992.

——. *Der Midrasch zur Eschatologie aus der Qumrangemeinde (4QMidrEschat[a,b]): Materielle Rekonstruktion, Textbestand, Gattung und traditionsgeschichtliche Einordnung des durch 4Q174 ('Florilegium') und 4Q175 ('Catena A') repräsentierten Werkes aus den Qumranfunden*. Studies on the Texts of the Desert of Judah 13. Leiden: Brill, 1994.

——. "Testimonia." Pages 936-38 in vol. 2 of *Encyclopedia of the Dead Sea Scrolls*. Edited by L. H. Schiffman and J. C. VanderKam. 2 vols. Oxford: Oxford University Press, 2000.

Stökl Ben Ezra, Daniel. *The Impact of Yom Kippur on Early Christianity: The Day of Atonement from Second Temple Judaism to the Fifth Century*. Wissenschaftliche Untersuchungen zum Neuen Testament 163. Tübingen: Mohr Siebeck, 2003.

Stone, Michael E. "Amram." Pages 23-24 in vol. 1 of *Encyclopedia of the Dead Sea Scrolls*. Edited by L. H. Schiffman and J. C. VanderKam. 2 vols. Oxford: Oxford University Press, 2000.

——. "Levi, Aramaic." Pages 486-88 in vol. 1 of *Encyclopedia of the Dead Sea Scrolls*. Edited by L. H. Schiffman and J. C. VanderKam. 2 vols. Oxford: Oxford University Press, 2000.

Stowers, Sidney G. *The Hermeneutics of Philo and Hebrews: A Comparison of the Interpretation of the Old Testament in Philo Judaeus and the Epistle to the Hebrews*. Zürich: EVZ-Verlag, 1965.

Strobel, August. *Der Brief an die Hebräer*. 4th ed. Das Neue Testament Deutsch 9. Göttingen: Vandenhoeck & Ruprecht, 1991.

Strugnell, John. "Notes en marge du volume V des 'Discoveries in the Judaean Desert of Jordan.'" *Revue de Qumran* 7 (1969-70): 163-276 and plates I-VI.

Stuckenbruck, Loren T. *Angel Veneration and Christology: A Study in Early Judaism and in the Christology of the Apocalypse of John*. Wissenschaftliche Untersuchungen zum Neuen Testament 2/70. Tübingen: Mohr Siebeck, 1995.

Sukenik, E. L., ed. *The Dead Sea Scrolls of the Hebrew University*. Jerusalem: Magnes, 1955. [Hebrew 1954]

Sullivan, Kevin P. *Wrestling with Angels: A Study of the Relationship between Angels and Humans in Ancient Jewish Literature and the New Testament*. Arbeiten zur Geschichte des antiken Judentums und des Urchristentums 55. Leiden: Brill, 2004.

Synge, F. C. *Hebrews and the Scriptures*. London: SPCK, 1959.

Talmon, Shemaryahu. "Types of Messianic Expectation at the Turn of the Era." Pages 202-24 in *King, Cult and Calendar in Ancient Judaism*. Jerusalem: Magnes, 1986.

Theißen, Gerd. *Untersuchungen zum Hebräerbrief*. Studien zum Neuen Testament 2. Gütersloh: Mohn, 1969.

Thompson, James W. *The Beginnings of Christian Philosophy: The Epistle to the Hebrews*. Catholic Biblical Quarterly Monograph Series 13. Washington: Catholic Biblical Association of America, 1982.

Tisserant, E. "Fragments syriaques du Livre des Jubilés." *Revue biblique* 30 (1921): 55-86, 206-32.

Trentham, Charles A. "Hebrews." Pages 1-99 in vol. 12 of *The Broadman Bible Commentary*. Edited by C. J. Allen. 12 vols. Nashville: Broadman, 1972.

Trotter, Andrew H., Jr. *Interpreting the Epistle to the Hebrews*. Guides to New Testament Exegesis 6. Grand Rapids: Baker, 1997.

VanderKam, James C. *The Book of Jubilees*. 2 vols. Corpus scriptorum christianorum orientalium 510-11. Scriptores Aethiopici 87-88. Louvain: Peeters, 1989.

——. "Book of Jubilees." Pages 434-38 in vol. 1 of *Encyclopedia of the Dead Sea Scrolls*. Edited by L. H. Schiffman and J. C. VanderKam. 2 vols. Oxford: Oxford University Press, 2000.

——. *The Book of Jubilees*. Guides to Apocrypha and Pseudepigrapha. Sheffield: Sheffield, 2001.
——. "Jubilees and the Priestly Messiah of Qumran." *Revue de Qumran* 13 (1988): 353-65.
——. "Jubilees, Book of," Pages 1030-32 in vol. 3 of *The Anchor Bible Dictionary*. Edited by D. N. Freedman. 6 vols. New York: Doubleday, 1992.
——. "Messianism in the Scrolls." Pages 211-34 in *The Community of the Renewed Covenant: The Notre Dame Symposium on the Dead Sea Scrolls*. Edited by E. Ulrich and J. VanderKam. Christianity and Judaism in Antiquity Series 10. Notre Dame, Ind.: University of Notre Dame Press, 1994.
——. "Sabbatical Chronologies in the Dead Sea Scrolls and Related Literature." Pages 159-78 in *The Dead Sea Scrolls In Their Historical Context*. Edited by T. H. Lim. Edinburgh: T. & T. Clark, 2000.
——. "Yom Kippur." Pages 1001-03 in vol. 2 of *Encyclopedia of the Dead Sea Scrolls*. Edited by L. H. Schiffman and J. C. VanderKam. 2 vols. Oxford: Oxford University Press, 2000.
VanderKam, James, and Peter Flint. *The Meaning of the Dead Sea Scrolls*. New York: Harper San Francisco, 2002.
Vanhoye, Albert. *Situation du Christ: Épître aux Hébreux 1 et 2*. Paris: Cerf, 1969.
Vaux, Roland de. *Ancient Israel: Its Life and Institutions*. London: Darton, Longman & Todd, 1961. Repr., Grand Rapids: Eerdmans, 1997.
——. *Archaeology and the Dead Sea Scrolls: The Schweich Lectures of the British Academy, 1959*. Rev. ed. London: Oxford University Press, 1973.
——. Review of J. A. Fitzmyer, *The Genesis Apocryphon of Qumran Cave I: A Commentary*. *Revue biblique* 74 (1967): 100-02.
Villalón, José R. "Sources vétéro-testamentaires de la doctrine qumrânienne des deux Messies." *Revue de Qumran* 8 (1972): 53-63.

Walter, Nikolaus. "Pseudo-Eupolemus (Samaritanischer Anonymus)." Pages 137-43 in vol. 1, part 2 of *Jüdische Schriften aus hellenistisch-römischer Zeit*. Edited by W. G. Kümmel. Gütersloh: G. Mohn, 1976.
Watson, Duane F. "Michael." Page 811 in vol. 4 of *The Anchor Bible Dictionary*. Edited by D. N. Freedman. 6 vols. New York: Doubleday, 1992.
Weiss, Hans-Friedrich. *Der Brief an die Hebräer*. 15th ed. Kritisch-exegetischer Kommentar über das Neue Testament 13. Göttingen: Vandenhoeck & Ruprecht, 1991.
Wenham, Gordon J. *Genesis 1-15*. Word Biblical Commentary 1. Dallas: Word, 1987.
Werner, Martin. *Die Entstehung des christlichen Dogmas*. Bern/Leipzig: Haupt, 1941.
Westermann, Claus. *Genesis 12-36*. Continental Commentary. Minneapolis: Fortress, 1995.
Williamson, Ronald. *Philo and the Epistle to the Hebrews*. Arbeiten zur Literatur und Geschichte das hellenistischen Judentums 4. Leiden: Brill, 1970.
Wilson, J. Christian. "Tithe." Pages 579-80 in vol. 6 of *The Anchor Bible Dictionary*. Edited by D. N. Freedman. 6 vols. New York: Doubleday, 1992.
Wilson, R. McL. *Hebrews*. New Century Bible Commentary. Grand Rapids: Eerdmans, 1987.
Windisch, Hans. *Der Hebräerbrief*. 2nd ed. Handbuch zum Neuen Testament 14. Tübingen: Mohr, 1931.
Wintermute, O. S. "Jubilees." Pages 35-142 in vol. 2 of *The Old Testament Pseudepigrapha*. Edited by J. H. Charlesworth. 2 vols. New York: Doubleday, 1983-85.

Woude, A. S. van der. "Melchisedek als himmlische Erlösergestalt in den neugefundenen eschatologischen Midraschim aus Qumran Höhle XI." *Oudtestamentische Studiën* 14 (1965): 354-73.

Wright, W. *Catalogue of Syriac Manuscripts in the British Museum Acquired Since the Year 1838: Part II*. London: Gilbert and Rivington, 1871.

Xeravits, Géza G. *King, Priest, Prophet: Positive Eschatological Protagonists of the Qumran Library*. Studies on the Texts of the Desert of Judah 67. Leiden: Brill, 2003.

Yadin, Yigael. "The Dead Sea Scrolls and the Epistle to the Hebrews." *Scripta hierosolymitana* 4 (1958): 36-55.

——. "A Note on Melchizedek and Qumran." *Israel Exploration Journal* 15 (1965): 152-54.

——. *The Scroll of the War of the Sons of Light against the Sons of Darkness*. Oxford: Oxford University Press, 1962.

Zimmermann, Johannes. *Messianische Texte aus Qumran: Königliche, priesterliche und prophetische Messiasvorstellungen in den Schriftfunden von Qumran*. Wissenschaftliche Untersuchungen zum Neuen Testament 2/104. Tübingen: Mohr Siebeck, 1998.

INDEX OF AUTHORS